ADVANCES IN AD HOC NETWORKING

IFIP – The International Federation for Information Processing

IFIP was founded in 1960 under the auspices of UNESCO, following the First World Computer Congress held in Paris the previous year. An umbrella organization for societies working in information processing, IFIP's aim is two-fold: to support information processing within its member countries and to encourage technology transfer to developing nations. As its mission statement clearly states,

> IFIP's mission is to be the leading, truly international, apolitical organization which encourages and assists in the development, exploitation and application of information technology for the benefit of all people.

IFIP is a non-profitmaking organization, run almost solely by 2500 volunteers. It operates through a number of technical committees, which organize events and publications. IFIP's events range from an international congress to local seminars, but the most important are:

• The IFIP World Computer Congress, held every second year;
• Open conferences;
• Working conferences.

The flagship event is the IFIP World Computer Congress, at which both invited and contributed papers are presented. Contributed papers are rigorously refereed and the rejection rate is high.

As with the Congress, participation in the open conferences is open to all and papers may be invited or submitted. Again, submitted papers are stringently refereed.

The working conferences are structured differently. They are usually run by a working group and attendance is small and by invitation only. Their purpose is to create an atmosphere conducive to innovation and development. Refereeing is less rigorous and papers are subjected to extensive group discussion.

Publications arising from IFIP events vary. The papers presented at the IFIP World Computer Congress and at open conferences are published as conference proceedings, while the results of the working conferences are often published as collections of selected and edited papers.

Any national society whose primary activity is in information may apply to become a full member of IFIP, although full membership is restricted to one society per country. Full members are entitled to vote at the annual General Assembly, National societies preferring a less committed involvement may apply for associate or corresponding membership. Associate members enjoy the same benefits as full members, but without voting rights. Corresponding members are not represented in IFIP bodies. Affiliated membership is open to non-national societies, and individual and honorary membership schemes are also offered.

ADVANCES IN AD HOC NETWORKING

Proceedings of the Seventh Annual Mediterranean
Ad Hoc Networking Workshop, Palma de Mallorca,
Spain, June 25-27, 2008

Edited by
Pedro Cuenca
Universidad de Castilla-La Mancha
Spain

Carlos Guerrero
Universitat de les Illes Balears
Spain

Ramon Puigjaner
Universitat de les Illes Balears
Spain

Bartomeu Serra
Universitat de les Illes Balears
Spain

 Springer

Advances in Ad Hoc Networking

Edited by Pedro Cuenca, Carlos Guerrero, Ramon Puigjaner
and Bartomeu Serra

p. cm. (IFIP International Federation for Information Processing, a Springer Series in Computer Science)

ISSN: 1571-5736 / 1861-2288 (Internet)

ISBN: 978-1-4419-3486-4   eISBN: 978-0-387-09490-8

Printed on acid-free paper

9 8 7 6 5 4 3 2 1

springer.com

Preface

This volume contains the proceedings of the Seventh Mediterranean Ad Hoc Networking Workshop (Med-Hoc-Net'2008), celebrated in Palma de Mallorca (Illes Balears, Spain) during June 25-27, 2008. This IFIP TC6 Workshop was organized by the Universitat de les Illes Balears in cooperation with the Asociación de Técnicos de Informática and sponsored by the following Working Groups: WG6.3 (Performance of Computer Networks) and WG6.8 (Mobile and Wireless Communications).

The rapid evolution of the networking industry introduces new exciting challenges that need to be explored by the research community. Aside the adoption of Internet as the global network infrastructure these last years have shown the growing of a set of new network architectures without a rigid and known a priori architecture using wireless techniques, like sensor and ad-hoc networks. These new types of networks are opening the possibility to create a large number of new applications ranging from domestic to nature surveying.

These new networks are generating new technical challenges like the capability of auto-reconfiguration in order to give the network an optimal configuration, the energy saving need when the nodes have not a source of energy other than a small battery, new protocols to access the network and to convey the information across the network when its structure is not completely known or should be discovered, new paradigms for keeping the needed information security and privacy in a quite uncontrolled environment, and others.

According to these trends, the intention of the conference was to provide a forum for the exchange of ideas and findings in a wide range of areas related to the above mentioned topics that were covered by the presentation of the papers accepted by the Programme Committee. The main program covered two days and included six sequential sessions. Also, the programme was enriched by a keynote speech offered by the prestigious and world-renowned researcher in the networking field that is Ian F. Akyildiz form the Georgia Institute of Technology (USA). Aside the paper presentation part, the workshop offered two tutorial given by: Guy Pujolle from the University of Paris 6 (France), on The Wi-xx family versus 4G generation and by Mario Gerla form the University of California at Los Angeles (USA) on Mobile P2P networks with applications to vehicles and health-nets.

June 2008

Pedro Cuenca
Carlos Guerrero
Ramon Puigjaner
Bartomeu Serra

Organization

GENERAL CHAIR

R. Puigjaner, Universitat de les Illes Balears (ES)

PROGRAM CHAIR

P. Cuenca, Universidad de Castilla-La Mancha (ES)

STEERING COMMITTEE

I. F. Akyildiz, Georgia Tech, (US)
K. Al Agha, Université Paris-Sud (FR)
M. Gerla, UCLA (US)
F. Kamoun, ENSI (TN)
G. Pau, UCLA (US)
G. Pujolle, Université Pierre et Marie Curie (FR)

FINANCIAL CHAIR

B. Serra, Universitat de les Illes Balears (ES)

PUBLICITY CHAIR

C. Guerrero, Universitat de les Illes Balears (ES)

PROGRAM COMMITTEE

O. Alintas, Toyota IT Center, JP
O. B. Akan, Middle East Tech. University, TR
A. Azcorra, Universidad Carlos III, ES
B. K. Bhargaya, Purdue University, US
C. Blondia, University of Antwerp, BE
A. Boukerche, University of Ottawa, CA
J. C. Cano, Universitat Politècnica València, ES
R. Cardell-Oliver, University of Western Australia, AU
M. Cesana, Politecnico Milano, IT
T. Chahed, INT. Evry, FR
S. Chandran, RF Consultant, MY
C. Chaudet, ENST, FR
M. Conti, CNR, IT

F. de Rango, Università di Calabria, IT
C. Douligeris, University of Piraeus, GR
B. Dudourthial, UTC, FR
E. Ekici, Ohio State University, US
A. Farago, University of Texas, Dallas, US
L. Fratta, Politecnico Milano, IT
S. Galmés, Universitat de les Illes Balears, ES
J. García-Vidal, Universitat Poliècnica Catalunya, ES
A. Garrido, Universidad de Castilla-La Mancha, ES
I. Guerin-Lassous, INRIA, FR
G. Haring, Universität Wien, AT
S. Heemstra de Groot, Delft University of Technology, NL
H. Hellbrück, Universität Lübeck, DE
O. Koné, Université Paul Sabatier–IRIT, FR
H. Liu, University of Ottawa, CA
M. López, UNAM, MX
M. Lenardi, Hitachi Europe, Sophia Antipolis Lab., FR
P. Lorenz, Université d'Haute Alsace, FR
M. Lott, Siemens AG, DE
P. Manzoni, Universitat Politècnica València, ES
C. Mascolo, University College London, UK
D. Meddour, France Telecom, FR
P. Minet, INRIA, FR
A. Murphy, Università di Lugano, IT
S. Nikoletseas, CTI/University of Patras, GR
L. Orozco-Barbosa, Universidad de Castilla-La Mancha, ES
M. Pérez, Universidad Miguel Hernández, ES
E. Rosti, Università di Milano, IT
P. Ruiz, Universidad de Murcia, ES
P. Santi, CNR, IT
B. Serra, Universitat de les Illes Balears, ES
D. Symplot-Ryl, Université de Lille, FR
V. Syrotiuk, Arizona State University, US
D. Turgut, University Central Florida, US
J. Villalón, Universidad de Castilla La Mancha, ES
L. Villaseñor, CICESE, MX
T. Watteyne, France Telecom, FR
S. Weber, Trinity College Dublin, IE
J. Wozniak, Technical University Gdansk, PL
H. Yomo, Aalborg University, DK

Table of Contents

Security and Privacy

MAC Protocols

Routing Algorithms and Protocols II

End To End QoS Mapping
Between Metroethernet and WiMAX

Leoncio Regal Dutra, Georges Amvame Nze, Cláudia J. Barenco Abbas,
Carlos Bon and Luciana Gomes.

[1]Universidade de Brasília.
{georges, leoncio}@redes.unb.br.

[2]Universidad Simón Bolívar.

barenco@ldc.usb.ve.

[3]Serviço Federal de Processamento de Dados

{carlos.bon, luciana.gomes}@serpro.gov.br.

Abstract. This work aims the implementation and analysis of an environment formed by WiMAX and MetroEthernet networks. WiMAX offers unwired broadband access with high capacity of data transmission for dispersed areas. This network allows the interconnection of MetroEthernet networks with connection up to 10Gbps. The study herein presented deals with a proposal of an end-to-end Quality of Service (QoS suitable not only for voice and video traffics but also for data traffic). Until the elaboration of this work, as far as we know, there is not a theoretical and practical study of the characteristics of real time traffic in WiMAX interconnecting MetroEthernet networks.

1 Introduction

Brazil is witnessing a radical change for network connections in metropolitan environment for public and research agencies. Twenty seven metropolitans networks will be created, one for each capital, where public and research organisms will divide modern optical infrastructure of high transmission capacity.

Although not being widely used in the market, the IEEE 802.16 network standard came to revolutionize the industry of wireless broadband access. It will offer ample transmission coverage for agricultural and metropolitans areas, with or without line of site. Such standard, known as WiMAX (*Worldwide Interoperability Microwave Access*), is defined by the IEEE group that deals with broadband access in dispersed areas. Although WiMAX does not create a new market, it should allow financial costs reduction and increase wireless communication usability. WiMAX sufficiently surpasses IEEE 802.11 limitations, such as bandwidth provision with the use of strong cryptography for data transmission.

Please use the following format when citing this chapter:

Dutra, L. R., Nze, G. A., Barenco Abbas, C. J., Bon, C., Gomes, L., 2008, in IFIP International Federation for Information Processing, Volume 265, Advances in Ad Hoc Networking, eds. Cuenca, P., Guerrero C., Puigjaner, R., Serra, B., (Boston: Springer), pp. 1-12.

With this scenario and the increasing demand for bandwidth to send and receive data, video, voice and television signal, an infrastructure with end-to-end Quality of Service (QoS) mapping is being proposed.

As the present scenery is to be heterogeneous at link layer, the implementation of an end-to-end QoS mapping is of great importance between both topologies. If one wants to guarantee a good end-to-end service, any kind of delay, delay variation (*jitter*) and data loss rate should obey strong QoS recommendation and implementation.

The topology herein presented includes link and network layer solutions, for effective end-to-end QoS guaranties, using IEEE 802.1p standard for frame priority in MetroEthernet and WiMAX QoS metrics for packet priority respectively. The overall end-to-end QoS would then be provided by the integration of WiMAX and MetroEthernet.

In this work we propose the implementation of QoS in MetroEthernet and WiMAX, based on measurements taken in laboratory and, suggested as a guide for future heterogeneous network implementations.

2   Diffserv

DiffServ is the abbreviation of Differentiated Services and is a technology that is scalable as to prevent the maintenance of flow state information inside the network.

At layer 3, inside and between networks, all flows having QoS guarantees are treated differently from other flows inside. A DS (Differentiated Services) field is present in the IP header protocol for a QoS metrics previously added by a border network node.

One of DiffServ's main functions is related to its behavior in analyzing a flow hop by hop (per-hop behaviors - PHB) inside a network. This behavior is the description of the treatment that is given to flows accordingly to their value mapped in the field DS (Differentiated Services).

PHB groups are implemented in each network node and are based essentially in scheduling and queuing management mechanisms.

The DiffServ model redefined the TOS (Type of Service) octet in the IPv4 header as DS octet. It contains two fields: the DSCP (Differentiated Services Code Point), with 6 bits, used in the determination of the PHB and two CU (Currently Unused) bits reserved for future use. Both fields must be ignored for the purpose of PHB election. Figure 1 shows what has been described previously.

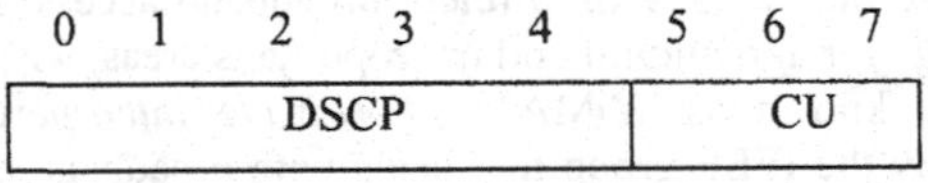

```
  0   1   2   3   4   5   6   7
┌───────────────────────┬───────────┐
│         DSCP          │    CU     │
└───────────────────────┴───────────┘
```

Fig. 1. DS byte structure in IP header.

DiffServ defines two PHB groups: *Assured Forwarding* [4, 12, 14] and *Expedited Forwarding* [4, 12, 14].

- PHB – AF
  - The AF group aims to supply distinct traffic class with varying levels of loss probability. For such, it praises the existence of four distinct AF classes, each one with proper resources attributed and treated independently. Inside each class there are three levels of loss precedence that correspond to a greater or minor loss probability inside the class queue.
- PHB – EF
  - The EF group is defined as a unique class with express forwarding. The EF PHB must be implemented when there is a necessity to transmit a traffic profile with low loss, low delay, little variation in the delay (low jitter) and guaranteed bandwidth. The EF PHB is used to identify and direct multimedia application traffic such as real time voice and video.

3   802.1p

To guarantee the transmission of information with good characteristics related to delay and its variation, as well as data loss rate, the 802.1p protocol can assist all type of traffic with QoS requirements.

The 802.1p specification introduces new mechanisms for traffic priority in IEEE 802 networks to support critical traffic and dynamic multicast filtering. Traffic volume limitation is implemented in LAN (*Local Area Network*) switches using these mechanisms. Although they both are interesting in performance, the 802.1p priorities mechanism has a direct impact in IEEE 802 quality of service networks [16].

In IEEE 802.3 (*Ethernet standard*), there is no existence of a priority header field for traffic priority mapping. So for Ethernet networks, IEEE 802.1q should be used to support the VLAN identification. The 802.1q should include a field of three bits for assigned user priority, as for future traffic aggregation requiring QoS mechanisms.

The 802.1p priorities mechanism is implemented at link layer. To make use of this mechanism, switches must have the capacity of mapping the traffic to different classes. This protocol defines eight priorities values, leaving to the network administrator the task to attribute values to the different types of traffic flows in the network.

Priority 7 mapping is the highest value raised and must carry critical traffic to the network, such as route update. Priorities 5 and 6 are indicated for applications sensible to the delay, such as voice and video. In turn, class 4 and 1 can carry from controlled load to low priority traffic.

Class 0 specifications are similar to best effort for packets with no special priority. Equipments do not have to implement eight different types of queuing disciplines on each port for the system to work properly [14, 15].

In Table 1, the recommended mapping is demonstrated for priority values that should apply for user applications and the queue it should hold to. This recommendation must be in agreement with the number of queues available in the equipment.

4   Leoncio Regal Dutra, Georges Amvame Nze, Cláudia J. Barenco Abbas, Carlos Bon and Luciana Gomes.

Although there is a mechanism of traffic differentiation capable of rearranging packets and guaranteeing a high priority delivery for critical applications, the 802.1p by itself cannot give any guarantee of how much latency has been introduce. The 802.1p becomes inadequate for applications that need rigid guarantees of such parameter. However, if used jointly with other QoS mechanisms, for example those implemented at network layer, the 802.1p can be vital in the integration of traffic differentiation in the same network [17].

Table 1. Mapping between the priority value and wait queue for different numbers of wait queue.

		Available number of Classes of Traffic							
		1	2	3	4	5	6	7	8
	0	0	0	0	1	1	1	1	2
	1	0	0	0	0	0	0	0	0
	2	0	0	0	0	0	0	0	1
User Priority	3	0	0	0	1	1	2	2	3
	4	0	1	1	2	2	3	3	4
	5	0	1	1	2	3	4	4	5
	6	0	1	2	3	4	5	5	6
	7	0	1	2	3	4	5	6	7

4   WiMAX Quality Of Service

To define the priority of MAC SDUs (*Medium Access Control Service Data Unit*) through the existing connections, each connection (defined as CID – Connection ID) is mapped in a daily pre-define class of scheduling. Each class has a set of parameters that quantifies QoS prerequisites. These parameters are managed through the management messages type DAS (*Dynamic Service Addition*) and DSC (*Dynamic Service Change*). Four classes of services are presented for QoS metrics implantation in WiMAX [3, 18 and 19]:

- *Unsolicited Grant Service* (UGS) – designated for real time traffic with constant rate flow, such as emulations circuits and ATM CBR.
- *Real Time Polling Service* (rtPS) – designated for real time traffic with variable rate flow rate (variable packet size), such as MPEG video.
- *Non-Real-time Polling Service* (nrtPS) – designated for stored traffic requiring low delay with variable flow rate (variable packet size), such as stored MPEG video.
- *Best Effort* (BE) – designated for variable traffic rate (variable packet size), such as TCP/IP.

5   QoS Mapping

From the techniques herein presented, the most significant scheduling mechanism defined for the IEEE 802.16 standard, was defined by Hawa [1 and 2]. His work presented a random analysis of scheduling mechanism based on the Fair Queuing technique with QoS support.

Another possibility in applying Quality of Service to IEEE 802.16 is using DiffServ. In networks implementing DiffServ, the admission control is based on *Bandwidth Brokers* (BBS) and *Service Level Agreement* (SLA) mechanisms. This solution does not fix the control flow congestion problem, where all flows having the same classification can be degraded. Admission Control solutions could be used to fix this problem.

The solution proposed by LCT - UC (*Laboratory of Communications and Telemetric of the University of Coimbra*) uses a metric to calculate an index of congestion of the network element to verify if it can admit a new flow [4, 5, 6, 7 and 8].

There are some techniques of probing the network using Packet Probing [9, 10 and 11] but they do not have applicability to a generic architecture of Quality of Service. Such conclusion elapses from the fact that they only can be applied on an IEEE 802.16 network, or either, they only deal with the possibilities to provide QoS in an IEEE 802.16 network.

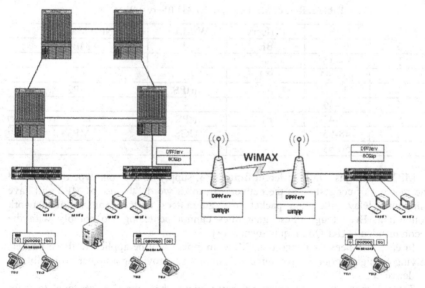

Fig. 2. Architecture of MetroEthernet – WiMAX networks.

These problems led us to consider a generic architecture of QoS, based on DiffServ, IEEE 802.1p and 802.16 standards, where MetroEthernet networks are connected through WiMAX wirelessly as shown in Figure 2, to extend the *Metropolitan Area Network* (MAN).

The proposal defined in this work, on one side, uses IEEE 802.1p as a mapping model defining link layer priorities and on the other, a group of DiffServ PHBs and Class of Services defined in IEEE 802.16. The proposal includes a static mechanism of admission control capable of reflecting the network state, guaranteeing all requirements considered essential for networks that implement QOS mechanisms. Requirements such as end-to-end delay, jitter and packet loss reduction.

The IEEE 802.1p standard implements 7 types of priorities, from the lowest to the highest priority (1...7), where each priority has an individual applicability.

To implement a QoS mapping between IEEE 8021.p and DiffServ (DSCP - COS) a ACLs (Extended Access List) will be used to maintain the priority parameters. These ACLs contain a table, where the DSCPs codes and their respective classifications are listed. The related list contains from 0 to 63 possibilities of PHBs mapping. Through this priority, is made the DSCP to COS mapping, as shown at Table 2 [12].

As an example, a packet having its DSCP value mapped to 6 will imply in having a packet mapped to class 6 by the IEEE 802.1p protocol.

In implementation terms, the support for MP3 mapping relies on the capacity to transmit other traffic aggregates, through priorities mechanisms. However, a limit for traffic debit must exist to prevent traffic congestion caused by other traffic aggregate. The packages that exceed this limit will have to be eliminated.

Table 2. Rule of Mapping 802.1p – DiffServ – WiMAX.

802.1p	PHBs	Diffserv	WiMAX	New Mapping
0	0 – 7	BE	BE	MP1
1	8 – 15	-	-	
2	16 – 23	BE	BE	
3	24 – 31	AF	nrtPS	MP2
4	32-39	-	-	
5	40-47	EF	rtPS	
6	48-55	EF	UGS	MP3
7	56-63	-	-	

MP2 mapping is a little different from MP3, supplying only one type of service at the moment of congestion in the network. In other words, the use of MP2 will have minimum delay, jitter and packet loss guarantees at the moment of network congestion. Even tough, these guaranties cannot be enough to comply with the recommended ITU-T QoS requirements [13].

In case of a network congestion, MP2 mapping will be applied to those packets relying on higher priorities recommendation and so, providing a higher probability to be delivered.

Table 2 shows two levels. For priority issues, where the COS is equal to 6 for example, traffic of higher importance will be mapped as more sensible to delay, jitter and packet loss.

For other types of network traffic sharing the same bandwidth, such as best effort, a MP1 mapping will be used.

6   The TestBed

The environment of development and chosen test is based on personal computers (PC) with the operational system Windows, configured with applications to generate traffic (called PC1, PC2, PC3 and PC4). Moreover, the architecture is composed for equipment such as switches and routers that will be shown in Figure 3.

An item of great importance in any system of quality test, is the traffic generator software, that must be capable to generate traffics with Internet flows characteristics and with support for QoS. These components are computers PC1, PC2 and PC4.

The receiving application will have to be capable of receiving the packets with no delay, so that the receiving interval of time does not affect the final results.

It will also have, to allow the attainment of statisticians who make possible the performance evaluation of the network, with respect to delay, jitter, packet loss percentage and data rate reception (throughput), PC3 being responsible for executing this function.

The network 1 is composed of two personal computers (PC1 and PC2), plugged in proper switch and router. The computers are connected to an interface with 1Gbps and full-duplex connection. The router has 5 Mbps - Full-Duplex of speed connection.

In the Network 2, switches are connected by two Pre-WiMax antennas, having a speed relatively low data transmission rate (something close to 3,5 Mbps Half-Duplex). It is important to say that all these values are difficult to the found in a MetroEthernet and WiMAX network standards, since the tests are carried through a test environment and not in a real world environment.

In relation to the antennas Pre-WiMAX, it is important to detach the item of configuration of them. Initially, an equal percentage of use of band for uplink and downlink was defined, that is, 50% of use for uplink and 50% of use for downlink. Later, the maximum tax supported of traffic for uplink and downlink was defined that it is of 20000Kbps for each one. In case that the traffic is bigger of what the supported one, a size of buffer was also configured to store these packages. The size of the buffer is of 20000kbits equally for uplink and downlink.

In the antenna a scheduling algorithm was configured, its proper implemented in the hardware, to prioritize channels that will treat better, all the packages marked with priority. Of this form, all the packages marked with COS up to 3 are considered by the antenna as a traffic of low priority, and all the packages marked with COS of 4 the 7, are considered by the antenna as a traffic of high priority.

It is important, the implementation of DiffServ Model in the antennas, to differentiate the packages marked with quality of service or not. In this implementation, packages without priorities will go to be treated by the PHBs with values between 0 and 7 (MP1). For mapping MP2, the packages they will be treated by the PHBs with values between 24 and 31 and for the mapping MP3, values between 48-55. With this we apply the Model of Diffserv Service in the antennas Pre-WiMAX.

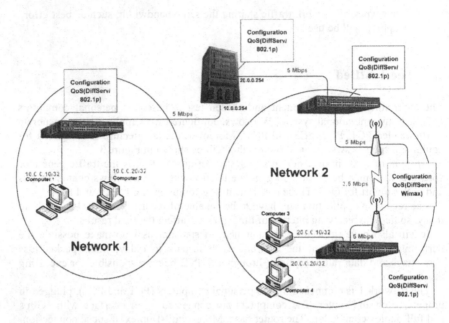

Fig. 3. Architecture of the Atmosphere of Test.

The configuration of IEEE 802.1p in the equipment is carried through in all the components that the architecture of the network composes in accordance with the service contracted for the user. Switch of network 1 will be the responsible one for marking the packages that will be generated in the network with corresponding values its priority, being the packages marked with 3 COS = referring to the model of Mapping MP2 and COS = 6 for the Model of Mapping MP3.

The others switchs will have the functionality of mapping the packages of DSCP for COS applying with this the priorities defined in the Model of Mapping. For this the ACLs was configured in the equipment the priority using (Extend Access List). Through the ACL, the packages they will be mapped of DSCP - COS and transmitted for its lines of priorities.

The Infovia Brasilia specifies up to 30 simultaneous VoIP calls. Of this form we configure the environment to support 30 simultaneous calls, that is, 30 traffics of VoIP at the same time.

Figure 4 represents the functioning of the mapping considered in the work.

In environment MP1, two standards of traffic had been defined: 1 VoIP and 1 competitor, in accordance with table 3.

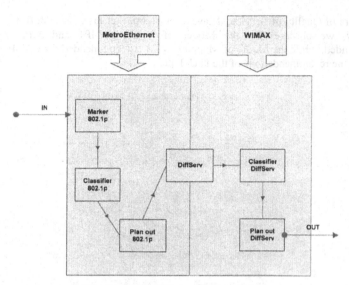

Fig. 4. Mapping 802.1p_DiffServ_Wimax.

Table 4. it shows the traffic defined for Mapping MP2. We continue with the two standards of traffic, only prioritizing the VoIP traffic.

Table 5. it shows the traffic defined for Mapping MP3. In this in case, traffic of VoIP is mapped with a higher priority.

Table 3. Flow of Traffic for MP1.

Speed	Class	Siza
64 Kbps	MP1	232 bytes
1000Kbps	MP1	1024 bytes

Table 4. Flow of Traffic for MP2.

Speed	Class	Siza
64 Kbps	MP2	232 bytes
1000Kbps	MP1	1024 bytes

Table 5. Flow of Traffic for MP3.

Speed	Class	Siza
64 Kbps	MP3	232 bytes
1000Kbps	MP1	1024 bytes

For better visualization of the Mapping, since Mapping MP1 until the Mapping MP3, figure 5, figure 6 and figure 7, compare to delay, jitter and packet loss for all types of mappings. In this visualization, we observe a significant improvement of the parameters of Quality of Service, delay, jitter and packet loss, for a VoIP traffic. In this way, we observe that the Model of Mapping MP1 and MP2 are not recommended, while the Model of Mapping MP3 is recommended for a VoIP traffic based on the recommendations of the ITU-T [13].

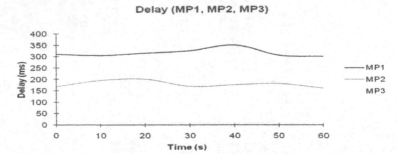

Fig. 5. Comparative of the Delay of Mapping (MP1, MP2, and MP3).

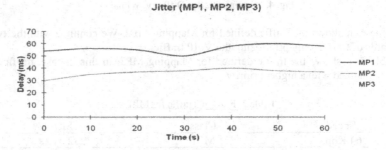

Fig. 6. Comparative of Jitter of Mapping (MP1, MP2 and MP3).

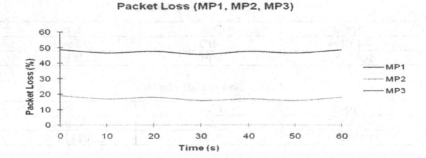

Fig. 7. Comparative of Packet Loss of Mapping (MP1, MP2 and MP3).

7   Conclusions and Future Works

In relation to the initial objective to implement a Quality of Service in a MetroEthernet and WiMAX networks, it can be said that the results were widely reached, based in the recommendations of the ITU-T. A recommendation of the Model of Mapping MP3 for the environment of the testbed can be defined to VoIP applications. With the implementation of the MP3 mapping ones can take care of higher traffic application sensible to delay, jitter and packet loss. Our implementation brought innumerable advantages for the integration of the IEEE 8021.p with the parameters of quality of service, if a transmission of VoIP of high quality has to be transmitted in the network, as proposed in this work.

Another advantage observed in this work is the integration of Diffserv as being the integrator in QoS mapping, since it is applied at the Network layer. DiffServ is much more flexible to the fact that it has great influence in the differentiation of any type of traffic service

The environment of tests, where exactly a small replica of the real world environment, called INFOVIA to build in Brasilia (Brazil) and, can be validated with all kind of QoS metric herein proposed.

In the near future, we can collect a real data information of the production environments and compare with the ones retrieved from the testbed environment.

Future works can give continuity to the improvement of the IEEE 802.16 QoS mapping and not by using a Pre-WiMAX equipment.

8   Reference

1. HAWA, M. Stochastic Evaluation of Fair Scheduling with Applications to Quality-of-Service in Broadband Wireless Access Networks. PhD's Thesis. Thesis University of Kansas. August 2003.

2. HAWA, M.; DAVID, W. Quality of Service Scheduling in Cable and Broadband Wireless Access Systems. In: Tenth International Workshop on Quality ofvService (IWQoS 2002). Miami, Florida, May 2002, pp. 247-255.

3. IEEE Std 802.16.2-2003. IEEE Standard for Local and metropolitan area networks. Part 16: Air Interface for Fixed Broadband Wireless Access Systems – Amendment 2: Medium Access Control Modifications and Additional Physical Layer Specifications for 2–11 GHz (Amendment to IEEE Std 802.16-2001). April 01, 2003.

4. G. Quadros, et al. "A QoS Metric for Packet Networks", in Proceedings of SPIE International Symposium on Voice, Video, and Data Communications Conference, Boston, USA, 1-5 Novembro, 1998.

5. G. Quadros, et al. "Measuring Quality of Service in Packet Networks", in Proceedings of the 2nd Conference on Telecommunications, Instituto de Telecomunicações (Portugal), Sesimbra, Portugal, 15-16 Abril, 1999.

6. QUADROS, et al. "Approach to the Dynamic Forwarding of Packets in a Differentiated Service Based Router", in Proceedings of SPIES Symposium on Voice, Video, and Data Communications conference on Quality of Service Issues Related to Internet II, Boston, USA, 19-22 Setembro, 1999.

7. QUADROS, et al. "An Approach to Support Traffic Classes in IP Networks", in Proceedings of QofIS'2000 - The First International Workshop on Quality of future Internet Services, Berlin, Germany, 25-26 Setembro, 2000.

8. QUADROS, et al. "The Role of Packet-dropping Mechanisms in QoS Differentiation", in Proceedings of ICON'2000 - IEEE International Conferences on Networks, National University of Singapore, Singapura, 05-08Setembro, 2000.

9. BRESLAU, et al. "Endpoint Admission Control: Architectural Issues and Performance", in Proceedings of ACM SIGCOM 2000, Stockolm, Suécia, Agosto, 2000.

10. ELECK,et al. "Admission Control Based on End-to-End Measurements", in Proceedings of IEEE INFOCOM 2000, Tel Aviv, Israel, Março, 2000.

11. BIANCHI, et al. A migration Path to provide End-to-End QoS over Stateless networks by Means of a probing-driven Admission Control, Internet Draft, draft-bianchi-blefari-end-toend-qos-01.txt, Julho, 2001.

12. HEINANEN, J. et al. "Assured Forwarding PHB Group", IETF RFC 2597, June 1999.

13. Internation Telecommunication Union – ITU, Recomendações G.711, G.723.1, G.726, G.728, G.729. Acesso em 14/06/2007. http://www.itu.int.

14. RFC 2998 - A Framework for Integrated Services Operation over Diffserv Networks. Acesso em 01/04/2007. http://www.faqs.org/rfcs/rfc2998.html.

15. IEEE 802.1 P,Q - QoS on the MAC level. Acesso em 02/05/2007. http://www.tml.tkk.fi/Opinnot/Tik110.551/1999/papers/08IEEE802.1QosIn MAC/qos.html.

16. A Bridging between IEEE 802.1Q VLANS. Acesso em 10/08/2007. http://www.cisco.com/univercd/cc/td/doc/product/software/ios121/121newft/121t/121t3/dtbridge.htm#xtocid114535

17. UBIK, S., VOJTECH, J. QoS in Layer 2 Networks with Cisco Catalyst 3550. CESNET Technical Report 3/2003. April 20, 2003.

18. DELICADO, j., BARBOSA, L.O., DELICADO, F., CUENCA, P. A QoS-aware protocol architecture for WiMAX. IEEE CCECCE/CCGEI, Ottawa, May 2006.

19. ALAVI, H.S., MOJDEH, M., YSZDANI, N. A Quality of Service Architecture for IEEE 802.16 Standards. Conference on Communications, Perth, Western Austraia, 3-5 October 2005.

A Mobility Model for Personal Networks (PN)

Yanying Gu, R. Venkatesha Prasad, Ignas Niemegeers

Center for Wireless and Personal Communication (CWPC),

Delft University of Technology, Delft, The Netherlands

Email:{y.gu, vprasad, I,niemegeers}@ewi.tudelft.nl

Abstract— Being highly user-centric, Personal Networks (PN) enable interconnection between various devices of a user (personal devices) in different geographic locations, such as home, office, car, etc., to form one secure network for the user. In this paper we analyze properties of node mobility in PNs first. We address typical PN scenarios where personal devices in the vicinity naturally form a small cluster and move in groups to support the demands of a user. Based on the PN mobility properties studied on the basis of the scenarios, a PN Mobility Model (PNMM) is proposed. PNMM can be used to evaluate the techniques and protocols designed for PN implementations. We evaluate PNMM, compare it with other mobility models, and show that PNMM applies better than other models with respect to the behaviors of nodes in PNs. Moreover, to evaluate mobility models some evaluation methods have been proposed to examine to what degree mobility model can represent the properties of a certain scenario. This includes node mobility, heterogeneity, relative node mobility in a group, and dynamics of group merge and split

Keywords—Personal Network (PN), ad hoc network, PN Mobility Model

1 Introduction

With the aim of supporting the future needs of a person, a Personal Network (PN) [1] [2] - shown in Fig. 1- interconnects all the devices belonging to a person to form a private and secure network. Thus a user can freely and safely use all his/her communicating and computing devices called personal nodes, and access personal or public services through them. All these personal nodes in PNs may be equipped with one or more communication technologies, such as WPAN, WLAN, UMTS networks, etc. And personal devices are separately involved in various networks using different kinds of communication technologies. By integrating all the personal nodes a PN should be designed to minimize the interference and take advantage of the coexistences of these existing technologies. As shown in Fig. 1, a Personal Area Network (PAN) includes all the devices within a range of a few meters around a person, whereas, a PN extends the range of a PAN beyond this boundary giving it a global scope. Personal nodes in different places, such as home, office,

Please use the following format when citing this chapter:

Gu, Y., Prasad, R. V., Niemegeers, I., 2008, in IFIP International Federation for Information Processing, Volume 265, Advances in Ad Hoc Networking, eds. Cuenca, P., Guerrero C., Puigjaner, R., Serra, B., (Boston: Springer), pp. 13-24.

14

vehicle, class room, etc., are covered by a PN. Thus personal nodes with different wired or wireless technologies in the same or different places should cooperate with each other to form one network to offer flexible personal services anywhere and at anytime. Some typical scenarios in PNs are explained in the next section to give an overview of the possible behaviors of a PN, which contain the detailed description of PN services and applications.

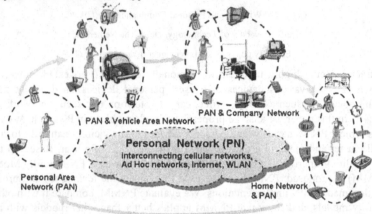

Fig. 1 Personal Network.

Since the actual mobility traces of personal nodes are not available at present, in order to evaluate the techniques and protocols designed for a PN, it is necessary to use a mobility model to describe the behavior of personal nodes in a PN as close to reality as possible. Moreover, different mobility models influence the performance of the designed protocols, and may offer entirely different results. A protocol may work well for a scenario with a particular mobility model; but perform poorly with another mobility model. Thus, a mobility model precisely representing the movement pattern of personal nodes (henceforth simply called as nodes) of a PN can predict whether the proposed techniques and protocols perform well in the future implementations.

Although some of the existing mobility models [3] can offer partial solutions to represent the behavior of mobile nodes in ad hoc networks, little has been done to model the mobility of nodes in a PN setting, especially in user-centric network which is different from simple ad hoc networks already studied in depth. A PN includes personal nodes in various wired and wireless networks, some of the nodes may never move, and others move, which makes the mobility model of a PN complex and different from the usual ad hoc network case studied in the literature [3]. Moreover, nodes naturally move in groups. For example, a person takes his/her mobile phone, PDA, laptop and some sensors on his body together which form a PAN; he/she moves from home to the work place thus these personal nodes move in a group along with the user. Unlike a group mobility model designed for particular scenarios, such as column mobility model [3], where a group of soldiers move together with less relative mobility inside a group, because they move along a given line and in one direction, a PN has a dynamic relative mobility within a group of nodes. For instance, a user may put his/her MP3 player in his/her left or right pocket, which makes a dynamic relative mobility between the MP3 player and his/her other personal devices. The behavior of nodes in a PN is different from the scenarios that have been already modeled [2]. Thus, a new mobility model specifically for PNs is indeed needed for the evaluation of PN protocols [1].

In this paper, we attempt to capture the various mobility aspects of PN nodes. The model evolved here would be useful in studying the PNs and studying its impact, usefulness and the pitfalls of the existing ideas of PN design. The remainder of this paper is organized as follows. In Section 2 we explain the requirements of a PN mobility model which are based on various PN scenarios and use cases. In Section 3 some existing mobility models are introduced and compared with the PN mobility model requirements to show the differences between them. In Section 4 the descriptions of the PN mobility model (PNMM) are highlighted. Section 5 also offers explanations of various evaluation results of the proposed PN mobility model and other existing mobility models. Finally, Section 6 summarizes our work with conclusions including the contributions and performance improvements of PN mobility model.

2 From PN Scenarios to PN Mobility Model Requirements

A mobility model for a PN should capture the features of the movement of nodes in a PN. Since PN is a user-centric design to support personal applications in various scenarios, personal services for different persons are to be defined first. In this section, we describe some PN services and applications for various scenarios, and from which we draw a picture of the nodes' mobility in a PN, and get the requirements for PN mobility model. Some of the use cases are as follows:

- A health-monitoring application:

Monitoring the health condition of a disabled or an elderly person is a potential personal service in a PN, which can collect useful data not only for emergency situations, but also for daily health monitoring and maintenance. Thus a PN incorporates sensing and actuating devices linked to a health-monitoring server at home. Some sensing devices are installed in various places at home to collect raw data for health applications. The user takes some wearable devices with him/her, which move together with the user. Thus we can draw the first PN mobility model requirement, which is the heterogeneous mobility nature of nodes: *some personal nodes never move, and some can move.*

While a person moves from room to room, some wearable and mobile devices moves in a group with him/her for the purpose of monitoring the user and support health applications. Thus we get another PN mobility model requirement: *person-*

al devices cooperate to support the demands of a user, they are not independent, and usually move in groups.

- Business environment

Considering the physical environment of a person, e.g., his/her home, office, car, etc., a person has some groups of personal devices in different places. A businessperson has a number of personal devices in different places for his/her social and private needs. While the businessperson, with his/her PANs, moves in these places, the number of personal devices in each place varies. Thus we conclude the third PN mobility model requirement: *the number of personal nodes in each group is not fixed.* In addition, the coverage areas of these places are also different. For example, the coverage areas of a room and a car are different. When personal nodes move in these places, they may cover the whole area to support the users. Thus the area covered by a group of personal nodes, such as an office, a vehicle, a bedroom, etc., is called group coverage area in this paper. So the fourth PN mobility model requirement is: *the coverage area of each group is not fixed, and we can set a maximum value.*

As the businessperson leaves his/her office and enters his/her car. Some personal devices are left in the office; other personal devices are carried by the person who moves into the coverage area of the on-broad car network. So the fifth PN mobility model requirement is: *group of nodes split.* When the person moves to his/her car, while he/she is making a conference call using his/her PDA, then the PN can enable the conference call seamlessly handing over to the on-broad car network, where on-board speakers, microphones and the PDA are used together to offer the conference call service. Thus the group of devices around the person and the group of personal devices in his/her car merge. The sixth PN mobility model requirement is: *two groups of personal nodes can merge into one group.*

- A remote babysitting application:

In the case of a mother visiting a friend's house her sleeping baby should be tracked. A PN can be designed for her need, thus she can divide her personal nodes into various groups according to the demands. For this application the mother can decide her nodes into two groups: one group is in the room monitoring her baby; and the other group of nodes carried by her to display the tracking data of her baby. Thus we get the seventh PN mobility model requirement: *the number of groups of personal nodes can be pre-set.* When the mother moves from her house to her friend's house by her car, the velocity of the group of personal devices in the car is dynamic and limited within a maximum value, because the vehicle velocity in a city is limited. So the eighth PN mobility model requirement is: *the group velocity is same for the member nodes, and can be limited by a maximum value.* After an hour, the mother comes back to home, and her baby is awake. At home, the two groups merge into one. The mother does housework and moves between different rooms; at the same time, she needs to keep her eyes on her baby and uses the baby monitoring service. Thus, the nodes carried by the mother and the devices near the baby should work together to support the baby monitoring service. And the devices move together with the mother have relative mobility with respect to other devices near the baby. Thus we can conclude the last PN mobility model requirement: *the personal devices included in the same group can have relative mobility with each other.*

Table 1 PN Mobility Requirements.

	Requirements
1	The mobility heterogeneity of personal nodes: some personal nodes never move, some can move
2	Personal devices cooperate to support the demands of a user, they are not independent, and usually move in groups.
3	The number of personal nodes in each group is not fixed.
4	The coverage area of each group is not fixed, and we can set a maximum value.
5	Group of nodes split.
6	Two groups of personal nodes can merge into one group.
7	The number of groups of personal nodes can be pre-set.
8	The group velocity is same for the member nodes, and can be limited by a maximum value.
9	The personal devices included in the same group can have relative mobility with each other.

Based on these examples of user scenarios, we conclude nine PN mobility model requirements, which are listed in the Table 1.

3 Related Work

In this section, we introduce some existing mobility models, and examine whether they can be used to model mobility in PNs.

- Random walk mobility model [4]:

Random walk mobility model is a simple mobility model developed to present the wandering movement of nodes. In this model, a mobile node randomly chooses a direction θ in the range $[0, 2\pi]$ and a speed in a pre-defined range $[V_{min}, V_{max}]$. A mobile node chooses a new direction and a new speed after traveling constantly for a time t.

- Random waypoint mobility model [5]:

Random waypoint mobility model is the most commonly used by researchers for simulating ad hoc networks with mobility. In this model, a mobile node travels towards a randomly chosen destination with randomly chosen speed in the range of $[V_{min}, V_{max}]$. After the node reaching the destination, it stops for a duration, and repeat the process again.

- Random direction mobility model [6]:

Similar to the random walk mobility model, a mobile node in this model chooses a random angular direction and a random speed. The difference is that a mobile node needs to travel to the edge of the simulation area, and then it can change direction and speed. The above three mobility models assume all the nodes are independent. Thus these mobility models do not meet most of the PN mobility requirements.

- Reference point group mobility model (RPGM) [7]:

Reference point group mobility model gives a solution to modeling group mobility. In this model, the movement of a group is represented by the logical center of the group moving along a series of pre-defined check points. However, this model assumes a group of nodes always move together, which does not meet the PN mobility model requirement 5 and 6.

- Reference region group mobility model (RRGM) [8]:

Reference region group mobility model defines a reference region as a destination to which a group of mobile nodes move. If a mobile node arrives at the reference region, it waits for the other mobile nodes to arrive. However, PN scenarios explained in the last section are different from the scenarios considered in RRGM. A group of personal nodes in PNs should have to move together to satisfy the need of a user at the same time. Thus the RRGM is not suitable for PNs.

Different mobility models typically focus on a specific scenario. Although some mobility models can meet part of the PN mobility requirements, none of them meets all the requirements. Thus a new mobility model for PNs is needed.

4 PN Mobility Model

A PN mobility model (PNMM) is explained in the following steps, and principles to meet each PN mobility model requirement (R1-R9) are highlighted.

- Step 1: Initialization

In order to meet R1, there are some non-moving nodes, and their positions are chosen randomly in the simulation area. To meet R3, each mobile node randomly selects one of M groups, where M is the mean value of the maximum and minimum number of groups (X and Y). In fact, setting a minimum and maximum limit is for practical reasons. That is PNs have limited number of devices and usually they have at least 1 to 3 groups (Home, office and car group). Each group covers a circular region with the center chosen randomly in the simulation area and a radius chosen randomly in the range of $[0, R_{max}]$, which satisfies R4. And the location of a node is chosen randomly in its group coverage area.

- Step 2: Movement of a group

In each time interval α, a group destination area is selected, to which a group moves. The center of the destination area is chosen randomly, which can be reached within a maximum value V_g meeting R8. The radius of the destination area is selected randomly and satisfies the rules explained in Step 1. For each node in the group, it randomly selects a point in the group destination area, and then moves towards it with a constant velocity. Thus all the nodes in a group move together at the same time, which meets R3. Moreover, the nodes in the same group have relative random mobility, because their position is re-chosen randomly inside the group coverage area in each time interval α, which meets R9.

- Step 3: Group merging

To meet R6, group merging is planned in each time interval $c \times \alpha$. When $c = 1$, the group merge interval is as the same as the group movement interval α. If two groups can reach each other within the maximum velocity V_g in a time interval α, they can merge into one group with the center randomly chosen in the area, where these two groups can arrive. To meet R7, the methods controlling the number of groups bigger than Y are given: if $n_{mp}^{(t)}$ pairs of groups can be merged, the maximum number of merged group pairs is m, where $m = Min\left(n_{mp}^{(t)}, \left(n_g^{(t)} - Y\right)\right)$, and $n_g^{(t)}$ is the group number. Thus the number of merged group pairs is chosen randomly in the range of $[0, m]$.

- Step 4: Group division

To meet R5, the group division is considered in every time interval $d \times \alpha$. When $d = 1$, the group merge interval is as the same as the group movement interval α. A group can be divided into two groups. The destination areas of the two groups should be chosen in the same way as described in Step 2. Each node in the original group can randomly choose one of the two groups. To control the number of groups smaller than X and meet R7, the number of divided groups is randomly chosen in the range $[0, (X - n_g^{(t)})]$.

- Step 5: Group merging and dividing at the same time

For a group chosen to be both merged and divided, the division is considered first. Some nodes chosen randomly move to another group (following Step 4). Other nodes undergo merging (following Step 3).

5 Evaluation

In this section, we evaluate mobility models with respect to the requirements of PNs. We divide the nine PN mobility model requirements into four categories, which describe different properties of node mobility in PNs: (1) the heterogeneity of node mobility (Requirement 1); (2) group mobility & node mobility inside a group (Requirements 2, 4, 8, 9); (3) group merging & dividing (Requirements 5,

6); (4) group numbers & number of nodes in each group (Requirements 3, 7). For each category, we discuss and compare the existing mobility models and our PNMM.

- The heterogeneity of node mobility:

Because nodes are equipped with different technologies, including different types of networks, and used for different kinds of applications for a user, heterogeneity is a key property in PNs. Personal nodes have heterogeneous mobility types as described in Section 2. In order to evaluate the heterogeneity of node mobility, we define a *Mobility Heterogeneity Value (MHV)*. Assume all the nodes considered have n levels of mobility; in each level, nodes have the same mean velocity v; the percentage of number of nodes in each level is q. Thus the mean velocity of all the nodes, $\overline{V}$, is

$$\overline{V} = \frac{1}{n}\sum_{i=1}^{n} v_i q_i \tag{1}$$

And *Mobility Heterogeneity Value (MHV)* is

$$MHV = \sum_{i=1}^{n} [(\overline{V} - v_i)^2 \times q_i] \tag{2}$$

A higher value of *MHV* means high node mobility heterogeneity.

For all the existing mobility models introduced in Section 3, their *MHV* are zero, because every node has the same maximum velocity; there is no velocity difference among the nodes. For our proposed PN mobility model, we separate all the personal nodes into two kinds: 'never move', n_s, and 'can move', n_m. Thus the $\overline{V}$ and *MHV* of the (PNMM) is

$$\overline{V}_{PNMM} = \frac{1}{2} \times \left(\frac{V_g}{2}\right) \times \left(\frac{n_m}{N}\right) \tag{3}$$

$$MHV_{PNMM} = \left(\overline{V}_{PNMM} - \frac{V_g}{2}\right)^2 \times \left(\frac{n_m}{N}\right) \tag{4}$$

Thus the node *mobility heterogeneity value (MHV)* of PNMM is higher than any other mobility model.

- Group mobility and node mobility inside a group:

Based on the PN mobility model requirement 2, 4, 8, 9, the mobility of groups of personal nodes and the mobility of nodes in each group should be represented. For the mobility of groups, in reference point group mobility model (RPGM), each group can freely move inside the considered area. However, in reference region group mobility model (RRGM), a group has a pre-specified destination area then the group moves to the destination along a curved route, because RRGM models *search or rescue* scenarios with groups of persons. In our proposed PN mobility model, random movement of groups can be modeled by randomly choosing the destination area of each group at every time interval α.

To meet the PN mobility model Requirement 9, nodes inside a group should have relative mobility. We define a *Relative Mobility in Group (RMG)*, δ to describe the relative mobility level of personal nodes in a moving group. Firstly, the *Average Possible Coverage Area of a Node (APCAN)* of node j, κ_j^N is defined as the total area, in which a node in a group may possibly reach, at any moment during the simulation time period. We define the *Average Possible Coverage Area of a Group (APCAG)*, κ^G as the total possible reachable area, in which all the nodes in a group move at any moment during the simulation time period. Assume n nodes are considered in a group then *RMG* is defined as

$$\delta = \left(\frac{1}{n \times \kappa^G} \right) \times \sum_{i=1}^{n} \kappa_j^N \tag{5}$$

With a bigger *APCAN* of every node in a group with respect to the *APCAG*, the relative mobility of nodes in that group is higher.

To compare the performance of relative mobility of nodes in a group, we calculate *RMG*, δ of RPGM, RRGM and our PNMM. We assume one group of n nodes, with the maximum group velocity V_g. In RPGM [7], there are n reference points (RP) for every node in a group. Each node can move randomly in the circular area with a specified radius with respect to its RP. Thus $\kappa_j^N \leq \kappa^G$, only then all the RPs of n nodes is the same, $\kappa_j^N = \kappa^G$ thus $\delta_{RPGM} \leq 1$. In RRGM [8] we assume the destination area of a group is κ^{Gd} and $\kappa_j^N = \kappa^{Gd}$. However, *APCAG* of RRGM is bigger than the destination area of a group, $\kappa^G \geq \kappa^{Gd}$, because each node in the group moves with a different velocity, when one node with a higher velocity arrives at the group destination area first, while another node with a lower velocity may still be moving towards the destination area. Thus $\delta_{RRGM} \leq 1$. In PNMM, since a node can randomly choose its location in the destination area of the group, $\kappa_j^N = \kappa^G$, and $\delta_{PNMM} = 1$. PNMM has the highest relative node mobility inside a group.

- Group merging & division

As explained in Section 2, in some PN scenarios, a group of personal nodes are divided into two groups, and two groups of personal nodes merge into one group. There are only two mobility models that can present the behavior of group merging and division, which are RRGM and our proposed PNMM. In RRGM, two groups can merge, if they meet two requirements: (1) they are small groups with a few nodes in each group; (2) the groups have paused at the destination for a pre-defined period of time. These two requirements are not suitable for the PN scenarios. Thus the cluster merge rules of RRGM can not be used in PNs.

In PNMM, group merging and division is performed randomly amongst all the groups. To show the dynamics of group merging and division from the view of each individual node, we define *Node Change Rate (NCR)* as the rate of number of nodes that join or leave a group. If the total simulation time is T, the time interval to plan group merge and division is α (we consider $c = d = 1$ in the evaluation part), there are m time slots considered, where $m = T/\alpha$, and $n_{md,i}$ represents the number of nodes that join or leave a group in the ith time interval.

$$NCR = \frac{\sum_{i=1}^{m}(n_{md,i}/\alpha)}{m} \tag{6}$$

Based on the rules of group merging and division as described in Section 4, the *NCR* of PNMM is,

$$NCR_{PNMM} = \frac{3N}{2}\left(\frac{X-Y}{X+Y}\right) \tag{7}$$

- Group numbers & number of nodes in each group

Since a PN belongs to a user and carry out the demands of the user, the user can organize his/her devices in a number of groups for his/her convenience. The number of groups can be decided by the user, and these groups can merge and separate, which results in the number of groups varying in the range of $[Y, X]$. Based on the rules of determining the number of pairs of groups to be merged, $n_m^{(t)}$, and the number of group pairs to be divided, $n_d^{(t)}$, the number of groups in PNMM is controlled and is in the range of $[Y, X]$. However, none of the other mobility model can give a solution of controlling the number of groups.

For the number of nodes in each group, in RPGM and RRGM, it should be pre-specified for each group. In PNMM, a node can randomly choose a group, thus for each case, the number of nodes in each group in a PN is different, which show the heterogeneity of the sizes of groups in PN and is suitable for PN scenarios explained in Section 2.

Based on the above evaluation, PNMM proves to be the best fit for R1-R9. However, in the current literature, ad hoc mobility models have been used in the evaluation of various protocols. The mobility in ad hoc networks offer an independent and random movement for each mobile node, while the mobility in PNs focuses mainly the heterogeneity in node movement and random group mobility. Because of these unique PN mobility properties, which are different from ad hoc networks, protocols and techniques proposed for PNs should be evaluated by PNMM to examine whether they work well in PNs.

6 Conclusion and Future Work

To model the node mobility in PN, the behaviors of the personal nodes are analyzed, and the desirable properties of PN node mobility are summarized as PN mobility model requirements in this paper. Based on nine PN mobility model requirements, PNMM is designed: it has high heterogeneity of node mobility; it enables group mobility and dynamic node mobility inside a group; it models group merging and division; it can control the number of groups; and it organizes groups with different number of nodes in each group. Another contribution in this paper is that we propose some mobility modeling evaluation methods: a *Mobility Heterogeneity Value (HMV)* for comparing the heterogeneity of node mobility, a *Relative Mobility in Group (RMG)* to present the relative mobility level of nodes in a moving group, and a *Node Change Rate (NCR)* to show the dynamics of group merging and division from the view of each individual node. These evaluation methods give a way of evaluating mobility models to test how realistic they can describe the mobility properties in the real situations.

The proposed PNMM can be used to evaluate the protocols and techniques designed for PNs, such as self-organization protocols [9], clustering protocols [10], context awareness [11], service discovery and management [12], network mobility (NEMO) [13] management protocols, etc. These protocols and techniques can be tested by using our PNMM to examine whether they can work well in PNs. Moreover, by considering the unique properties of mobility in PNs, the protocols and techniques designed for PNs should be equipped with some special mechanisms to fit the PN scenarios.

Additional work must still be done to deeply analyze the influence of the environments on the mobility for PNs, such as collision avoidance, congestion avoidance [14], etc. Moreover, PNs contains devices involved in different types of networks, such as UMTS, ad hoc networks, sensor networks [15], etc. The particular behaviors of personal devices in these networks should be considered in the future work of mobility modeling for PNs. For example, swarm behaviors [16] of devices in mobile sensor networks should be investigated to address the details of personal nodes mobility in PNs.

Acknowledgment

This work is partially funded by the EU IST MAGNET Beyond Project and the Dutch Freeband PNP2008 Project.

References

[1] Niemegeers, I., & Heemstra de Groot, S., (2003). Research issues in ad-hoc distributed personal networking. *Wireless Personal Communications*, 26(2), 149–167.

[2] Lu, L., et al. (2005). D1.2 Initial Architecture of Personal Networks. *IOP GenCom Project QoS for Personal Network at Home Deliverable.*

[3] Camp, T., Boleng, J., Davies, V., (2002). A Survey of Mobility Models for Ad Hoc Network Research. *Wireless Communication & Mobile Computing (WCMC)*, 2(5), 483-502.

[4] Sanchez, M., Manzoni, P., (2001). A java based simulator for ad-hoc network. *Future Generation Computer Systems*, 573-583.

[5] Johnson, D., Maltz, D., (1996). Dynamic source routing in ad hoc networks. *Mobile Computing*, 153-181.

[6] Royer, E., Melliar-Smith, P.M., Moser, L., (2001). An analysis of the optimum node density for ad hoc mobile networks. *IEEE International Conference on Communications.*

[7] Hong, X., Gerla, M., Chiang, C., (1999). A group mobility model for ad hoc wireless networks. *ACM International Workshop on Modeling and Simulation of Wireless and Mobile Systems (MSWiM).*

[8] Ng, J.M., Zhang, Y., (2005). Reference Region Group Mobility Model for Ad Hoc Networks. *Wireless and Optical Communications Networks (WOCN).*

[9] Lu, W., Gu, Y., Prasad, R.V., Lo, A., Niemegeers, I., (2007). A Self-organized Personal Network Architecture. *3rd International Conference on Networking and Services (ICNS'07).*

[10] Gu, Y., Lu, W., Prasad, R.V., Lo, A., Niemegeers, I., (2007). Clustering for Ad Hoc Personal Network Formation. *International Conference on Computational Science (ICCS).*

[11] Sanchez, L., Lanza, J., Olsen, R., Bauer, M., Girod-Genet, M., (2005). A Generic Context Management Framework for Personal Networking Environments. *3rd Annual International Conference on Mobile and Ubiquitous Systems.*

[12] Stephen, H., & Aruna, S., (2006). Service Composition for Mobile Personal Networks. *3rd Annual International Conference on Mobile and Ubiquitous Systems.*

[13] Devarapalli, V., Wakikawa, R., Petrescu, A., Thubert, P., (2005). RFC 3963: Network Mobility (NEMO) Basic Support Protocol. IETF, NEMO Working Group, January.

[14] Williams, S., & Huang, D., (2006). A group force mobility model. *9th Communications and Networking Simulation Symposium.*

[15] Ren, H., & Meng, H., (2006). Understanding the Mobility Model of Wireless Body Sensor Networks. *IEEE International Conference on Information Acquisition.*

[16] Anthony, B., Lamont, G.B., (2002). A particle swarm model for swarm-based networked sensor systems. *ACM Symposium on Applied Computing.*

Replicated Random Walks for Service Advertising in Unstructured Environments

Dimitris Kogias, Konstantinos Oikonomou, and Ioannis Stavrakakis

Abstract Service advertisement is a key design issue in modern dynamic and large-scale networking environments such as unstructured peer-to-peer networks. The intrinsic capability of a *single random walker* of *stretching* the information dissemination over widely spread network areas (compared to *flooding*), is explored and exploited in this paper, along with the introduction of random walkers which can *replicate* themselves. Two *replication policies* are also introduced in this paper: the *Topology Independent Policy* that creates replicas according to an exponentially decreasing probability (creating more replicas at the beginning of the advertising process), and the *Topology Dependent Policy* in which replication decisions are based on some locally available topological information (aiming at creating replicas at the dense network areas). The discussion and the results in this paper reveal intrinsic comparative properties of flooding and the single random walker, as well as the advantages that the random walker replication can bring in improving the overhead, speed and coverage of the advertising process.

Acknowledgements This work has been supported in part by the project ANA (Autonomic Network Architecture) (IST-27489), the PENED 2003 program of the General Secretariat for Research and Technology (GSRT) co-financed by the European Social Funds (75%) and by national sources (25%) and the NoE CONTENT (IST-384239).

Dimitris Kogias · Ioannis Stavrakakis
National And Kapodistrian
University of Athens, Department of Informatics & Telecommunications
Panepistimiopolis, Ilissia 15 784, Athens, Greece
Tel: +30 210 7275315, Fax: +30 210 7275333
e-mail: {dimkog, ioannis}@di.uoa.gr

Kostantinos Oikonomou
Ionian University
Department of Informatics
Corfu, Greece
e-mail: okon@ionio.gr

Please use the following format when citing this chapter:

Kogias, D., Oikonomou, K., Stavrakakis, I., 2008, in IFIP International Federation for Information Processing, Volume 265, Advances in Ad Hoc Networking, eds. Cuenca, P., Guerrero C., Puigjaner, R., Serra, B., (Boston: Springer), pp. 25-36.

1 Introduction and Motivation

The evolution of the *Peer-to-Peer* (P2P) networks has attracted a great deal of attention lately, becoming an environment suitable for numerous networked services (e.g. file or service sharing) mostly due to their low cost sharing of these services. These environments are highly dynamic and of large scale since a great number of users join and leave the network at any time, exchanging a large amount of data and sharing a huge number of services/files. *Unstructured* P2P networks, e.g. Gnutella, [1], have become popular, mostly because they are easily formed without the need for any sophisticated configuration methods. These environments present some major design challenges due to the aforementioned lack of structure. One key challenge (that is actually the focus of this paper) is *service discovery*. That is, the design of the mechanism that allows user nodes to *discover* the *service location* or, equivalently, the location of a *service node* (i.e., the node that hosts a particular service).

The effectiveness or the required intensity of a service discovery mechanism depends strongly on the service location information availability within the network. If only the service node knows about the service location, then the service discovery mechanism should launch a service location search process that will need to "hit" the service node itself in order to retrieve the service location information. If, on the other hand, more nodes in the network are aware of the service location, then the *service searching* task during the service discovery can be less intense or more effective (e.g., time-wise), as it would be sufficient for the searching agent (or packet) to hit one of the (more than one) nodes that possess the service location information. Informing other than the service node of the location of the service is the function of the *service advertising* process or mechanism that basically disseminates the service location in the network.

At the end of a service advertising process a number of network nodes becomes aware of the service location. This set of (informed) nodes will be referred to here as the *advertising network* that has been generated by the specific advertising process. It is important to emphasize that the effectiveness or efficiency of the service discovery process will depend not only on the size of the advertising network but also on its *stretch*; loosely speaking (to be defined in a specific way later), the stretch of an advertising network would reflect how spread out within the network are the nodes of the advertising network. It would, also, reflect the distance in hops of an average network node (which could decide to search for the service location and look for a node of the advertising network) from the advertising network (the smaller the distance the larger the stretch). Between two advertising networks with the same number of nodes, the one with the larger stretch would be considered to be more effective than the one that generated the advertising network of smaller stretch.

The focus on this paper is to explore service advertising (or information dissemination, in general) schemes for unstructured, large scale networks. More specifically, this paper investigates the effectiveness of (multiple) random walkers or *agents* in spreading the service location information effectively, with respect to certain criteria to be introduced later. One way to carry out service advertising is through traditional *flooding*, e.g., [2], [3]. In this case, the advertising network is the entire network (largest coverage possible) and the *advertising network completion time* is small (upper bounded by the network diameter); on the negative side, though, flooding induces large message overhead. To reduce the large message overhead of traditional flooding, *probabilistic flooding* (where a message is forwarded with some probability less than 1) can be employed , [4], [5], [6], [7], [8], [9]. This scheme is capable of reducing the number of messages, at the expense of some increase in the advertising network completion time and possible decrease in the size of the advertising network, compared to (traditional) flooding, [6]. Another way to reduce the overhead of the traditional flooding is through *controlled flooding*, where the advertisement is confined to an area of some (predefined) number of hops (say K) away from the service node; if K is very large this scheme approaches the traditional flooding.

A very different - from flooding – approach to implementing service advertising is through the employment of a *single random walker*, e.g. [10], [11], [12]. Under this approach, a single agent moves randomly in the network informing the network nodes on its path about the service location. As it will be discussed later, this approach tends to create advertising networks of typically larger stretch than those generated by some equivalent (in terms of overhead) flooding approach. On the other hand, completion time is higher (equal to the number of messages).

Flooding and single random walker can be viewed as two rather "extreme" dissemination approaches. For example, when the amount of affordable messages in the network (denoted as H) - to be viewed also as the amount of the "advertising budget" – is large (larger than the number of network links), flooding is the best choice (the advertising network is the entire network with small completion time), as opposed to the single random walker. On the other hand, when H is relatively small, a single random walker is expected to create advertising networks of larger stretch than under flooding at the expense of larger completion time.

This good performance of flooding for a large advertising budget, as discussed above, may be attributed to the large number of "agents" that work in parallel and independently in order to create the advertising network. On the other hand, only one agent undertakes the task of creating the advertising network under the single random walker approach, which makes the creation slow; furthermore, it does not facilitate the wider spreading of the coverage (that could materialize due to the large advertising budget), as it would need to be implemented through one agent only in a sequential manner.

The introduction of "multiple" random walker approaches could enhance the performance of single random walker, in the sense that the size, the stretch and the completion time of an advertising network could be improved. To this end, the idea of *agent replication* is introduced in this paper that allows an agent, moving in the network according to the random walker paradigm, to create a replica or a *child* of itself. The introduction of a new agent in the network is expected to cover (probabilistically) a different area (by initiating its independent path) than that of its *parent* agent. For a given advertising budget, the larger the number of agents generated, the smaller their individual advertising budget would be, since it would be a portion of the original and the coverage would be limited to nearby areas only. Consequently, the effective number of replicas should depend on the total advertising budget and increase with it. Clearly, the employed *agent replication policy* shapes accordingly the resulting advertising network and its completion time.

In view of the above discussion, a replication policy, to be referred to hereafter as *Topology Independent Policy* or *TI-Policy*, is proposed in this paper under which agent replication takes place according to some probability that decreases exponentially after each replication. When the initial value p of this probability is relatively large, it would create replicas relatively soon; the exponential decrease ensures, though, that replications will be rare afterwards, thus allowing agents to move for some time and cover wider network areas. On the other, small values of probability p would result in a behavior similar to the single random walker case.

Another replication policy that would make sense could be one that creates replicas in the *dense* network areas (i.e., network areas of nodes with relatively high number of neighbor nodes). In such areas it is reasonable to assume that new agents are more likely to follow a different "network direction" compared to that of their parent agent, thus potentially increasing the stretch and size of the coverage area. On the other hand, in less dense network areas, replication should be avoided since it is likely to result in an (undesired) "overlapping" of the covered network areas by different agents. To this end, the *Topology Dependent Policy* or *TD-Policy* is also presented in this paper.

The performance of the proposed algorithms is evaluated through simulations and compared to that of single random walker and flooding. It is shown that, as long as advertising budget H is not extremely high (in which case flooding should be employed) or low (in which case single random walker should be employed), there is a range of values for q and p for which the proposed policies are capable of covering a certain part of the network faster (i.e., smaller completion time) and more efficiently (i.e., stretched).

For the rest of the paper, a formal definition of the network system is given in Section 2. The proposed replication policies are described in Section 3 and simulation results are presented in Section 4. Finally, a summary and the conclusions can be found in Section 5.

2 System Definition

Let the undirected connected graph $G(V, E)$ represent a network with a certain set of nodes V and a set of bidirectional edges E among nodes. Let $d(u, v)$ denote the number of hops over a shortest path between node u and node v; obviously, $d(u, u) = 0$. Let S_u denote the set of neighbor nodes of node u. Let $|X|$ denote the number of elements or size of a particular set X. The number of nodes $|V|$ in the network will also be noted as N ($N = |V|$).

The service location node, denoted by s, is the initiator of the associated service advertising process aiming at disseminating service location information over a subset E_a of the network links E ($E_a \subseteq E$) and eventually informing a subset V_a

of the network nodes V ($V_a \subseteq V$). The network consisting of nodes in V_a and links in E_a, denoted as $G_a(V_a, E_a)$ is the advertising network. Obviously, $G_a(V_a, E_a)$ is a connected network.

Many different advertising networks can be defined in a certain network, depending on the algorithm employed by the advertising process. The interest is to *stretch* the advertising network in order for the disseminated information to come as close as possible to all network nodes. Of course, in the exceptional case that information reaches all network nodes, the meaning of stretching becomes obsolete and no service searching is needed. In the general case, however, not all network nodes are part of the advertising network and, thus, a searching mechanism needs to be employed. A simple searching process that is assumed here, is implemented through controlled flooding of depth of L hops away from the node initiating the search. Clearly, if the advertising process is capable of creating an advertising network such that $\min d(u, v) \leq L$, for some node $u \in V$ and at least one $v \in V_a$, then the searching process of node u will be successful.

Let the *L-property* of any network node u be defined as the existence of at least one node of the advertising network in at most L hops away from the particular node u. Let *coverage* of a particular advertising process for a certain L, denoted as $C(L)$, be defined as the proportion (%) of the network nodes for which the L-property is satisfied. For two different advertising networks (e.g., $G_a(V_a, E_a)$ and $G'_a(V'_a, E'_a)$) of the same number of nodes ($V_a \neq V'_a$, and $|V_a| = |V'_a|$), if $C_1(L) > C_2(L)$, then the advertising network $G_a(V_a, E_a)$ is more stretched than the advertisement network $G'_a(V'_a, E'_a)$, since the information is closer (under the L-property notion) to more network nodes.

For example, under flooding if the advertising budget is large (exceeds a minimum value that depends on the network topology and size), all network nodes will be part of the advertising network. Under a single random walker, though, previous statement is not true, since no matter how large the advertising budget is, the "full" coverage cannot be guaranteed. For example, when the requirement is $C(0) = 100\%$, ($L = 0$), and the available number of messages H is high, then under flooding it is "deterministically" assured that $C(0) = 100\%$, as well as a small completion time. Under single random walker on the other hand, a large completion time would be required (equal to the number of messages H) but it is not guaranteed (only with high probability) that $C(0) = 100\%$.

There are some interesting properties about the L-property and coverage $C(L)$. For example, if for a node the L_1-property is satisfied for some L_1, then the L_2-property is also satisfied for any $0 \leq L_1 < L_2$. If the 0-property is satisfied for some node u, then node u belongs also to the advertising network ($u \in V_a$). If the L-property is satisfied for all network nodes, then $C(L) = 100\%$, and vice versa. Furthermore, for any two values of L, $0 \leq L_2 < L_1$, $C(L_1) \geq C(L_2)$. Since $L = 0$ is an exceptional case that has been addressed extensively in the literature, e.g., [10], [11], [12], the focus in this paper is mainly on $L > 0$.

The number of messages H used to create an advertising network as well as its completion time are two performance metrics (along with coverage) that will be used in the remaining of this paper. An interesting observation is that for the exceptional case of $C(L) = 100\%$ (for some value of $L > 0$) if minimization of the number of messages is required, the resulting advertising network is a *connected L-distance dominating set*, [13], of the initial $G(V, E)$ network. The creation of such a set in a graph, is a *NP*-complete problem that requires *global knowledge*. Obviously, such solutions are not suitable for the considered unstructured, large-scale, and dynamic network environment. In any case, dominating sets are not within the scope of this paper.

3 Replication Policies

The service advertising policies presented in this section employ the *random walk* paradigm in order for an agent e, carrying information about the service location to be forwarded in the network, thus, creating an advertising network. The initial agent (denoted as e_0) is created at the source node s. When an agent moves from a node u to another neighbor node $v \in S_u$, it is assumed that this particular movement takes place in one time unit (or time slot) and it corresponds to one message. When an agent arrives at node v from node u ($v \in S_u$), it does not choose node u as its next hop destination, unless node u is the only neighbor node of v. Note that this rule does not prevent the agent from re-visiting a certain network node in the future. The initial agent has an advertising budget of H hops (corresponding to H messages). After each movement the remaining budget for agent e, denoted by h_e, is decreased by 1.

The core idea behind the policies proposed in this section is to allow for *creating replicas* of the agents (only one replica each time in this paper). Any new agent e_x (referred to as *child* agent) continues to move in the network just like its *parent* agent e_y. The number of allowed messages of the parent agent h_{e_y} (i.e., its advertising budget), is divided equally (or almost equally since h_{e_y} is an integer) among the child and the parent agent.

When only one agent is employed in the network, it is expected to achieve a certain value of coverage, $C(L)$, for some $L > 0$ and for a certain number of messages H, in (completion) time equal to H time units. If a child agent is created (assuming half of the allowed number of messages of its parent agent), the completion time is expected to be reduced, while coverage $C(L)$ may: (a) remain the same – for example, when both agents cover the same coverage area as the single agent; (b) increase – for example, when the agents cover different coverage areas and therefore, are capable of stretching the advertising network more than the case when a single agent was employed; (c) decrease – for example, when both agents cover the same coverage area but for a shorter time due to the division of the number of messages.

From the previous discussion it becomes evident that the coverage and/or completion time can be improved through agent *replication*. It should also be noted that *replication* may also have undesired results (e.g., coverage is decreased). For example, replication should not be too frequent but also not too rare. Frequent replications results in agents with small advertising budget (since h_e is divided after the replication of agent e) that is mostly spent to move in largely overlapping, small areas. On the other hand, rare replication results in a behavior that is similar to a single random walker (i.e., large completion time, etc).

A reasonable approach is to allow replication to take place frequently at the beginning when they will have enough "steam" to move and create a stretched advertising network, while becoming rarer afterwards (giving multiple agents sufficient time to create stretched and less overlapping coverage areas). A second approach would be to allow frequent replications to take place in the "dense" areas of the network (assuming that it would be more likely for a child agent to cover different coverage areas than that of its parent agent), while not allowing for frequent replicas in the less "dense" areas of the network (otherwise, most likely both the parent and the child agent would cover the same area). The replication policies presented in the sequel employ the aforementioned approaches.

3.1 The Topology Independent Policy (TI-Policy)

A simple first idea is to have the agents replicate themselves according to some fixed probability p. If p is large, replication would be rather excessive, as each agent would have limited budget (i.e., initial budget is divided to them) and cover mostly overlapping areas. On the other hand, if p is very small replication would occur after a considerably long time, when no messages (budget) are left for the new agent to take advantage of. As already mentioned, a reasonable approach would be high replication at the initial stages of the advertising process and lower afterwards.

The proposed TI-Policy allows for the replication of an agent e according to the *replication probability* $p(k_e) = p^{2^{k_e}}$, where p is a constant probability (as before), and k_e is the number of replications that have taken place in the past for agent e and all its parent agents. For the initial entity e_0, $k_{e_0} = 0$. Obviously, as the number of replications increases, the probability for a new replication decreases rapidly. This particular policy is easily applied requiring only that k_e is maintained along with agent e and made available to its child agents (if any).

3.2 The Topology Dependent Policy (TD-Policy)

The main aim under the TD-Policy is to exploit information that can be easily gathered by an agent during its movement in the network, in order to decide whether to replicate or not. As already mentioned, the goal is to allow replication in dense network areas and avoid it in non-dense areas. The information related to the topology, that is used under the TD-Policy, is actually the number of neighbor nodes $|S_u|$ of the particular node u that is agent's e current location. Agent e updates during its movement a certain parameter Q_e that corresponds to the total number of neighbor nodes for all nodes that agent e has visited so far during its walk in the network.

Initially, for any agent e, $Q_e = 0$. When agent e moves to some node u that does not belong to the advertising network V_a (but it will eventually become part of it since the agent just moved to it), Q_e is increased by $|S_u| - 1$ (-1 has the meaning that the link over which the agent arrived should not be considered). If node $u \in V_a$, this implies that at least one agent (maybe the same one) has already visited node u and the corresponding number of neighbor nodes has already been taken into account for replication purposes and therefore, Q_e does not change its value. Replication of an agent e takes place if at some node u, Q_e becomes larger than a threshold value q. When replication takes place for entity e, a child entity e' is created and $Q_e = Q_{e'} = 0$.

The particular value of threshold q is to be explored. Small values of q result in frequent replications resulting in an advertising network that would not be stretched, as already mentioned. On the other hand, large values of q would keep the number of replications low but they may occur late in the sense that replication may take place long after the agent is outside the dense area.

4 Simulation Results

In this section simulation results are presented evaluating the previously presented algorithms. For the simulation purposes, a simulation program that has been written in C programming language is used for topologies of 500 nodes according to the *Random Geometric Graph* model. Each node is randomly put in the $[0, 1] \times [0, 1]$ area, and communication radius r is selected so as to create a connected network ($r = 0.08$); the resulting network has 2323 links among its 500 nodes. For the rest of this section $L = 2$. The presented results correspond to average values for 10 runs for each experiment.

In Table 1 simulation results regarding coverage and completion time are presented for flooding and single random walker. There are a number of conclusions that may be drawn from these results. As expected, as the advertising budget H increases, the coverage and the completion time increase. When it is sufficiently large (e.g., $H \geq 2000$), both approaches achieve high coverage but the completion times are dramatically shorter under flooding. Consequently, when H is very large (e.g., $H \geq 4000$), flooding is to be preferred, as it achieves about as high coverage as under the single random walker with drastically shorter completion time.

Referring again to Table 1 one can notice that when H is small (e.g., $H \leq 1000$) the single random walker achieves drastically higher coverage compared to flooding. This clearly demonstrates and is due to the larger stretch of the advertising network created by the single random walk compared to flooding. Consequently, when the advertising budget is small and completion time not as critical, the single random walker is to be preferred. This holds true in general for larger amounts of advertising budgets as well, but the difference in the stretch diminishes (e.g., $H = 3000$) or it could be reversed (e.g., for $H = 4000$ flooding achieves a bit higher coverage) due to the dominating impact of the "noise" in (or probabilistic impact of) the spreading processes when coverage reaches its limit.

Table 1 Coverage $C(L)$ (%) and completion Time for $L = 2$ for the Flooding and Single Random Walker (both running until H expires).

H	C(L) (%)						Completion Time					
	100	500	1000	2000	3000	4000	100	500	1000	2000	3000	4000
Flooding	6.8	32.4	47.8	81.8	98.2	100	3	8	11	14	18	22
SRW	24.9	56.5	85.5	95.4	99.3	99.4	100	500	1000	2000	3000	4000

Another conclusion is that the completion time under a single random walker is fairly high (in fact it coincides with H). The main conclusion drawn from the results shown in Table 2 (where results under TI-policy are presented) is that the introduction of replicas in the random walk helps reduce the completion time significantly at a generally very small loss (or occasionally no loss or even gain) in coverage. Thus, when both coverage and completion time are of interest and the advertising budget is neither very small nor very large, the proposed policies that introduce replicas of the random walker are more effective. Notice that for $H = 500$ and $p = 0.05$ the achieved coverage is 68.5% and completion time is 238.7, compared to 56.5% and 500, respectively under the single random walk. Thus, for small H both the completion time and coverage are improved, indicating that the generated replicas not only yield the benefits of faster built up of the advertising network due to the multiplicity of the agents, but they also help build a stretcher advertising network. For $H = 4000$ the completion time decreases significantly (1030.6 versus 4000 in the single random walker case) at a slight loss in coverage (97.2% versus 99.4%), indicating a slight reduction in the stretchiness of the advertising network that may be attributed to the increased chance that the replicas cover some overlapping areas when the "virgin" area in which to move and cover decreases for large H. Finally notice from Table 2 that as expected, both coverage and completion time increase as H increases. Furthermore, for the same H, the coverage of the network is smaller for large values of p (e.g., $p = 0.9$) than the corresponding values when p is small (e.g., $p = 0.05$), as expected. This trend is also reflected in the completion time, which decreases as p increases due to the increased number of replicas.

Table 3 presents the results under the TD-Policy approaches for various values of q and H. Both coverage and completion time increase as H increases. The coverage of the network for the same H is generally smaller for small values of q (i.e., where more replicas are created) as is expected. When the values of q become large enough (in which case replicas are very unlike to be created), then the performance is similar to the single random walk. The observation made regarding the TI-policy and the results on Table 2 are also valid here, where a small p in the TI-policy corresponds to large q in the TD-policy.

Table 4 presents a comparison between the single random walker and the TI-Policy and TD-Policy from another perspective. This time the resources are not

Table 2 Coverage $C(L)$ (%) and completion time under the TI-Policy for $L = 2$ and various values of p and H.

p/H	C(L) (%)						Completion Time					
	100	500	1000	2000	3000	4000	100	500	1000	2000	3000	4000
0.05	13.3	68.5	79.5	94	98.6	97.2	64.7	238.7	453.6	724.1	1030.6	1362.9
0.1	20.2	56.8	80.5	91.7	98.2	98.5	54.3	240.8	346.9	601.5	862	1069
0.3	19.1	52.3	77.6	91.1	96.9	99.3	35.7	133.8	246.7	427.9	511.9	658
0.5	15.2	45.3	68.5	90.9	94.5	96.4	29.3	82.1	148.4	264.6	380.9	456.7
0.7	14.7	38.6	58.4	82	90.7	98.5	21	61.2	91.2	156.6	214.4	280
0.9	11.6	24.1	38.3	57.4	73.7	80.4	13.5	30.1	47	76.1	103.4	128.4

Table 3 Coverage $C(L)$ (%) and completion time under the TD-Policy for $L = 2$ and various values of q and H.

q/H	C(L) (%)						Completion Time					
	100	500	1000	2000	3000	4000	100	500	1000	2000	3000	4000
10	12.3	30.9	49.8	75.6	87.3	94.6	22.2	74.3	121.9	287.9	343.4	366.4
20	9.8	38.1	61.8	83.2	93.4	98.4	29.6	103.4	154.4	286.4	421.9	516.1
30	14.3	44.6	70.8	86.5	95.2	98.9	32.5	120.5	214.6	299.3	496.5	651
50	16.4	45.6	66.5	92.2	97.5	98.1	48.5	157.3	249.3	344.1	577.8	755.5
150	25.2	55.3	80.6	95.5	97.1	99.1	65.5	214.5	337	483.9	659	797
250	18.3	65.3	77.7	91	98.3	99.2	91.8	241.3	350.3	555.1	782.8	931.9
400	17.4	67.1	86.2	95.8	98.3	99.3	99.8	291.6	409	667.1	971.6	1186.5
600	19.6	64.5	77.7	94.9	97.2	99.1	100	374.7	548.3	791.2	1107	1421.3
2000	28.5	68.2	82.1	95.8	96.9	99.9	100	491.6	885.1	1315.4	1852.6	2371.5

kept constant, but the time and the coverage are kept constant instead. In more details, the first column (labelled: SRW *ct*) corresponds to the completion time of the single random walker. The coverage under the TI-Policy and the TD-Policy for the same completion time is shown in the next two columns. The fourth column (labelled: SRW $C(L)$%) corresponds to the coverage under the single random walker for the completion time of the same row and the first column. The last two columns correspond to the completion time under the TI-Policy and the TD-Policy, in order to achieve the same coverage as the one corresponding to the single random walker case.

Table 4 clearly shows that for same completion time both proposed policies outperform the single random walker with respect to coverage. For example, for completion time 500 (SRW *ct* = 500) the coverage is 82.6%, 94.6% and only 56.5% under the TI-policy, TD-policy and the single random walker, respectively. Similarly, for the same coverage both proposed policies outperform the single random walker with respect to completion time. For example for coverage 99.3% (SRW $C(L)$% = 99.3) the completion time is 709.8, 541.6 and as high as 3000 under the Ti-policy, TD-policy and the single random walker. The increased coverage for the same completion time demonstrates again the larger stretchiness of the advertising network that can be achieved within a given available completion time. For applications for which service advertisement needs to be done in a (strict) timely manner (i.e., completion time is bounded), the proposed policies can achieve significantly higher coverage. It should be noted that the advertising budget actually utilized is not the same under the three policies, though. Nevertheless, it is for lower than flooding.

Table 4 Coverage $C(L)$ (%) for various values of the completion time (column: SRW ct) and coverage (column: SRW $C(L)$%) under Single Random Walker, TD-Policy and TI-Policy ($p = 0.1$ and $q = 250$).

| SRW ct | $C(L)$ (%) | | SRW $C(L)$% | Completion Time | |
	TI-Policy	TD-Policy		TI-Policy	TD-Policy
100	29.82	36.12	24.9	70.6	60.4
500	82.6	94.6	56.5	172.4	202.6
1000	99.16	99.96	85.5	374.4	367
2000	100	100	95.4	506.8	379.6
3000	100	100	99.3	709.8	541.6
4000	100	100	99.4	972.6	572.2

Eventually, the simulation results presented in this section have shown in the first place that a single random walker is a suitable alternative to flooding, when the number of allowed messages is limited. This is due to the capability of the single random walker to create stretched advertising networks. For both proposed replication policies it was shown that an improvement in the completion time is achieved generally at the expense of a slight decrease in coverage, when the number of messages is kept constant; sometimes, though, coverage may also be improved in addition to the completion time. Finally it has been shown that the proposed policies improve the coverage of the single random walker when completion time is fixed, or they can achieve a given coverage in shorter completion time.

5 Summary and Conclusions

In this paper the problem of service advertising is studied for unstructured network environments. An advertising process disseminates information to the network nodes in an attempt to make information about a certain service location a priori available in as wide (or stretchable) network area as possible, to ease searching for it. A generic, simple, service searching approach is subsumed here: each node is considered as capable of employing a simple searching mechanism that searches for the particular information at most L hops away from the particular node.

Flooding and single random walk were shown to be at rather extreme points with respect to coverage, completion time and number of required messages. However, as shown in this paper, a single random walker is capable of creating a more "stretched" advertising network than flooding, especially when the advertising budget is small, resulting in improved completion times and sometimes even coverage.

This capability of the random walk approach was exploited further in the sequel in the context of two proposed policies, by allowing agents to move in the network according to the random walk paradigm and replicate themselves when certain criteria are met (with some probability p that decreases exponentially or by using information related to the topology).

Simulation results, for both proposed replication policies when compared to single random walker, have shown that an improvement in the completion time is achieved generally at the expense of a slight decrease –or even increase– in coverage, when the number of messages is kept constant. Finally it has been shown that the proposed policies improve the coverage of the single random walker when completion time is fixed, or they can achieve a given coverage in shorter completion time.

References

1. Gnutella. Gnutella rfc. http://rfc-gnutella.sourceforge.net/, 2002.
2. A.Segall, "Distributed network protocols", *IEEE Transactions on Information Theory*, vol. IT-29, pp.23-35, 1983.
3. B.Williams, T.Camp, "Comparison of broadcasting techniques for mobile ad hoc networks", MOBIHOC 2002, pp.194-205, 2002.
4. F.Banaei-Kashani and C.Shahabi, "Criticality-based analysis and design of unstructured peer-to-peer network as "complex" systems", in *Proceedings of the Third International Symposium on Cluster Computing and the Grid*, pages 351-358, 2003.
5. V. Dimakopoulos and E.Pitoura, "On the performance of flooding-based resource discovery", *IEEE Transactions on Parallel and Distributed Systems*, 17(11):290-297, November 2006.
6. K.Oikonomou and I.Stavrakakis, "Performance analysis of probabilistic flooding using random graphs", in *The First International IEEE WoWMoM Workshop on Autonomic and Opportunistic Communications (AOC 2007)*, Helsinki, Finland, 18 June, 2007.
7. Y.Sasson, D.Cavin, and A.Schiper, "Probabilistic broadcast for flooding in wireless mobile ad hoc networks", in *Swiss Federal Institute of Technology (EPFL), Technical Report IC/2002/54*, 2002.
8. D.Tsoumakos and N.Roussopoulos, "Adaptive probabilistic search for peer-to-peer networks", in *3rd IEEE International Conference on P2P Computing*, 2003.
9. M.Bani Yassein, M.Ould-Khaoua and S.Papanastasiou, "On the Performance of Probabilistic Flooding in Mobile Ad Hoc Networks", in *11th International Conference on Parallel and Distributed Systems (ICPAD '05)*, 2005.
10. N.Alon, C.Avin, M.Koucky, G.Kozma, Z. Lotker, M.Tuttle, "Many Random Walks Are Faster Than One", *ArXiv e-prints. Vol. 705*, May 2007.
11. C.Gkantsidis, M.Mihail and A.Saberi, "Random Walks in Peer-to-Peer Networks", *in Proceedings of IEEE INFOCOM*, 2004.
12. C.Gkantsidis, M.Mihail and A.Saberi, "Hybrid Search Scemes for Unstructured Peer-to-Peer networks", *in Proceedings of the 24th Annual Joint Conference of the IEEE Computer and Communications Societies (INFOCOM '05), vol. 3, pp. 1526-1537, Miami, Fla, USA*, March 2005.
13. T. Haynes, S. Hedetniemi and P.Slater, "Fundamentals of Domination in Graphs", *Marcel Dekker, New York*, 1998.
14. P.B. Mirchandani and R.L. Francis, "Discrete Location Theory", John Wiley and Sons, 1990.

ACF: An Autonomic Communication Framework for Wireless Sensor Networks

Jingbo Sun and Rachel Cardell-Oliver

Abstract The performance of wireless sensor networks in the field has been shown to be both unreliable and unpredictable. One reason for this is that radio links between pairs of nodes are often unstable, with significant variation in performance over both time and space. Timeout-based, streaming and ExOR protocols, which represent three mechanisms used in improving the reliability in data delivery, are analysed and areas of good and poor performance are identified for certain combinations of packet delivery probabilities on the communication links. A new autonomic communication framework (ACF) is proposed for sensor networks, which is able to adapt to changing environments. Experimental results show that our framework optimises performance under different environmental conditions for performance measures including link efficiency and energy consumption.

1 Introduction

The performance of sensor network protocols in the field has been shown to be both unreliable and unpredictable [4, 20, 19, 9], leading to low delivery rates and high delivery costs [10]. The main reason for this problem is that sensor nodes use low-power short-range radio links to communicate with each other. The characteristics of this kind of radio links are significant variation and asymmetry over both time and space [24, 6, 19], which can cause long periods of poor to no connectivity.

Autonomic systems are those with the ability to self-configure to suit varying and unpredictable conditions, that can monitor themselves constantly for optimal functioning, that are able to find alternate ways to function when they encounter problems, and that are able to adapt to varying environments. The goal of our work

Jingbo Sun and Rachel Cardell-Oliver
School of Computer Science & Software Engineering and Cooperative Research Centre for Plant-based Management of Dryland Salinity, The University of Western Australia, M002, 35 Stirling Highway, Crawley, Western Australia, 6009, Australia. e-mail: jingbo,rachel@csse.uwa.edu.au

Please use the following format when citing this chapter:

Sun, J., Cardell-Oliver, R., 2008, in IFIP International Federation for Information Processing, Volume 265, Advances in Ad Hoc Networking, eds. Cuenca, P., Guerrero C., Puigjaner, R., Serra, B., (Boston: Springer), pp. 37-48.

is to develop autonomic sensor networks. Although researchers have proposed many protocols to improve the data delivery reliability in wireless sensor networks [2, 3, 8, 18, 21], no one alone can really adapt to changeable environmental conditions. For autonomy, different data delivery strategies are required for different radio link conditions.

The technologies used to guarantee reliable data delivery using single path usually are *retransmissions*, which include *retransmissions* based on positive acknowledgements and *retransmissions* based on negative acknowledgements. *Multiple paths delivery* is another mechanism used for providing reliable data delivery over wireless links.

In this paper, we choose three protocols: timeout-based protocol [10], streaming protocol [3] and ExOR protocol [2], which represent the above three technologies respectively. In choosing optimal protocol, we need to consider memory cost (buffer size), latency to successfully deliver a packet and energy expended per packet delivered. For space, we only analyse the *energy consumption* of these three protocols in different environments in this paper. Our results help to identify situations in which we should use each of these protocols to optimise reliability in wireless sensor networks. We find streaming performs better than ExOR when forward link quality is good (above 0.5); while ExOR performs better when forward link quality is from medium to low (below 0.5).

Based on analysis results, we propose an autonomic communication framework (ACF) for sensor networks that can change its behaviour according to different environments. ACF includes *protocol library*, *monitor* module, *scheduler* module and *central control service*. The *central control service* decides the protocol used in the running sensor network based on the gathered information from the *monitor* module, and controls the node behaviour by using *scheduler* module. Thus, the network can use different mechanisms under different situations so that the network performance can be improved. Experimental results show that our framework performs better than ExOR in terms of *link efficiency* and *energy consumption*.

We focus on sensor networks that require reliable transmission of batches of data, for example data gathered by periodic monitoring, for which delivery delays can be tolerated. In this paper we focus on single hop communication, for example between nodes and cluster heads. Many sensor network applications, such as environmental monitoring, satisfy these criteria.

The reminder of this paper is organized as follows. Section 2 analyses the performance of the timeout-based protocol, streaming protocol and ExOR protocol in different environmental conditions. In Section 3 we propose an autonomic communication framework (ACF) for sensor networks based on the analysis from Section 2. The experiment setup and results are presented in Section 4. Section 5 describes related work. Section 6 concludes this paper and outlines our future work.

2 Protocol Performance Analysis

In this section, we briefly introduce three reliable protocols: timeout-based protocol, streaming protocol and ExOR protocol, then point out limitations of these three protocols in terms of *energy consumption*.

2.1 Protocol Overview

In the timeout-based protocol [10], the source node relies on a timer to control retransmissions. The source sends one packet at a time and sets a timer. If the source receives an acknowledgement from the destination, the next packet can be transmitted. Otherwise, the source retransmits the packet one or more times when the timer expires, up to some limit or an acknowledgement is received, before the packet is declared lost.

In streaming [3], the source node sends packets in sequence. The destination replies with a Retransmission Request Packet (RRP) if it finds a sequence gap in the received packets. Streaming is more efficient than the timeout-based protocol since the destination only sends a negative acknowledgement (NACK) for every lost packet, instead of sending a positive acknowledgement for every received packet, which reduces the amount of transmissions. However, streaming still needs to wait a NACK for every transmitted packets. Thus, using aggregated NACKs or batch transmissions can improve the efficiency of streaming. The buffer size of streaming is unpredictable. When the link quality is getting worse, its buffer size should be increased in order to store all non-sequence packets.

In ExOR [2], source sends a batch of packets to destination via a named multihop path and those packets may be overheard by potential forwarder nodes. The destination replies with multiple copies of its acknowledgement. The forwarder then forwards packets which are received by itself but not by the destination. After that, the source retransmits remaining packets. This procedure is repeated until all packets are received by the destination. ExOR is a multihop protocol in which source has global information about routes. In this paper we use ExOR as single link. ExOR is more suited to bad link quality environments than streaming because it uses multiple paths to improve reception. However, when link quality is good, it consumes more energy because of its redundant paths.

2.2 Energy Consumption Analysis

In this section, we compare the performance of the timeout-based protocol, streaming protocol and ExOR protocol in terms of *energy consumption*. Formally, we define *link quality* between two nodes in terms of the probability of successful packet delivery from one node to the other. For sensor nodes A and B, link quality, LQ_{AB},

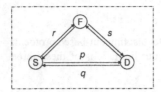

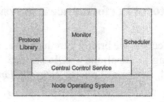

Fig. 1 Timeout, Streaming and ExOR
Protocol Network Architecture

Fig. 2 Autonomic Communication
Framework Architecture

at a given time is denoted by a pair (p,q) giving the probability of successful packet delivery from A to B and B to A respectively. Figure 1 shows nodes and links used for timeout (SD), streaming (SD) and ExOR (SDF).

Energy Consumption is an important criteria to be considered in the design of sensor network protocols. It can be measured by *average energy consumption per delivered packet* (*AEC* for simplicity in the following) that depends on the time used for successfully delivering one packet from source to destination.

Suppose each node uses the same energy. The following parameters are used for calculating *AEC*.

- TxD_i: the time used for node i to transmit or listen for a batch of data packets;
- TxA_i: the time used for node i to transmit or listen for acknowledgement(s);
- CN: the electrical current of a node when its radio is on;
- VN: the battery voltage of a node;
- N: the number of nodes participating in the protocol;
- BS: the number of data packets transmitted in one cycle.

For each node, *energy consumption* is the energy (that is *volts* $\times$ *amperes*) times the time of its radio turned on in order to deliver or listen for a packet. The total energy consumption is the sum of the energy used by each participating node. Therefore, the *AEC* is the total energy consumption of all participating nodes divided by the number of data packets transmitted during this period:

$$AEC = N \times (CN \times VN \times (TxD_i + TxA_i))/BS \qquad (1)$$

In the timeout protocol, both source and destination have the same radio on time. Suppose the batch size is one. The packet delivery success ratio for the source is pq because success means both data packet and acknowledgment are successfully received. Therefore, the source sends $1/pq$ times on average to know one packet has been successfully received. The average duration per packet is $(TxD_S + TxA_D)/pq$. The *AEC* of the timeout protocol is therefore:

$$AEC_{timeout} = 2 \times CN \times VN \times \frac{1}{pq}(TxD_S + TxA_D) \qquad (2)$$

Using the same assumption as the timeout protocol, in streaming, the possibility of packet loss is $1 - p$ and the average number of RRPs sent by the destination node is $1/pq$. The average number of retransmissions for a lost packet sent by the source is $(1-p)\frac{1}{pq} \times q = \frac{1}{p} - 1$. The total transmission times (including retransmissions) is $1/p$. Therefore, the AEC is:

$$AEC_{streaming} = 2 \times CN \times VN \times \frac{1}{p}(TxD_S + TxA_D) \qquad (3)$$

The AEC of streaming is not related to backward link quality because lost packets are detected as long as the network runs long enough and the buffer is large enough to store all out of order packets. However, its energy is still wasted by listening for a NACK even when none is transmitted. We also note that the cost of streaming's energy use is high buffer requirement and high packet delivery latency when the link quality is low. The energy efficiency of streaming could be improved by sending data packets in batches. Because of the limited space, we do not give a detailed analysis in this paper.

In ExOR, the AEC depends on how many total transmissions are used by the source and forwarder to successfully transmit a batch of packets to the destination. Here, we do not consider the backward link quality because the destination sends multiple copies of acknowledgments (10 in [2]) in order to make sure source or forwarder is able to receive at least one. Three nodes, source, forwarder and destination, are used in this single-hop network with radios turned on at all times. The average number of transmission times, including retransmissions is $\frac{1}{p+rs-prs}$. Suppose the data transmission time of the forwarder is the same as that of the source, the estimated AEC of the ExOR protocol is:

$$AEC_{ExOR} = 3 \times CN \times VN \times \frac{1}{p+rs-prs}(TxD_S + TxD_F + TxA_D)/BS \qquad (4)$$

The electrical current of Fleck nodes [17],which are used in our implementation, is measured in terms of different states. Table 1 from [1] shows that node uses most of its energy when its radio is on. In its low power mode, the energy consumption is negligible, which supports our AEC estimation.

Table 1 Power Usage Table for Fleck Nodes [1]

Mode	Current (mA)
Low Power	0.4
Sensing Only	14.0
Radio Only	35.8

In order to get a clear view of the energy consumption for three protocols, we graph Equation (2), (3) and (4) based on parameters in Table 2. Since ExOR sends 10 copies of the acknowledgement, the TxA_D for ExOR is 10 times as that for the timeout and streaming protocol.

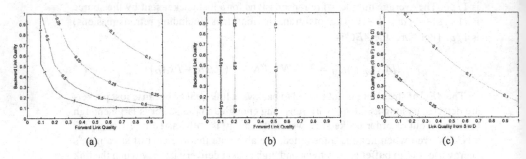

Fig. 3 Distribution of *AEC* (Joule): (a) Timeout; (b) Streaming; (c) ExOR.

Table 2 Parameters Used for Calculating *AEC*

	TxD (ms)	TxA (ms)	CN (mA)	VN (V)	N	BS
Timeout	200	100	35.8	2.4	2	1
Streaming	200	100	35.8	2.4	2	1
ExOR	2000	1000	35.8	2.4	3	10

Figure 3 shows the distribution of energy consumption of three protocols measured in units of Joule. Comparing Figure 3(b) with Figure 3(c), we observe that the energy consumption of streaming is better than that of the ExOR protocol when its forward link quality is above 0.5. However, ExOR is better when forward link quality is below 0.5 even though it uses three nodes instead of two. The forwarder is indeed able to help increase the delivery speed without consuming much energy. The energy consumption of the timeout protocol is worst according to Figure 3(a), 3(b) and 3(c), because it needs good quality of both forward and backward links in order to reduce the number of retransmissions.

3 Autonomic Communication Framework for Sensor Networks

Based on the above analysis, we observe that in order to adapt to varying environments, different mechanisms should be used under different situations. Only an autonomic network, which can alternate its behaviour, can really perform well in time varying environments. Therefore, we propose an autonomic communication framework (ACF), where nodes can dynamically change their behaviour according to current environmental conditions.

The architecture of ACF contains four modules: *protocol library, monitor, scheduler* and *central control service*, shown in Figure 2. The *protocol library* has protocols which may be needed in different situations. The *monitor* module is used to monitor the change of the situation, which will result in the change of the protocol.

Node behaviour controlled by the *scheduler* module, includes sending, receiving, waking up and sleeping. All the information is passed to nodes by the *central control service* module. We will specifically describe the function of these modules in the following.

Protocol Library

The *protocol library* contains implementations of protocols to be used under different environmental conditions. The *protocol switching time* is decided by the *monitor* module based on the *protocol switching threshold*. That threshold is defined by users before the start of the experiment. Our library implements versions of the streaming and ExOR protocols. When nodes use these protocols, they transmit batches of packets since this strategy increases transmission speed and reduces waiting time. Acknowledgements are aggregated in one packet for every batch. The number of the acknowledgements for both protocols is changed dynamically based on the current link quality.

Monitor Module

The *monitor* module is used to monitor current conditions, such as battery level, sensor temperature, link quality and solar power. In our experiments, we use link quality as the main metric to decide if the node's behaviour should be changed. We can use any existing link quality estimation method, such as ETX [7] or window mean with EWMA [22]. In our implementation, we use a simple estimation method in order to reduce the complexity of the implementation and avoid using much memory and calculation energy. Each node estimates link quality by counting packets received from neighbours during a fixed time window.

Scheduler Module

This high-level *scheduler* is used to decide upon the node behaviour, such as transmitting, receiving, listening, waking up and sleeping for every node in the network. It can be used to schedule communication over multiple links. Every node has its own time slot to transmit and receive packets. We have implemented a simple fixed schedule. The schedule frame of each node is built as follows. Each node is assigned a transmitting slot by the base station and listens to the traffic from its neighbours during other slots. Then the node marks the specific slot as listening for one of its neighbours when it hears traffic from that neighbour during that slot. Transmitting and listening slots have the same length. In our implementation, each node has a 5-second time slot in the schedule frame to transmit a batch of packets, and uses the other two slots for listening or sleeping.

Synchronization is also controlled by the *scheduler* module. We integrate a lightweight synchronization scheme in which data packets carry a time stamp and children update their times to match their parents [14].

Central Control Service

The *central control service* receives information from the *monitor* module and decides which protocol should be chosen from the *protocol library* based on the predefined *protocol switching threshold*. A *threshold indicator* is integrated in the data packets. The *scheduler* module uses the *threshold indicator* to control node behaviour. In our implementation, based on the previous analysis, when the link quality is below 0.5, the ExOR protocol is chosen, otherwise streaming is selected. When using ExOR, the *central control service* also passes information to *scheduler* that one more node should be woken up during the source transmission slot.

4 Results

4.1 Experiment Set Up

We implemented our autonomic communication framework ACF and ExOR using TinyOS/nesC [15] with TinyOS Blocking Library [13]. We evaluated their performance in a single hop network using CSIRO Fleck motes [17].

Our experiments used a source, a destination and a helper node, with a fourth node with high gain antenna as the base station. The base station was connected to a personal computer and the three nodes were placed in two different rooms, with the destination in a separate room from the source and the helper. We put nodes in different angles in order to get different link qualities.

The schedule slot was 5 seconds and the size of the schedule frame was 3. The *monitor* module performed every 30 minutes to calculate link quality between the source and the destination. The batch size was 10. The *protocol switching threshold* was 0.5 based on bidirectional link quality according to the above three protocol analysis. The destination node sent 2 copies of acknowledgements when link quality was above the threshold, otherwise it sent 6 copies. The base station recorded all packets it heard from the three nodes.

In our experiments, the length of the data packet was the same as the length of the acknowledgement packet (33 bytes), although in practice the length of the acknowledgement could be much shorter. The smaller acknowledgements only affect the best performance of the network, but do not affect the trend of the performance over varying link quality.

We repeated each experiment at least 3 times in different days in order to enlarge the range of link quality. Two experiments ran total 46.5 hours together. In order to get fair comparison, data chosen in Table 3 was the average from data that had the first two same decimal digits. The forwarder was in the middle of the source and the destination and so its link quality to these two nodes were good enough to fit for our purpose. The experimental results are with 95% confidence interval.

Table 3 Link Quality: Autonomic Communication Framework (ACF) and ExOR

Link	Protocol	L1	L2	L3	L4	L5	L6	L7	L8	L9	L10	L11	L12
SD	ACF	0.241	0.314	0.375	0.408	0.505	0.666	0.752	0.762	0.778	0.803	0.823	0.892
	ExOR	0.242	0.312	0.378	0.416	0.507	0.669	0.755	0.761	0.779	0.808	0.826	0.890
DS	ACF	0.659	0.758	0.747	0.751	0.785	0.867	0.895	0.702	0.878	0.899	0.983	0.952
	ExOR	0.350	0.769	0.859	0.575	0.933	0.960	0.796	0.998	0.801	0.912	0.913	0.828

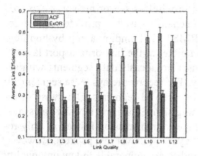

Fig. 4 Link Efficiency: ACF and ExOR

Fig. 5 Energy Consumption: ACF and ExOR

4.2 Experimental Results

In this section, we analyse the performance of our framework ACF from two aspects: *link efficiency* and *energy consumption*.

The x-axis of Figure 4 and 5 corresponds to categories in Table 3. From Figure 4 we observe that the *link efficiency* of ACF is better than that of ExOR, especially when link quality is above 0.5. It improves the link efficiency than ExOR up to 119%. The main reason is that it changed its behaviour by using 2 nodes instead of 3 nodes in the ExOR protocol when the bidirectional link quality between the source and the destination is above the predefined threshold. Another reason is that the number of acknowledgements used in our framework is dynamically changed to adapt to its environment, which decreases the total number of packets transmitted in the network.

We also compared the energy consumption of ACF with ExOR shown in Figure 5. It shows that ACF performs better than ExOR when link quality is above the threshold and has almost the same performance as the ExOR when link quality is below the threshold. We also notice that the energy consumption of our framework is worse than that of ExOR when link quality is around the threshold in Figure 5. That may be because of the bias of the estimated link quality or because the current threshold may not be optimal. However, the overall performance of our framework is still better than that of ExOR.

Based on the above analysis, our autonomic communication framework ACF has the optimal overall performance based on the analysis of its *link efficiency* and *energy consumption*.

5 Related Work

Reliable delivery is one of important issues in wireless sensor networks explored by researchers. *Retransmission* is a major mechanism used to provide reliable delivery in sensor networks. PSFQ [21] and RMST [18] employ a hop-by-hop negative acknowledgement (NACK) mechanism either at the link or transport layer to increase network reliability. In PSFQ, the user broadcasts data segments with sequence numbers to its neighbors periodically. The receiver relays these segments to its neighbours if there is no sequence gap in received segments. Otherwise, it requests immediate retransmission of the missing segments using a NACK message. RMST improves on PSFQ by using MAC layer retransmission instead of only relying on explicit NACKs from the transport layer to recover lost packets. However, both of them route data along a single path and so are vulnerable to low link quality anywhere in that path.

Multiple path delivery protocols improve on the reliability of single path protocols. ReInForM [8] provids reliable data delivery to adapt to the channel error rate by using multiple copies of the same packet delivered through multiple edge-disjoint paths from source to sink. Nodes themselves decide their forwarding directions without explicit paths. However, the ReInForm's requirement of the existence of multiple edge-disjoint paths in connected unit disk graphs of uniform density is unrealistic in the real world. The main idea of GRAB [23] is that a packet is forwarded through interleaved multiple paths from source to sink. The number of paths is determined by the required reliability, which is used to control the degree of path redundancy. Because of multiple paths are created on the fly, all nodes in GRAB have to listen to packets from their neighbours, this increases the overall energy use.

Several self-healing approaches exist for ad hoc and sensor networks, such as CATS [16] and the autonomic routing framework (ARF)[12]. CATS is a cross-layer approach to help routing protocol maintain network reliability. It uses a Management Plane to gather information in order to identify and react to network failure. However, the amount of information from each of the seven layers of the OSI Reference Model generates too much traffic for a sensor network setting. The ARF aims to improve the adaptivity of routing services in sensor networks by adapting to the application and network dynamics. The aim of ARF is different from ours. ARF maintains some feature functions that are decoupled from the routing service. Feature functions have a set of parameters to tune to fit application and network changes. ARF uses its monitor module to collect state information and make adaptation decision. However,ARF is implemented on a Linux PC and its total code size is around 180KB, and so it is not suited to memory constrained sensor nodes. Our Fleck nodes only have 128KB programmable flash memory.

ASCENT [5] is a topology-adaptive protocol, which uses redundancy to extend network lifetime. A minimum set of nodes is selected to establish a routing backbone. In ASCENT, each node assesses its connectivity and adapts its participation in the multihop network topology based on the measured operating region. ASCENT is neither a routing nor data dissemination protocol. It only decides upon the network topology. Gu *et al.* proposed a dynamic switch-based forwarding protocol (DSF) [11] that reduces end-to-end latency over unreliable links. DSF uses multiple potential forwarding nodes at each hop that in turn receive packets from the source. This strategy overcomes unreliable links and reduces transmission delay. Although DSF also uses extra nodes for forwarding, its aim minimising latency is different from our aim minimising energy use.

6 Conclusion

Reliable energy efficient data delivery is an important function of wireless sensor networks, particulary in harsh environments. Our goal is to build a reliable, adaptive data delivery approach which maximises the field life of environmental monitoring sensor networks.

We analysed the performance of existing reliable protocols: timeout-based protocol, streaming protocol and ExOR protocol in order to find out if current technologies used for improving the reliable data delivery alone can really adapt to varying environments. Analysis of *energy consumption* shows that none of these protocols is able to optimise its performance by adapting completely to varying environments.

In this paper, we present an autonomic communication framework (ACF) for sensor networks that is able to optimise its performance for time-varying links. ACF uses different mechanisms based on the different environmental conditions in order to achieve an optimal performance. We implemented this framework and ExOR on CSIRO Flecks to test their real world performance. Experimental results show that the overall performance of our framework is better than that of ExOR. In the future, this framework will be extended for multi-tier networks and tested in the field at different sensor network scales.

References

1. Wireless sensor networks project wiki. URL http://www.csse.uwa.edu.au/~mkranz/wiki/index.php/Fleck:Fleck_Power
2. Biswas, S., Morris, R.: ExOR: opportunistic multi-hop routing for wireless networks. In: SIGCOMM '05: Proceedings of the 2005 conference on Applications, technologies, architectures, and protocols for computer communications, pp. 133–144 (2005)
3. Cao, Q., He, T., Fang, L., Abdelzaher, T., Stankovic, J., Son, S.: Efficiency centric communication model for wireless sensor networks. In: IEEE INFOCOM (2006)

4. Cardell-Oliver, R., Smettem, K., Kranz, M., Mayer, K.: A reactive soil moisture sensor network: Design and field evaluation. International Journal of Distributed Sensor Networks pp. 149–162 (2005)
5. Cerpa, A., Estrin, D.: ASCENT: Adaptive self-configuring sensor networks topologies. IEEE Transaction on Mobile Computing 3(3), 272–285 (2004)
6. Cerpa, A., Wong, J., Potkonjak, M., Estrin, D.: Temporal properties of low power wireless links: Modeling and implications on multi-hop routing. In: Proceedings of the 6th ACM international symposium on Mobile ad hoc networking and computing, pp. 414–425 (2005)
7. Couto, D.S.J.D., Aguayo, D., Bicket, J., Morris, R.: A high-throughput path metric for multi-hop wireless routing. In: MobiCom '03: Proceedings of the 9th annual international conference on Mobile computing and networking, pp. 134–146 (2003)
8. Deb, B., Bhatnagar, S., Nath, B.: ReInForM: Reliable information forwarding using multiple paths in sensor networks. In: LCN '03: Proceedings of the 28th Annual IEEE International Conference on Local Computer Networks, p. 406 (2003)
9. Falchi, A.: Sensor networks: Performance measurements with motes technology. Master's thesis, Dept. of Information Engineering, Uni. of Pisa (2004)
10. Gnawali, O., Yarvis, M., Heidemann, J., Govindan, R.: Interaction of retransmission, black-listing, and routing metrics for reliability in sensor network routing. In: Proceedings of the First IEEE Conference on Sensor and Adhoc Communication and Networks (2004)
11. Gu, Y., He, T.: Data forwarding in extremely low duty-cycle sensor networks with unreliable communication links. In: SenSys '07: Proceedings of the 5th international conference on Embedded networked sensor systems (2007)
12. He, Y., Raghavendra, C.S., Berson, S., Braden, R.: An autonomic routing framework for sensor networks. In: Cluster Computing, Specical Issue on Autonomic Computing (2006)
13. Kranz, M.: Tinyos blocking library. URL http://wsnwiki.csse.uwa.edu.au/index.php/Software
14. Lee, W.L.: Flexible-schedule-based tdma protocols for supporting fault-tolerance, on-demand tdma slot transfer, and peer-to-peer communication in wireless sensor networks. Ph.D. thesis, The University of Western Australia (2007)
15. Levis, P., Madden, S., Polastre, J., Szewczyk, R., Whitehouse, K., Woo, A., Gay, D., Hill, J., Welsh, M., Brewer, E., Culler, D.: Ambient Intelligence, chap. TinyOS: An Operating System for Sensor Networks, pp. 115–148. Springer Berlin Heidelberg (2005)
16. Sadler, C.M., Kant, L., Chen, W.: Cross-layer self-healing mechanisms in wireless networks. In: Proceedings of the World Wireless Congress (2005)
17. Sikka, P., Corke, P., Overs, L.: Wireless sensor devices for animal tracking and control. In: Proceedings of the 29th Annual IEEE International Conference on Local Computer Networks, pp. 446–454 (2004)
18. Stann, F., Heidemann, J.: RMST: Reliable data transport in sensor networks. In: Proceedings of the First International Workshop on Sensor Net Protocols and Applications. IEEE (2003)
19. Sun, J., Cardell-Oliver, R.: An experimental evaluation of temporal characteristics of communication links in outdoor sensor networks. In: ACM REALWSN'06, pp. 73–77. Uppsala, Sweden (2006)
20. Szewczyk, R., Mainwaring, A., Polastre, J., Anderson, J., Culler, D.: An analysis of a large scale habitat monitoring application. In: Proceedings of the 2nd International Conference on Embedded Networked Sensor Systems, pp. 214–226 (2004)
21. Wan, C.Y., Campbell, A.T., Krishnamurthy, L.: PSFQ: a reliable transport protocol for wireless sensor networks. In: WSNA '02: Proceedings of the 1st ACM international workshop on Wireless sensor networks and applications, pp. 1–11 (2002)
22. Woo, A., Tong, T., Culler, D.: Taming the underlying challenges of reliable multihop routing in sensor networks. In: Proceedings of the 1st international conference on Embedded networked sensor systems, pp. 14–27 (2003)
23. Ye, F., Zhong, G., Lu, S., Zhang, L.: GRAdient broadcast: a robust data delivery protocol for large scale sensor networks. Wirel. Netw. 11(3), 285–298 (2005)
24. Zhao, J., Govindan, R.: Understanding packet delivery performance in dense wireless sensor networks. In: Proceedings of the 1st international conference on Embedded networked sensor systems, pp. 1–13 (2003)

An Autonomous Energy-Aware Routing Scheme: a Supplementary Routing Approach for Path-Preserving Wireless Sensor Networks

Fang-Yie Leu, Guo-Cai Li and Wen-Chin Wu

Department of Computer Science and Information Engineering,
Tunghai University, Taiwan

{leufy, g942815}@thu.edu.tw, altosax.tw@gmail.com

Abstract One of the hottest research topics is how to reduce energy consumption to prolong the lifetime of a WSN. Some nodes of a WSN may be isolated from others, particularly when all their neighbors have crashed or run out of energy, and are thus no longer helpful in collecting and relaying messages, even though their batteries still retain some level of energy. To avoid this, in this paper, we propose a supplementary routing approach, named Energy-aware routing (EnAR in short), which can help to extend the lifetime of a WSN by integrating itself with the routing scheme of the host WSN. With the EnAR, a node in a given WSN (denoted by host WSN) checks the amount of its remaining energy, each time the node receives a request, to see whether it should reject or accept the request. The WSN routes messages through other communication paths when nodes on the original path have consumed too much energy under the condition that alternate paths truly exist. One of the alternate paths will be chosen to relay messages to prevent nodes along the original path from exhausting all their energy so that the WSN can last longer. Our experimental results show that this scheme is applicable to and suitable for an environment with decentralized control, and is able to effectively prolong the lifetime of a WSN.

Keywords: wireless sensor networks; energy-aware routing; supplemental routing scheme; energy consumption; path-preserving routing scheme

1. Introduction

Due to the rapid advancement and development of manufacturing techniques, sensor nodes (sensors in short) have become tinier and cheaper. Those that work autonomously can be used in place of human workers to sense and monitor environmental change. In a wireless sensor network (WSN), sensors are usually put in locations that people can not or seldom reach. Hence, their batteries can not be replaced or can only be replaced infrequently. That is why prolonging the lifetime of batteries has become a hot research topic recently. Researchers have proposed ways to solve this problem, e.g., by decreasing message relaying counts, shortening communication distance, or using nodes with more energy to handle energy consuming tasks. LEACH [1], directed diffusion [2], SPIN [3], and SAR [4] concentrate on routing affection, whereas SMACS/EAR (Self-organizing Medium Access Control for Sensor networks/ Eavesdrop And Register) [4] uses a self-organizing and asynchronous approach to improve MAC protocols. All of these methods

Please use the following format when citing this chapter:

Leu, F.-Y., Li, G.-C., Wu, W.-C., 2008, in IFIP International Federation for Information Processing, Volume 265, Advances in Ad Hoc Networking, eds. Cuenca, P., Guerrero C., Puigjaner, R., Serra, B., (Boston: Springer), pp. 49-60.

50

decrease the energy consumption of a node and prolong system life. But let us consider the following situation.

The topology shown in Fig. 1 roughly consists of sections A, B and C. If too many events have occurred or there are many hot nodes in section B, nodes in this section will soon use up their batteries. This will isolate sections A and C. About two-thirds of the nodes still retain some level of energy, but only one-third of them (i.e., section C) are now in service. In other words, checking the total remaining energy in all nodes of a system will not enable us to estimate the remaining life of the system. The focus should be on whether system service is able to proceed or not, which can more accurately reflect the real situation. For example, when using sensors to monitor whether a forest/house is on fire, we do not consider that the system is still working if 30% of nodes have failed. Even if only 1% of nodes are not working, no one knows whether the forest/house is on fire if the fire occurs in the 1% unmonitored area. Hence, prolonging system service is more important than prolonging the life of a node, particularly when an entire monitored area should be completely sensed all the time. In the following, we consider that a system's service become unreliable when at least one node exhausts its energy.

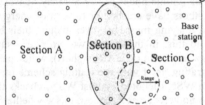

Fig. 1 Topology of a wireless sensor network in which there is an isolation section B

In this research, we propose a routing approach, named energy-aware routing (EnAR), which, as a supplemental mechanism, should be integrated with a path-preserving routing scheme of a WSN to effectively extend the WSN's service time. A node in such a system can reject service requests issued by other nodes, particularly when it has consumed too much energy since system start up. We call the original routing scheme the EnAR integrates with a host routing scheme. In the following, we use the terms routing and relaying messages interchangeably, even though some researchers define them differently. Also, a host routing scheme X, e.g., on-demand, after being integrated with the EnAR, is called X-EnAR, e.g., on-demand-EnAR, and the WSN that deploys an X-EnAR routing scheme is called EnAR-WSN.

2. Related Work

Several types of energy saving methods have been proposed for WSNs. The first type focuses on remaining energy, e.g., E-SPAN (energy-aware spanning tree algorithm) [9] considers energy that each device currently has when building a routing tree as an energy-saving topology. The one with the greatest amount of residual energy will be the root. Others choose one of their neighbors as the parent based on the residual energy the neighbor has and the distance between the underlying node and the root.

The second type emphasizes reducing the number of packet transmissions and receptions. LEACH [1] adopts a cluster-based routing approach in which nodes of a WSN are clustered into groups. Groups are self-organized in each round of data collection. Packets generated by nodes of a cluster (group) are centralized to their cluster head which is responsible for transmitting these packets to a base station. Therefore, how to choose cluster-heads is a critical issue in saving energy. The focus of MECH [5] is on the remaining energy in that, the more energy a node currently has, the higher probability the node will be chosen as a cluster-head. TEEN (threshold sensitive energy efficient sensor network protocol) [6], LEACH-C (LEACH-centralized) [7] and PEGASIS [8] all refine LEACH. TEEN defines a clustering algorithm to classify WSNs into two types, proactive and reactive which are described above, and for saving energy. LEACH-C determines which nodes will be chosen as cluster-heads based on global information collected by base stations, including geographical topology and remaining energy. In PEGASIS, only one designated node rather than all cluster-heads sends aggregate data to a base station. It uses a greedy algorithm to establish a chain that includes all nodes of a WSN. Nodes transmit messages through a downstream chain for upstream nodes in each round of data collection.

The third type conducts sleeping-mode to nodes. Idle devices enter sleeping-mode in which devices turn off their antennas and some system components to save energy. S-MAC [10] added a sleeping-mode and a random schedule to IEEE802.11 MAC. Each sensor has a probability of entering its sleeping-mode [11] extended system life by preserving coverage and letting some system components go to sleep. LDS (linear distance-based scheduling) [12], BS (balanced-energy scheduling) [17], RS (randomized scheduling) [18], and DS (distance-based scheduling) [13] involve cluster-based routing and focus on a sleeping-mode algorithm. DS and LDS determine whether a sensor should go to sleep or not by calculating the distance between the sensor and its cluster-head. BS prolongs a system's life time by balancing system energy consumption.

The fourth type focuses on energy consumption and its impact on sensing coverage of sensor nodes. The DAPR protocol (distributed activation based on predetermined routes) [10] was proposed based on an application plane that considers the relationship between coverage area and available energy. Reducing power consumption may prolong the lifetime of whole WSNs, but the effective coverage area may not be in proportion to the number of surviving nodes due to the high density of remaining nodes. A CPCHSA algorithm (coverage-preserving cluster-head selection algorithm) [14] was devised to modify the LEACH [1] by deploying a threshold-adjusting formula based on effective coverage area to select a better cluster-head, which is one with a smaller effective coverage area. Those with larger effective coverage areas have lower probability of being a cluster-head. Carefully selected cluster-heads can physically extend the system lifetime and help a WSN maintain a higher effective coverage area.

3. System Model
3.1 Modification of routing

Table-driven and location-aware routing schemes maintain routing tables/paths at all times. Such maintenance consumes much energy and is harmful to system life. During routing, a node only needs to know the type of packets it is requested to relay or send. Routing paths are maintained or established periodically. This type of routing scheme is different from the on-demand approach in that a node with on-demand approach, before sending data, submits a path-discovery packet, that carries source and destination addresses, to find a routing path so that messages generated can reach a base station in its following stage, i.e., data transmission stage. To cope with all probable path-preserving routing schemes that host WSNs may deploy, the EnAR adopts on-demand's routing steps. A node in a EnAR-WSN can autonomously determine whether it should reject relaying messages for other nodes, continuously relay messages for other nodes, or reject a path-discovery request.

3.2 Modes

Fig. 2 shows the layer structure of the EnAR in which a node has two modes, normal and rejection. A node in its normal mode performs the designated tasks normally, including sensing environmental changes and relaying/transmitting message, etc. A node R enters its rejection mode when its remaining energy is less than a threshold, or in some WSNs (e.g., S-MAC, and LDS) it enters sleeping mode. R disappears when it enters rejection mode or leaves the WSN (e.g., failure or exhausting its energy). If a path-preserving WSN can accept that its nodes will disappear during its life time, the EnAR as a supplementary routing mechanism can then be smoothly integrated with the WSN. There are two cases when R will reject the request it receives. The first is if R, after entering its rejection mode, receives a path-discovery request. It rejects the request by replying with no messages, which will force the EnAR-WSN to choose another path that excludes R. The second is if R is now on a routing path. After receiving a packet, it finds that its remaining energy is insufficient to process (e.g., relay) the packet, R then switches itself to rejection mode. Such will cause the host routing scheme to issue a path-discovery request. Whether R should enter its rejection mode and the activities performed before and after entering rejection mode are all autonomously determined and done by R itself, i.e., it is a fully distributive and autonomous way without any central control (e.g., base station's interference and global information collected by base station).

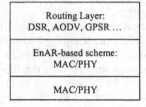

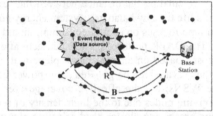

Fig. 2 The layer structure of the EnAR

Fig. 3 Data generated in an event field is sent to a base station through different paths when a node R along a routing path refuses to relay packets. Neighbor which will receive a packet sent by node S is autonomously determined by S itself, which is either a source node of or an intermediate node along a routing path.

3.3 Isolation problem

How does an EnAR-WSN work? As shown in Fig.3, if a node R on path A enters its rejection mode, path A will be replaced by another path, e.g., by path B. For instance, DSR establishes path B, excluding R, with the least hop counts as the alternate shortest routing path. Although path B is farther away with longer delay, it may (may not) consume more energy than those nodes on path A if the bandwidth of the two paths is the same [19]. This is helpful not only in prolonging the life time of an entire system, but also in preventing node R from running out of energy too quickly in transmitting packets from the event field (data source) to a base station, thus avoiding the occurrence of isolation sections. A path-discovery request to establish path B is initiated by, e.g., node S in Fig. 3, which may be either the data source node or the disappearing node's upstream neighbor depending on the re-routing policy of the host WSN. The former (the latter) is the case when the host routing scheme is a static (dynamic) routing.

3.4 Types of packets

Node energy is often consumed by sensing environment, transmitting data and relaying packets. In this research, we divide total energy E_{total} that a node currently has into four types E_x, E_y, E_z and E_u , which are defined in Table 1 where $E_{total} = E_x + E_y + E_z + E_u$, in which the initial energy allocated to E_u will be described later. The way to allocate remaining energy $E(= E_{total} - E_u)$ is as follows. Transmission priorities of type x, y and z, denoted by $Pri(x)$, $Pri(y)$ and $Pri(z)$ respectively, are $Pri(x)>Pri(y)>Pri(z)$. The allocation function of the three types' initial energy E_i is defined as $E_i = E \times C_i$ where C_i is the weight of type i, $i = x, y, z$ and $\sum_{\forall i} C_i = 1$, i.e., a node reserves E_i for processing and transmitting type i packets on receiving a request Req. Before relaying (when Req is type y or z), transmitting (when Req is type x), or replying with a packet, a node, e.g., node R, along a routing path checks which type the request is and how much energy it currently has. If E is less than a predefined threshold δ, R rejects the request. Otherwise, if the request is type x, y, or z, R further checks to see whether there is enough of the corresponding type of energy to serve the request. If not, a reallocation is performed. We assume that $E_p = E_{pi}$ where E_{pi} is the energy required to transmit a packet of type i, i=x,y,z. The reallocation policy is that when a node runs out E_x, $(E_y + E_z) \times C_x$ is then allocated to type x constrained on the fact that new $E_x \geq E_p$.

Table 1 Energy consumption types on a node R

Type	Energy consumption description
E_x	energy for sensing environmental data and transmitting data, which is the quota for node R itself, i.e., data source is node R.
E_y	energy for relaying packets for neighbors, which is the quota for neighbors. Data source is a neighbor of R.
E_z	energy for relaying packets for others, which is the quota for those other than node R and R's neighbors. Data source is neither node R nor R's neighbors.
E_u	energy for processing, including receiving and transmitting/relaying/replying, a path-discovery packet.

As the node runs out E_y , E_z will be reallocated to types y and z as

$$E_y' \; (= E_z \times \frac{C_y}{C_y + C_z}) \quad \text{and} \quad E_z' \; (= E_z \times \frac{C_z}{C_y + C_z}),$$ respectively, also constrained on $E_y' \geq E_p$. A node (e.g., node R), when running out E_z , will reject type-z requests. If R rejects a request, either due to $E < \delta$ or since E_j is less than E_{pj} of a type j request, even if reallocation has just been completed, j=x, y or z, re-routing will be performed. If node R is a throat point of the underlying WSN, the new path-discovery request, carrying the source and destination node addresses which are the same as those either of a previous

path-discovery request rejected by R or of a previous connection for the continuous relaying of messages going through R that R rejected for some reason, reaches R again. This time the node, except for exhausting E after receiving the request, should accept this request and relay the following arriving packets to make the WSN robust enough to serve requests. Therefore, a parameter that records a node's routing history should be referred to.

3.5 Working algorithm

We assume that in an EnAR-WSN each packet carries destination and source addresses and all packets are of the same size because a WSN is an event report system and data conveyed on a packet is very often fixed in size. That is why we assume $E_{px} = E_{py} = E_{pz}$, which can simplify the following algorithms, their analyses, and the calculation of the energy consumed by a packet. A node, when receiving a request, checks to see whether its remaining energy is larger than a given threshold or not by invoking ChkReq(). If yes, the EnAR updates its energy by executing ChkServ(). ChkServ() will call ReallocEngy() to reallocate its remaining energy when E_x or E_y is used up. Furthermore, ChkReq() checks to see whether a request that a node receives has been rejected by the node within a period pre-defined of time or not by involving a timer. If yes, R should accept the request since re-routing after rejection selects R again.

ChkReq (p)

/* When node R receives a request (i.e., a packet) p which may be a path-discovery request (type u) or a packet of type i either from its upstream node M (i.e., type y or z) or from itself (i.e., type x), it checks to see whether p is acceptable or not; Also, assume that a node maintains a list L to keep its routing history */

1.   {Let Sa and Da be the source and destination addresses of p, respectively, and L be a list of source and destination pairs (Sa, Da) with a counter count$_{Sa\_Da}$ and a timer t$_{Sa\_Da}$. /*the counter counts the times having been rejected */

2.   if ((Sa, Da) is not in L) { L = L ∪ {(Sa, Da)} ; count$_{Sa\_Da}$=1; starts timer t$_{Sa\_Da}$} else

       if (t$_{Sa\_Da}$ times out) count$_{Sa\_Da}$=0; /*(Sa, Da) already exists but the timer times out*/

3.   if ((E > threshold δ) or ($E > E_p$ and count$_{Sa\_Da} \geq 1$))

       {Deci=ChkServ(p, count$_{Sa\_Da}$,t$_{Sa\_Da}$);

3.1. switch(Deci)

3.2. case (accepted): if p is a type-u packet, then reply to the request with an accept-ACK;

       else {deliver the packet received/generated to the downstream node toward Da;
       count$_{Sa\_Da}$ =0;}

3.3. case (rejected): {reject the request; count$_{Sa\_Da}$++; enter rejection mode; start t$_{Sa\_Da}$;}

3.4. default: output an error message; /* p is a type other than u, x, y and z */ }

4.   Else {reject p; count$_{Sa\_Da}$++; /* E < δ , or the time point that R rejected last request was not within the pre-defined period of the time from right now */}

ChkServ(p, count$_{Sa\_Da}$, t$_{Sa\_Da}$) /*E_p is the energy required to transmit a packet p */

1.   { switch (type(p))

2.   case(u): if(count$_{Sa\_Da} \geq 1$ and t$_{Sa\_Da}$ does not time out) return(accepted); /*a path-discovery request*/

3.   case(x): if ($E_x \geq E_p$){ $E_x = E_x - E_p$;return (accepted);}

       else{ ReallocEngy(E_x , E_y , E_z , x, Decision); return(Decision);}

4.　　case(y): if ($E_y \geq E_p$){ $E_y = E_y - E_p$; return (accepted);}

　　　　else{ReallocEngy(E_x , E_y , E_z , y, Decision); return (Decision);}

5.　　case(z): if ($E_z \geq E_p$){ $E_z = E_z - E_p$; return (accepted);}

　　　　else return (rejected);

6.　　default: return (error);}

ReallocEngy(E_x , E_y , E_z , Q, Decision) /* to reallocate energy */

1.　　{if (Q==x) {

　　　　case($E_p \leq E < 2 \cdot E_p$):{ $E_x = E$; E_y =0; E_z =0; Decision=accepted;}

　　　　/* $E = E_x + E_y + E_z$ *is only sufficient to transmit a packet, then allocate energy to*

　　　　E_x */

　　　　case($2 \cdot E_p \leq E < 3 \cdot E_p$):{ $E_x = 0.5 \times E$; $E_y = 0.5 \times E$; $E_z = 0$; Decision=accepted;} /*E *is only sufficient to transmit two packets* */

　　　　default: /* $E \geq 3 \cdot E_p$, *Distributed energy to* E_x , E_y *and* E_z *based on their*

　　　　weight C_x , C_y *and* C_z */

　　　　{ $q = E - 3 \cdot E_p$; $E_i = q \times C_i + E_p$, $\forall i = x, y, z$; Decision=accepted;}}

2.　　else /* Q==y */

　　　　if ($E_p \leq E_y + E_z < 2 \cdot E_p$){ $E_y = E_p$; $E_x = E - E_p$; E_z =0; Decision=accepted;}

　　　　/* $E_y + E_z$ *is only sufficient to transmit a packet, so give* E_p *to* E_y *and remaining en-*

　　　　ergy to E_x */

　　　　else /* $E_y + E_z \geq 2 \cdot E_p$ */

　　　　$$q = E_y + E_z - 2 \cdot E_p ; \; E_j = q \times \frac{C_j}{C_y + C_z} + E_p, \forall j = y, z ;$$

　　　　Decision=accepted; }}}

4.　Experimental Results and Discussion

Three experiments were performed in this research. The first studied the difference between the lifetime of a WSN and an EnAR-WSN when different extreme amounts of initial energy are allocated to types x, y and z where system lifetime is the time period from the beginning of a system to the time point when the first node of the system dies. The second illustrated the ways to allocate initial energy to a node in a uniformly distributed WSN. The third compared system service time (in rounds) when different initial energy allocation approaches are used.

4.1　System Life Time

In the first experiment, each sensor was given only enough energy to transmit and receive 100 packets. The energy required for reallocation computation is one-tenth of that for transmitting a packet. In Fig. 4, *a-b-c* along x-axis means the energy reserves for types *x, y* and *z* of a node are *a*%, *b*% and *c*%, respectively, where *a+b+c*=100. It shows that the lifetimes of clustering approaches with EnAR and without EnAR (cluster with EnAR and cluster without EnAR, in short, respectively) are similar on 0-0-100 because most nodes in both approaches exhausted most of their energy relaying packets for others (excluding a node itself and its neighbors). As compared with the cluster with EnAR in the cases of 0-100-0 and 100-0-0, the cluster with EnAR on 0-0-100 consumed the least energy (i.e., the difference between two poles of a pair, with and without the EnAR) to issue and process path-discovery packets. Its lifetime thus was longer than that of the other two.

The worst case occurs at 100-0-0. Because after a node enters its rejection mode, each time it receives a type-y or type-z request, a path-discovery request will be issued. Unfortunately, requests of these two types are the majority, particularly for those nodes near their base station. Such a node consumes a lot of energy to run ChkReq() and ChkServ(), and the system of such an allocation issues more path-discovery requests than 0-0-100 and 0-100-0. Both of these operations are harmful to system life. Our conclusion is that initial energy allocation significantly affects energy consumption.

To improve the situation, we deployed the *Pareto principle*, with which 20% of energy is reserved for a node itself and 80% for neighbors (30%) and others (50%). System lifetime (see 20-30-50 in Fig.4) was longer than that of the cluster approach without EnAR. Theoretically, its optimal initialization occurs when C_i (recall, weight of type i) is the probability that a node will receive a type-i request, $i=x,y,z$, during its lifetime. Formula (1) is an estimation.

$$C_i(t_k) = \frac{P_i(t_k)}{\sum\limits_{j \in \{x,y,z\}} P_j(t_k)}, i = x, y, z \tag{1}$$

where $p_j(t_k)$ is the amount of type j requests received during the period of time from time points t_{k-1} to t_k, j=x, y, or z, and $\sum\limits_{j \in \{x,y,z\}} P_j(t_k)$ is the total amount of requests of types x, y, and z received in this time period. The energy initially allocated to E_u is

$$E_u = E_{total} \times \frac{P_u}{\sum\limits_{j \in \{x,y,z\}} P_j + \sum P_u} \tag{2}$$

where $\sum P_u(\sum\limits_{j \in \{x,y,z\}} p_j)$ is the total amount of type-u (types x, y and z) packets a node has received in its historical records.

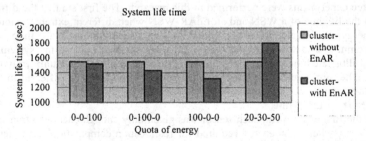

Fig. 4 a-b-c in x-axis means energy reserved for types x, y and z of a node is a%, b% and c%, respectively, and $a+b+c=100$. The difference between two poles of a pair (with and without the EnAR) is the energy consumed for reallocation and path-discovery.

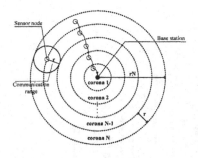

Fig. 5 Delineation of an EnAR-WSN for initial energy allocation

Fig. 6 Topology of a simulation environment of 200x200m² in which nodes are uniformly distributed and node 51 (at the center of this field) is a base station

4.2 Initial Energy Allocation

In the second experiment, we assume that there is a uniform distribution system of which, as shown in Fig. 5, the communication range of a node is r geographical distance units, and the data stream is forwarded to a base station hop by hop, i.e., a node in a corona, e.g., corona c, relays packets generated by nodes in outer corona, i.e., corona c+1, c+2, ..., N, to its direct inner corona, i.e., corona c-1, where c=1,2,3 ..., N-1 and corona 0 is a base station, This framework is the same as that illustrated in [20]. Assume that the probability of data generation is equal to all nodes, if we can preload different ratios of initial energy to sensor batteries in different coronas, the sensor network should have a better balance energy consumption model as we expect, so that initial energy allocated to a node is a function of c, i.e., $E_i = f_i(c)$, $i = x, y, z$.

Let r_y and r_z be respectively the numbers of neighbors and others which a node has to relay packets for. When sensor density in the underlying field is high, r_y and r_z can be expressed as

$$r_y = \frac{(r(c+1))^2 - (rc)^2}{(rc)^2 - (r(c-1))^2} = \frac{2c+1}{2c-1} \tag{3}$$

$$r_z = \frac{(rN)^2 - (r(c+1))^2}{(rc)^2 - (r(c-1))^2} = \frac{N^2 - (c+1)^2}{2c-1} \tag{4}$$

Here, c also means that a node is c hops (c coronas) away from a base station and N is the total number of circles in the underlying system. Then, theoretically the optimal initial energy allocated to a node is as follows.

$$E_x = \frac{E}{1 + r_y + r_z} \tag{5}$$

$$E_y = \frac{r_y E}{1 + r_y + r_z} \tag{6}$$

$$E_z = \frac{r_z E}{1 + r_y + r_z} \tag{7}$$

58

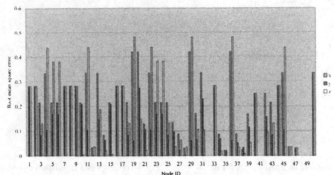

Statistics of energy consumption

Fig. 7 Root mean square errors between simulated results by deploying formulas (5) to (7) and their theoretically optimal values in a static network topology deploying AODV without EnAR

In this experiment, we deployed 51 nodes for a sensing/event field and relayed packets generated by using static AODV without EnAR. The topology shown in Fig. 6 is produced by using QualNet [15], and is a field in which nodes are uniformly distributed. Fig. 7 illustrates the root mean square errors (RMSEs) of energy physically consumed by a node for processing requests of types x, y and z when initial energy is individually allocated by using formulas (5) to (7) and by using the theoretically estimated optimal values (i.e., formula (1)) where RMSE(x)=0.14317, RMSE(y)=0.132233, and RMSE(z)=0.18803, showing that the RMSEs do not very approximate to zero, owing to the steady path of static AODV. Some nodes one hop (circle) or a few hops (circles) away from a base station do not relay packets for other nodes, e.g., nodes 29 and 36 in Fig. 6, since most packets generated by their upstream nodes flow through nodes 30 and 28, respectively.

To simplify the following description, we again assume that the probabilities of data generation of all nodes in a WSN are the same, and the information required, i.e., the total number of packets that a node has received within a period of time or since the system started up, can be gathered from the system in some ways so that we can accordingly allocate initial energy to a node. For example, Fig. 8 shows that the number of packets that a node has received during a given period of time can be obtained by analyzing its system topology. Hence, the node can realize how to allocate its initial energy, e.g., initial energy allocated to types x, y and z for node A is $(\frac{1}{7},\frac{2}{7},\frac{4}{7})$ since it has two neighbors and four others. Actually, the information gathered from a real static WSN is often general enough to meet all cases, no matter which distribution (e.g., normal, uniform or Poisson) nodes in the WSN are? That means the information is better than that derived from a uniform distribution, i.e., formulas (5) to (7), since it can help to allocate more accurate initial energy so as to prolong the system life of the WSN.

4.3 System Service Time

In the third experiment, we compared the two schemes, formulas (5) to (7) and formula (1), to see how they affect the system service time of a WSN. The simulation environment deployed AODV routing scheme and 50 nodes which are randomly distributed in system field. For simplicity, we assume the energy consumption of generating and relaying a packet is the same, even it is not always true in real world. Fig. 9 shows the service time before the first node exhausts all its energy. It is clear that AODV-EnAR using formulas (5) to (7) outperforms AODV without EnAR, but does not perform as well as AODV-EnAR using formula (1). The reasons are mentioned above.

Unfortunately, collecting packet statistics for deriving formula (1) sometimes is infeasible since the collection always consumes energy and should be performed system wide. Also, before allocating initial energy, we have to know the value of the denominator of formula (1). Furthermore, some routing schemes can not predict or obtain their routing topologies beforehand, e.g., direct diffusion [16], particularly when the system is a decentralized-control WSN. Our conclusion is that formulas (5) to (7) are feasible if r_y and r_z can be derived from system topology, e.g., based on the number of upstream hops which a node has to relay packets for.

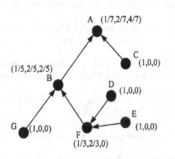 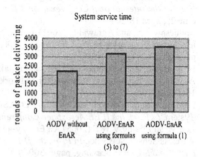

Fig. 8 A routing topology deploying AODV where (x,y,z) of a node represents the ratios of types x,y and z requests the node will receive

Fig. 9 Comparison of system service time when different initial energy allocation approaches are used

5.   Conclusion and Future Research

In this study, we propose an energy-aware supplemental routing scheme, named the EnAR, to prolong a WSN's system life by routing packets through alternate paths with a decentralized approach. Nodes along the alternate paths will take over the task of relaying packets to prevent nodes on the original path not only from exhausting their energy quickly, but also from forming an isolated section no sooner after system start up. The EnAR should collaborate with path-preserving routing schemes. Experimental results showed that the collaboration can effectively prolong an underlying WSN's system lifetime. Also, the ways to allocate initial energy have been proposed and discussed. Among them formulas (5) to (7) are suitable for uniform distribution. Even if a base station is located at or near the edge of a field, they are still applicable. Formulas (1) and (2) can be applied to different distributions, uniform, normal, Poisson and so on, if the number of packets a node will receive can be obtained or predicted.

Our future work includes analyzing the cost and reliability models such as integrating the EnAR with different routing schemes, and studying other appropriate methods that can optimally allocate initial energy to requests of types x, y and z, besides the Pareto principle and formulas (1) and (2), particularly when nodes are distributed to a system field with different distributions, e.g., normal distribution and the stochastic approach, since in a WSN it is very difficult to collect global information, which also consumes a lot of energy and bandwidth. Furthermore, we will try to integrate MAC layer protocols, like sleeping mode scheduling, with the EnAR to further improve its system efficiency so as to save as much energy as possible, especially when the node density of a sensor network is high.

6. References

[1] Heinzelman W, Chandrakasan A, and Balakrishnan H (2000) Energy-Efficient Communication Protocols for Wireless Microsensor Networks (LEACH). *In Proc. the 33rd Hawaii International Conference on Systems Science*, volume 8, pages 3005-3014.

[2] Intanagonwiwat C, Govindan R, Estrin D, Heidemann J, andSilva F (2003) Directed Diffusion for Wireless Sensor Networking. *IEEE/ACM Transactions on Networking*, 11(1):2-16.

[3] Heinzelman W, Kulik J, and Balakrishnan H (1999) Adaptive Protocols for Information Dissemination in Wireless Sensor Networks. *In Proc. the Fifth Annual ACM/IEEE International Conference on Mobile Computing and Networking*, pages 174-185.

[4] Sohrabi K et al (2000) Protocols for Self-Organization of a Wireless Sensor Network. *IEEE Personal Communication*, 7(5):16–27.

[5] Chang R, and Kuo C (2006) An Energy Efficient Routing Mechanism for Wireless Sensor Networks. *In Proc. the International Conference on Advanced Information Networking and Applications*, volume 2, pages 18-20.

[6] Manjeshwar A, and Agrawal D (2001) TEEN: a Routing Protocol for Enhanced Efficiency in Wireless Sensor Networks. *In Proc. the International Parallel and Distributed Processing Symposium*, pages 2009-2015.

[7] Heinzelman W B, Chandrakasan A P, and Balakrishnan H (2002) An Application-Specific Protocol Architecture for Wireless Microsensor Networks. *IEEE Transactions on Wireless Communication*, 1(4):660-670.

[8] Lindesy S, and Raghavendra C (2002) PEGASIS: Power-Efficient Gathering in a Sensor Information System. *In Proc. the IEEE Aerospace Conference*, volume 3, pages 1125-1130.

[9] Lee M, and Wong V W S (2005) An Energy-aware Spanning Tree Algorithm for Data Aggregation in Wireless Sensor Networks. *In Proc. the IEEE Pacific Rim Conference on Communications, Computers and Signal Processing*, pages 300-303.

[10] Perillo M and Heinzelman W (2004) Dapr: A Protocol for Wireless Sensor Networks Utilizing an Application-based Routing Cost. *In Proc. the IEEE Wireless Communications and Networking Conference (WCNC 2004)*, volume 3, pages 1540–1545.

[11] Tian D, and Georganas N D (2002) A Coverage-Preserving Node Scheduling Scheme for Large Wireless Sensor Networks. *In Proc. the first ACM International Workshop on Wireless Sensor Networks and Applications*, pages 32-41.

[12] Deng J, Han Y S, Heinzelman B, and Varshney P K (2005) Scheduling Sleeping Nodes in High Density Cluster-based Sensor Networks. *Mobile Networks and Applications*, 10:825-835.

[13] Deng J, Han Y S, Heinzelman B, and Varshney P K (2005) Balanced-Energy Sleep Scheduling Scheme for High Density Cluster-based Sensor Networks. *Computer Communications*, 28(14):1631-1642.

[14] Tsai Y R (2007) Coverage-Preserving Routing Protocols for Randomly Distributed Wireless Sensor Networks. *IEEE Transactions on Wireless Communications*, 6:1240-1245.

[15] Scalable Network Technologies, http://www.scalable-networks.com

[16] Intanagonwiwat C, Govindan R, Estrin D, Heidemann J, and Silva F (2003) Directed Diffusion for Wireless Sensor Networking. *IEEE/ACM Transactions on Networking*, 11(1):2-16.

[17] Chamam A and Pierre S (2007) Optimal Scheduling of Sensors' States to Maximize Network Lifetime in Wireless Sensor Networks. *In Proc. the IEEE International Conference on Mobile Ad-hoc and Sensor Systems (MASS 2007)*, pages 1-6.

[18] Eryilmaz A, Modiano E, and Ozdaglar A (2006) Randomized Algorithms for Throughput-Optimality and Fairness in Wireless Networks. *In Proc. the 45th IEEE Conference on Decision and Control*, pages 1936-1941.

[19] Leu F Y, and Li G C (2007) A Scalable Sensor Network Using a Polar Coordinate System. *Signal Processing*, 87(12):2978-2990.

[20] Yang Y and Cardei M (2007) Movement-Assisted Sensor Redeployment Scheme for Network Lifetime Increase. *In Proc. the 10th ACM Symposium on Modeling, analysis, and simulation of wireless and mobile systems (MSWiM '07)*, pages 13-20.

FlowerNet - How to design a user friendly Sensor Network

Bjoern Gressmann and Horst Hellbrueck

Abstract Today, sensor networks are on the way from simulation and short term measurements in the laboratory to real long term applications where devices operate for several weeks without administration. In this paper we describe the design, development and evaluation of a suitable application for further measurements of sensor network protocols and applications where users can benefit from the services of this network in daily life. Energy efficiency, reliability and adaptability are key features to fulfill the requirements of the users. We decide to develop a monitoring system for potted flowers at our institute and support the users with automatically generated decisions for watering the flowers. We perform long term measurements and evaluate the whole system including the benefit that the users experience. In this paper we present first results and the long term evaluation of the system.

1 Introduction

Simulations were standard in the Mobile Ad Hoc Network (MANET) and sensor networks research community in the past for years. First experimental results show that simulation models for sensor networks are far from being realistic and protocols developed in simulations might fail in real world environments.

Reference implementation of protocols and their evaluation in MANET or sensor network testbeds help to improve the confidence in protocols. The research focus of these testbeds is evaluation of protocol and variants which does not require long term measurements in many cases. In these field experiments data and information transferred as well as user interaction were only of secondary interest.

Bjoern Gressmann
Institute of Telematics, University of Luebeck, e-mail: gressmann@itm.uni-luebeck.de

Horst Hellbrueck
Institute of Telematics, University of Luebeck e-mail: hellbrueck@itm.uni-luebeck.de

Please use the following format when citing this chapter:

Gressmann, B., Hellbrueck, H., 2008, in IFIP International Federation for Information Processing, Volume 265, Advances in Ad Hoc Networking, eds. Cuenca, P., Guerrero C., Puigjaner, R., Serra, B., (Boston: Springer), pp. 61-72.

Before sensor networks can be deployed in real world application new challenges need to be solved. A very practical issue is the required interaction with individuals. Systems under test need to offer a real user benefit, so that users ideally voluntarily utilize these systems regularly.

In this paper, we introduce *FlowerNet* as a suitable application to conduct protocol evaluations as well as user acceptance surveys in a simple setup. *FlowerNet* allows long term evaluation with a multi hop radio network and is based on the ESB sensor network platform ([1]) that provides a convenient programming environment, a simple radio interface and an extension connector for additional sensors.

The user acceptance for sensor network applications poses important challenges for such a system. Acceptance depends on the reliability and correctness of the system as well as the service and the way the service is offered. Systems like *FlowerNet* should provide the user with recommendations and detect faults and recover from them silently instead of dominating the user with instructions that might be even wrong.

The rest of the paper is organized as follows. Next section introduces related work. Section 3 lists all the user requirements and some prerequisites and constraints given by the hardware. In the next sections we will discuss design decisions where we focus on the adaptability of the application. We will finish the paper with a first evaluation of the system and an outlook for the future work.

2 Related Work

Environmental monitoring and in-situ habitat monitoring are two main applications of Wireless Sensor Networks.

Possible applications besides monitoring of plants in private environment are the improvement of agricultural production, monitoring of animal populations or climate data acquisition.

A project also addressing monitoring of plants is the Botanicalls project ([2]) based on ZigBee. A main feature of this application is the creation of a new communication channel between a plant and its owner using Voice over IP. The user can call plants to get information about their condition and the plants call the user to ask for water.

On Great Duck Island a population of Ceach's Storm Petrell is monitored by a WSN consisting of Mica Nodes ([3],[4]).

A research group at Agrosphere Institute, Forschungszentrum Juelich, is working on a project called SoilNet ([5]), in which a WSN based on the ZigBee Standard acquires soil moisture data in areas of 100's of meters.

The Computational Modeling Laboratory of the National Agricultural Research Center in Japan developed a system which acquires data of different environmental parameters in paddy fields and tries to improve the crops ([6]).

Within the MarathonNet project a monitoring system for runners in a running event presents various data of the participants to the interested audience, even in the Internet ([7],[8],[9]). Besides the implementation and evaluation of the system the application puts the main focus on usability and the special requirements of the devices in a sports event.

Practical approaches to animal tracking have been developed in the ZebraNet-project ([10]) and in the Electronic Shepherd-project ([11]).

In the Heathland experiment network characteristics have been evaluated in practical application ([12]) to collect experimental results about connectivity and data loss rates.

These examples of related work mainly focus on the network properties and the data collection itself. The collected data is provided to research people so that user friendliness in the first place is not that important. Researchers for soil measurements are interested in fine granular, long term raw data for a certain region. However, *FlowerNet* focuses on getting experience and results in the acceptance of the use of WSN technology in everyday life and not on the new network protocols as many other related work. Users of *FlowerNet* expect valuable information instead of raw data, which calls for a different focus of the project. The user expects the sensors to be self-adaptive and self-learning, so that they support the watering of cactuses in sandy soil as well as roses in humus. We will discuss the requirements of the users for a support system for flower care in the next sections.

3 Requirements

FlowerNet as a typical wireless application requires flexibility, fault tolerance, usability, reliability and a long life time.

As the user will not be interested in the technical aspects of the application, the presentation of data and the notification of the events has to be user friendly and appealing. Although routing is not the focus of this work the routing algorithm needs to support moving of flowers without user interaction to the system. When events of interest occur, the system sends an email to the user. The user can monitor his flowers by visiting a website which presents the acquired data graphically. Configuration and deployment of the network must be easy and intuitive. Thus, another aspect to achieve user friendliness is the adaptability of the event detection mechanism. Thereby the system adapts to the watering behavior of the user and special knowledge of the characteristics of the plants is not required for using *FlowerNet* .

Besides the technical requirements, the enclosure of the nodes should not affect the decorative function of the flowers and should be nearly invisible. The risk of damaging the roots of the flowers by inserting the measurement contacts into the soil should be minimal. There is a need for mechanisms to filter double events or wrong notification by incorrectly detected events. The nodes have to be protected by a housing from water and physical damage but still allow for easy battery change. An e-mail sent to the user in order to replace batteries is also a must in the system.

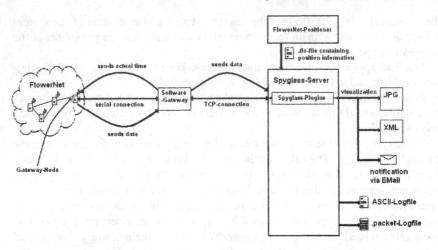

Fig. 1 *FlowerNet* Components

4 Network Design

This section describes the most important network design decisions that were made to fulfill requirements of *FlowerNet* .

The *FlowerNet* -application consists of several components (Figure 1). Data is collected in *FlowerNet* and routed to the gateway node, which propagates data to a software gateway. This software gateway also acts as a time server for the synchronization. The SpyglassServer ([13]) processes the data and creates the graphical output, an XML/XSLT file with the actual state of the plants. Additionally, log files are written, containing the acquired data since system start. Also, it sends the notification emails to the users.

For an easy configuration of the application, the tool *FlowerNetPositioner* has been developed. This tool enables easy configuration of positions of the flowers and create the graphical representation of the building map to achieve a nice graphical presentation of the collected data to the user. Furthermore, it allows the administrative users to enter email addresses of users in charge of each flower for the system notifications that are sent. The user receives e-mails in case of low battery to change the batteries and if the gateway node detects that nodes do not send packets for a long time period. This allows the user to react to error situations.

To assure a long life time, the system operates very energy efficient and nodes avoid collisions on the medium. The used routing protocol assures flexibility of positioning the nodes and achieve reliability of data transmission (Subsection 4.2). Figure 1 depicts the important components as described so far.

4.1 Schedule-based Time Division Multiplexing

This section presents the MAC layer of *FlowerNet*, which is determined as a schedule based time division multiplexing (STDM) with fixed intervals in which the radio transceivers are set into sleep mode to reduce energy consumption. As the number of nodes is known in advance and there are no real-time requirements, this simple solution fits well to the application.

For STDM, suitable time synchronization between the nodes is mandatory. *FlowerNet* synchronizes periodically. Each synchronization event is initiated by the gateway node which receives the actual time from the Software-Gateway. Each node has an interval of ONPERIOD seconds in which the transceiver is active as shown in Figure 2. This interval is called sending period. Afterwards the radio interface is switched off for OFFPERIOD seconds. During the sending period, all nodes have to be active too, as data forwarding to the gateway node is performed in a single sending interval. The duty cycle can be reduced by adapting the parameters ONPERIOD and OFFPERIOD. During the sending period, the node has a power consumption of 7.15mA. When the receiver is turned off, the power consumption reduces to 1.5 mA. So, the theoretical life time of a node using batteries with an energy of $E_{battery}$ in mAh is calculated by formula (1).

$$\frac{E_{battery}}{\frac{ONPERIOD}{OFFPERIOD} \times 7.15mAh + (1 - \frac{ONPERIOD}{OFFPERIOD}) \times 1.5mAh} \tag{1}$$

In our tests, we used 2000mAh batteries and set ONPERIOD to 6 and OFFPERIOD to 66, which results in a theoretical lifetime of 41.4 days. Although we know that this approach does not scale for large sensor networks, in *FlowerNet* with about tens of nodes it is appropriate.

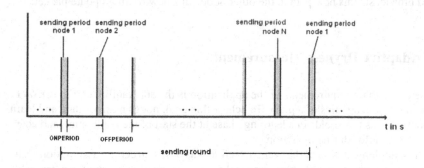

Fig. 2 Time Division Multiplexing scheme

There are several situations in which nodes need to connect to the network. In this case, nodes are not synchronized with the network yet. After the system start, a node stays active and periodically sends SIGN-Requests which indicate that this node is not synchronized yet. When the node receives network synchronization response messages it sets its own time and multiplexing information accordingly. This approach offers flexibility in deployment of the nodes, as there is no need to deploy any node at any special point of time.

4.2 Routing

As robustness of the system is a key requirement, we decided to use a routing protocol based on link qualities in the local neighborhood of the nodes as routing metric.

A suitable link metric has been presented in [14] and is implemented in *FlowerNet* . When a node receives a packet, it calculates a link quality for the link from the neighboring node and itself. This quality metric is calculated from sequence numbers in the data packets. After each interval of 32 packets sent by a neighbor the packet delivery rate is calculated and defines the downstream link quality. For further details we refer to [14].

The routing is organized in rounds triggered by the gateway node as a central component. It initiates a new routing round periodically, where nodes build a spanning tree on top of the existing meshed network graph. For this purpose, the gateway node broadcasts a routing update packet that is forwarded within the network These routing update packets contain the actual parent node and the sum of the link quality on the optimal path to the gateway node. When a node receives a routing update packet, it compares its actual quality of the routing path with the sum of the received path quality plus the quality of the link to the sending neighbor. If the new offered path has better quality the receiving node updates its routing information and broadcasts this new path to the other nodes in a new routing update packet.

5 Adaptive Dryness Measurement

One of the main requirements of the application is the adaptability of *FlowerNet* to specific characteristics of a plant. To achive this goal, nodes monitor data and learn about dryness thresholds in a learning phase at the start of the application and adapt these thresholds during operation.

The implementation of the event detection was based on certain assumptions. The dryness of ground increase with time and a watering will have a sudden measurable effect on the dryness of the soil.

There are several uncertainties that affect the measurement. For instance, the electric conductivity of different soil types can vary and different plants need different humidity levels in the soil which requires adaptability of the system. The

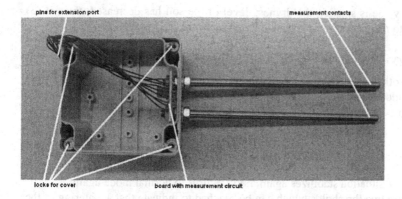

Fig. 3 Enclosure of the nodes

measured value depends on the insertion position of the contacts. So, the system will experience sudden changes in the measured values if the user repositions the plant. After the node has collected steady data again it gets back into a stable mode.

To measure the dryness we charge a capacitor through the soil with a current of 1mA. The soil acts a resistor in that case. The raw value is the time in milliseconds until the capacitor reaches a threshold voltage. The lower the resistance of the soil, the lower is this measured time, so we measure the dryness of the soil.

Measurements are repeated ten times and averaged to reduce the influence of variations due to measurement errors. This averaged value is called a dryness measurement (*dryness*) in the following.

Nodes detect on their own several events:

- The flower has been watered.
- The flower has to be watered because the soil is dry.
- The flower has to be watered because it's time.
- The flower has been watered, but the system did not detect a necessity for it.
- An error has been detected, no valid measurements possible at the moment.
- Node left error state, node collects valid dryness data again.

After a measurement has been executed, the node forecasts the next dryness value by using the delta between two measurements (*diff*). Diff is adapted by using exponential smoothing first order:

$$diff_{n+1} = (1 - \alpha_{diff}) \times diff_n + \alpha_{diff} \times new\_diff \tag{2}$$

The parameter $\alpha_{diff} \in [0..1]$ controls the filtering. The forecast dryness value is then $dryness_{forecast} = dryness_n + diff_n$.

If new dryness value differs from this forecast value more than a threshold, a watering event or an error is detected, depending on the new value. If the actually measured value is smaller, the dryness level of the soil has decreased, thus, if (3) evaluates to *true*, the system detects a watering event:

$$dryness_{n+1} \leqslant DRY\_FRAC \times dryness_{forecast}, \quad DRY\_FRAC \in [0..1] \qquad (3)$$

On the other side, if actual measurement value is larger, the dryness level of the soil has suddenly increased, possibly by changing the position of the two contacts, thus, if (4) evaluates to *true*, the node enters an error state:

$$dryness_{n+1} \geqslant ERROR\_FRAC \times dryness_{forecast}, \quad ERROR\_FRAC > 1 \qquad (4)$$

When the situation stabilizes again, node returns to normal mode again.

There are two thresholds which can be reached to indicate that a watering of the flower is necessary. The robustness and adaptability of the measurement is achieved by learning the initial thresholds during operation in a monitoring mode. The dryness threshold is set to the measured value immediately at the point of time of watering. The time threshold is initialized to the time interval between the first two watering events.

After a detected watering, the dryness threshold and the time threshold are adapted according to the following formula.

$$threshold_{n+1} = (1 - \alpha_{threshold}) \times threshold_n + (\alpha_{threshold}) \times dryness_n \qquad (5)$$

$$timeThreshold_{n+1} = (1 - \alpha_{time}) \times timeThreshold_n + \alpha_{time} \times time_n \qquad (6)$$

The parameters $\alpha_{threshold} \in [0..1]$ and $\alpha_{time} \in [0..1]$ describe how strong the new threshold is adapted.

The dryness threshold is the marker at which the plant should be watered when dryness level of the soil rises. If (7) evaluates to *true*, the user is notified that the flower has to be watered because the soil is dry.

$$dryness_{n+1} \geqslant THRESHOLD\_FRAC \times threshold_n, \quad THRESHOLD_FRAC \in [0..1] \qquad (7)$$

THRESHOLD_FRAC is the fraction of the dryness threshold that the measured dryness value has to exceed for notifying the user to water the plant.

Because of errors that lead to an irregular decrease in the dryness level of the soil we add another condition (8) to notify the user. This condition is true when a period of time has elapsed since the last watering. Then the user is notified that it is time to water the plant again.

$$time_{actual} \geqslant (timeThreshold_n + (TIME\_INTERVAL \times 3600)) \qquad (8)$$

A delay for the notification can be set by TIME_INTERVAL. There are several parameters to configure the event detection and the adaptation of the thresholds that have to be set in a proper way to achieve a coorect behavior of the system.

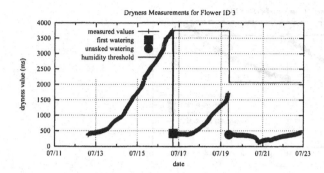

(a) dryness measurement

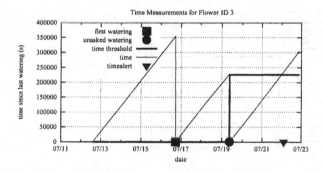

(b) time measurement

Fig. 4 Test run number 1; node with id 3

6 Evaluation

As described so far the design and implementation focus on robust and simple solutions. In this section we will present first evaluation results. Therefore, we started 2 test runs for approximately 2 weeks, where we apply the above described algorithm and analyzed the gathered data from the server across the network. The network runs stable for a period of 2 weeks time until nodes run out of battery power.

The diagrams Figure 4(a) and Figure 5(a) illustrate the measured dryness values and the dryness thresholds. The diagrams Figure 4(b) and Figure 5(b) show the time since the last watering and the time threshold after the second watering. Additionally

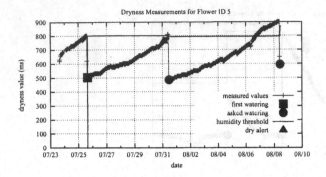

(a) dryness measurement

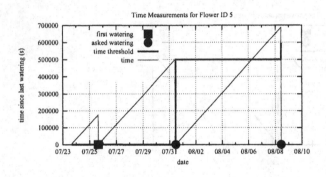

(b) time measurement

Fig. 5 Test run number 2; node with id 5

the diagrams display the events detected by the system. A watering of the flowers results in one of the three events:

- The flower is watered for the first time, then the node detects a first watering event.
- The flower is watered after it sent a notification for need of water to the user, then the system detects an asked watering event.
- The flower is watered, but sent no notification to the user, then the system detects an unasked watering event.

Events that trigger a notification are dry alerts which are detected if dryness values have reached the dryness threshold and time alerts if the time since last watering has exceeded the time threshold.

As can be seen in Figure 4 and Figure 5 in the first days, the system just monitors and collects dryness values. The measured value increases slowly due to loss of humidity until the plant is watered for the first time by the user. Then the sensor node sets a first threshold for a dry alert to inform the user when this state is reached again in the future. A dry alert can be seen in Figure 5 at day 07/31. The time threshold is learned after the second watering, as can be seen in Figure 4(b) and Figure 5(b). The user is informed to water his flower because of a time alert in Figure 4(b) at day 07/22. This is reasonable because the measured dryness values after the second watering differ a lot from the measured dryness values before the first and after the first watering (Figure 4(a)) and the dryness threshold might be reached lately in the future. Furthermore, the sensor nodes detect also extra watering and adapt the threshold to a new value as can be seen in Figure 4 at day 07/19. The different characteristics of the soils in Figure 4(a) and Figure 5(a) result in completely different ranges of the dryness values and show the necessity of a self-learning event detection mechanism.

For the proof of reliability we created the following test cases:

- Switch off sensor nodes simulates device failures
- Move plant with sensor node out of range simulates transient network failures
- Pull sensor nodes out of the pot to produce dryness measurement errors
- Run until end of battery to test battery replacement messages

FlowerNet had passed all test cases as nodes created error messages accordingly that were sent as e-mails to the user and successfully recovered from the errors again.

The test users respond in a positive way to e-mails about detected watering events as a helpful feedback for the correct operation of the system. As the user has to perform regular watering first so that the system can learn the threshold values, the system is not able to give reasonable decision support for users who just water their plants in a random fashion. The system was also confused be the effect that users water their plants before some days of vacation as *FlowerNet* is not aware of the days of a week.

7 Conclusion

In this paper we described a robust implementation of a sensor network where users communicate interactively with the system. Sensors detect watering and anomalies, set thresholds themselves and forward this data backwards along a spanning tree to a central server where e-mails are generated to remind users to water the plants. The system adapts to new situations where for example the sensor is moved or the user decides to change the watering behavior of the plant. The measurement is very accurate, so that even the daily (temperature) cycles are visible in the dryness mea-surements. For the future we work on the improvement of the lifetime of the system, so that the system is not discontinued every two weeks. This is even more important as users do not water a plant in very regular fashion. The use of replacement batteries could rise the lifetime up to six weeks and makes longer studies possible. There are certain situations like weekends or vacations where users change the watering behavior unpredictable such as increase the amount of water or water the plant too early in time. This shows that sensor networks need to take into account the needs of the users to offer an optimal service. With too many false positives, users will ignore the support, and will even be annoyed by "wrong" support decisions. We address these issues at the moment.

References

1. "Scatterweb," http://cst.mi.fu-berlin.de/projects/ScatterWeb/.
2. "The botanicalls project," http://www.botanicalls.com.
3. A. Mainwaring, D. Culler, J. Polastre, R. Szewczyk, and J. Anderson, "Wireless sensor networks for habitat monitoring," in *WSNA '02: Proceedings of the 1st ACM international workshop on Wireless sensor networks and applications.* New York, NY, USA: ACM Press, 2002, pp. 88–97.
4. R. Szewczyk, A. Mainwaring, J. Polastre, J. Anderson, and D. Culler, "An analysis of a large scale habitat monitoring application," in *SenSys '04: Proceedings of the 2nd international conference on Embedded networked sensor systems.* New York, NY, USA: ACM Press, 2004, pp. 214–226.
5. "Soilnet - a zigbee based soil moisture sensor network," http://www.fz-juelich.de/icg/icg-4/index.php?index=739.
6. "Field server - a wireless sensor network for plant and field condition monitoring," http://www.agnet.org/library/pt/2004033/.
7. H. Hellbrueck, M. Lipphardt, D. Pfisterer, S. Ransom, and S. Fischer, "Praxiserfahrungen mit marathonnet - ein mobiles sensornetz im sport," *PIK - Praxis der Informationsverarbeitung und Kommunikation*, vol. 29, no. 4, 2006.
8. D. Pfisterer, M. Lipphardt, C. Buschmann, H. Hellbrueck, S. Fischer, and J. H. Sauselin, "Marathonnet: Adding value to large scale sport events - a connectivity analysis," in *Proceedings of the International Conference on Integrated Internet Ad hoc and Sensor Networks (InterSense)*, May 2006.
9. M. Lipphardt, H. Hellbrueck, D. Pfisterer, S. Ransom, and S. Fischer, "Practical experiences on mobile inter-body-area-networking," in *Proceedings of the Second International Conference on Body Area Networks (BodyNets'07)*, 2007. [Online]. Available: http://www.bodynets.org/
10. P. Zhang, C. M. Sadler, S. A. Lyon, and M. Martonosi, "Hardware design experiences in zebranet," in *Proceedings of the 2nd international conference on Embedded networked sensor systems.* ACM Press, 2004, pp. 227–238.
11. B. Thorstensen, T. Syversen, T.-A. Bjornvold, and T. Walseth, "Electronic shepherd - a low-cost, low-bandwidth, wireless network system," in *MobiSys '04: Proceedings of the 2nd international conference on Mobile systems, applications, and services.* New York, NY, USA: ACM Press, 2004, pp. 245–255.
12. V. Turau, C. Renner, M. Venzke, S. Waschik, C. Weyer, and M. Witt, "The heathland experiment: Results and experiences," in *Proceedings of the REALWSN'05 Workshop on Real-World Wireless Sensor Networks*, Stockholm, Sweden, Jun. 2005.
13. C. Buschmann, D. Pfisterer, S. Fischer, S. P. Fekete, and A. Kröller, "Spyglass: A wireless sensor network visualizer," in *SIGBED Review, Vol. 2, No. 1, 2005*, 2005.
14. M. Yarvis, W. Conner, L. Krishnamurthy, J. Chhabra, B. Elliott, and A. Mainwaring, "Real-world experiences with an interactive ad hoc sensor network," 2002. [Online]. Available: citeseer.ist.psu.edu/yarvis02realworld.html

Distributed Policy Management Protocol for Self-Configuring Mobile Ad Hoc Networks

Mouna AYARI, Farouk KAMOUN and Guy PUJOLLE

Abstract Mobile ad hoc networks (MANETs) are fundamentally different from wired networks. They are autonomously formed with a collection of mobile nodes without any preexisting infrastructure or administrative support. In the last few years, Policy-Based Network Management (PBNM) has gained a considerable interest in order to reach adaptive and automated management goals in MANETs. Previous work in this field either cluster-based or hierarchical architectures are highly dependent of the network topology. A distributed approach with a high degree of autonomy and self-management is still lacking. In this paper, we give an overview of existing policy-based management solutions and we focus on some of their limitations. We outline the need of incorporating self-configuration property in the design of MANETs. Then, we present a new protocol for distributing policies and high-level goals over all nodes in the network. Simulation-based performance evaluation results are described and analyzed.

1 Introduction

A mobile ad hoc network (MANET) consists of a collection of mobile wireless nodes that dynamically create a network without any existing infrastructure or ad-

Mouna AYARI
CRISTAL lab, National School of Computer Sciences, ENSI, 2010, Manouba, Tunisia and
LIP6 University of Paris-VI, 104, Avenue Pd Kennedy, 75016, Paris, France e-mail: mouna.ayari@lip6.fr

Farouk KAMOUN
CRISTAL lab, National School of Computer Sciences, ENSI, 2010, Manouba e-mail: frk.kamoun@planet.tn

Guy PUJOLLE
LIP6 University of Paris-VI, 104, Avenue Pd Kennedy, 75016, Paris, France e-mail: guy.pujolle@lip6.fr

Please use the following format when citing this chapter:

Ayari, M., Kamoun, F., Pujolle, G., 2008, in IFIP International Federation for Information Processing, Volume 265, Advances in Ad Hoc Networking, eds. Cuenca, P., Guerrero C., Puigjaner, R., Serra, B., (Boston: Springer), pp. 73-84.

ministrative support. Some of the features that characterize ad hoc networks are the dynamic topology and the limitation of resources [1, 2]. Mobile nodes are also operating under severe constraints (limited battery power, variable link quality, limited storage capacity, etc.), which makes the network management process more difficult [3]. We aim in this work to improve self-configuration capabilities in MANETs management. We believe that it is very useful to incorporate this property of autonomic computing into the design of MANETs since these networks are self-creating and operate without a centralized control. The first initiative towards autonomic computing was proposed by IBM through the eLisa project [4]. After that, many researches have been carried out in this area [5, 6]. An autonomic network consists of autonomous network elements. These entities are able to adapt themselves to the changes that can affect their environment while respecting high-level policies. One of the defined properties of these networks is the self-configuration. The network will be able to configure and automatically reconfigure itself under varying conditions and changes in its environment. Human intervention will be limited to guiding the network behavior by defining high-level directives.

Policy-Based Network Management (PBNM) has been adopted by the IETF (Internet Engineering Task Force) mainly to provide automation in network configuration process [14, 15]. This approach allows the definition of high level objectives based on a set of policies that can be enforced in the network. Policies are defined as a set of rules to manage and control access to network resources [7]. An efficient network management system for MANETs can be realized through a reliable distributed policy-based management approach. However, traditional PBNM systems are originally conceived to be used in a centralized LAN-like network environment. We note that the idea to use a fully distributed policy-based management has been proposed the first time in [8]. This paper proposes a new protocol named DPMP for Distributed Policy Management Protocol enabling policies and high-level directives distribution in a fully distributed manner.

The remainder of this paper is organized as follows. Section 2 describes and reviews the related work in policy-based network management. In section 3, we present the basic idea of our proposed system, its components and an overview of a new protocol named DPMP for Distributed Policy Management Protocol. In particular, we provide a detailed description of the proposed policy distribution process. Simulation experiments and results are presented in section 4. Finally, section 5 concludes the paper and presents future work.

2 Overview of Policy-Based Management solutions

Many researches have been carried out in the area of policies for the network management. In this section, we provide an overview of architectures and the commonly used protocols for policy-based management.

The IETF (Internet Engineering Task Force) has defined a policy framework to the admission control. As shown in Figure 1, the proposed architectural model for policy framework consists of the following four tiers: a policy management tool, a PDP or Policy Decision Point, a PEP or a Policy Enforcement Point and a Policy Repository. The policy management tool is an interface between a network manager and the PBNM system through which policies may be edited, modified and deleted. The PDP is a component responsible for high-level decisions making. A PEP represents the network element where decisions will be enforced. The PDP's decision is based on network level information collected from network devices and policies retrieved from the policy repository (a location where policies are stored in a structured way).

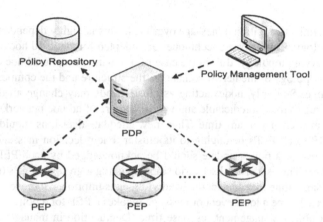

Fig. 1 Policy-Based Management System

Based on information collection and communication strategy, we can distinguish in the literature two types of policy-based management architectures: centralized and cluster-based. The IETF framework [17] is based on a centralized approach. System components are operational within a single domain administrated and managed using a common set of policy rules. There is a single PDP that controls and manages the network. It is clear that this approach is not designed for dynamic and distributed environments, such as MANETs. On one hand, the PDP is a single point of failure that manages and controls entire network devices. The performance of the system deteriorates rapidly when the number of PEPs connected to the PDP increases [16]. On the other hand, ad hoc networks have a frequently varying-topology. So, the network may get partitioned periodically and nodes will become disconnected frequently. In this case, disconnected partitions will be left without any management control.

In order to extend policy-based management to MANETs, cluster-based architectures have been adopted. As shown in Figure 2, several PEPs are grouped into clusters. Each cluster is managed by a PDP [9]. The system management can be also hierarchical [18, 12, 13]. In this case, PDPs in turn are managed by an upper PDP. Clustering techniques transform the ad hoc network to a logical centralized system within each cluster. However, the process of forming and maintaining clusters may

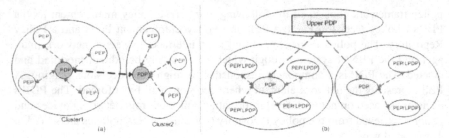

Fig. 2 Cluster-Based architectures

produce a significant additional message overhead. This is highly dependent on the network topology. Cluster-based techniques are adapted for static ad hoc networks with a low varying topology. But, in the case of a dynamic mobile ad hoc environment, as the topology of the network changes, the structure and the composition of clusters change. Similarly, nodes acting as clusterheads may change all the time. In addition, due to the unpredictable and varying nature of ad hoc networks, policy information may change at any time. Thus, new adequate decisions should be sent from the PDP to all PEPs belonging to its cluster. Each decision message issued due to a request or a policy update should be acknowledged by each PEP with a report message. This is a critical scenario since updating a group of PEPs (possibly large) at the same time may impact the bandwidth consumption. Moreover, contacting the PDP each time a local event or message invokes a PEP for a policy decision, would affect policy management response time. Degradation in management system performance is observed as the number of hops between a policy server and client increased [9]. Furthermore, a policy transfer between PDPs is required each time a PEP leaves its domain or cluster to another one. So, the problem of interdomain policy transfer is further exacerbated by the high degrees of mobility in ad hoc networks.

Different protocols have been used to distribute policies over MANETs. In [9], COPS-PR (COPS for Provisioning) protocol [10] was used to exchange policy information and decisions between PDPs and PEPs. COPS-PR was originally conceived as an extension to COPS (Common Open Policy Service) protocol [11] to support differentiated service policies over wireline fixed Internet. So, extensions to the COPS-PR protocol [9] were proposed in order to allow delegation and redirection capabilities in MANETs. However, the use of COPS-PR may affect the limited ad hoc network resources. This protocol was designed for a centralized policy management system where bandwidth is not a critical resource. It is a heavyweight connection-oriented protocol.

In [12], several protocols (YAP (Yelp Announcement Protocol), AMPS (Ad hoc Mobility Protocol Suite), DRCP/DCDP (Dynamic and Rapid Configuration Protocol/Dynamic Configuration Distribution Protocol) were used jointly in order to distribute, control and collect policy management information. However, this may limit the adoption of such a solution. Besides, DRCP/DCDP protocols have been designed for IP-address configuration and assignment in MANETs.

3 Distributed Policy Management Protocol

3.1 Basic idea

The basic idea is to distribute the functionalities of the manager PDP among ad hoc nodes as LPDP. However, the use of a fully-distributed approach within a policy based network management system can encounter some difficulties. In fact, if multiple autonomous management entities (LPDP) are making independent decisions, a lack of consistency between them may occur. In order to regulate and coordinate LPDP's decision making, we propose to use predefined proactive policies. Initially, the human network manager defines policies and high level directives to manage the network and introduces them into at least one node. Policies are expressed as event-condition-action rules. A specific action can be taken at the observation of an event or/and when a particular condition occurs. These policies will be automatically distributed and replicated in the policy repository of each node. They regulate the access to resources and govern dynamic reconfigurations in function of network condition changes.

Each mobile ad hoc node will contain LPDP, PEP, local policy repository and a monitor. The MANET will be formed with a set of autonomous elements that know how to operate in a cooperative way. The LPDP makes local decisions to be enforced by the PEP. The monitor is responsible for collecting monitoring information and changes in environment conditions.

3.2 Protocol Description

Based on requirements expressed in previous sections, we have proposed a distributed protocol that we called: DPMP (Distributed Policy Management Protocol).

3.2.1 DPMP Messages

Firstly, we present different DPMP messages.

- *DPMP_DISCOVER*: a one-hop broadcast message sent by a non-configured LPDP to neighboring nodes in the network to request proactive management policies.
- *DPMP_OFFER*: a unicast message sent by a configured LPDP in response to a DISCOVER message. A policy requester can receive more than one OFFER message. An OFFER message does include neither policies nor decisions. It simply indicates a service availability.
- *DPMP_DECISION*: this message includes policy decisions. It is a unicast message sent by a LPDP to another LPDP. It is used also as a local message sent by the LPDP to its local PEP.

- *DPMP_ACCEPT*: a unicast message sent by a LPDP in order to accept an OFFER or DECISION message from another LPDP.
- *DPMP_REJECT*: a unicast message sent by a LPDP in order to refuse or reject an OFFER or DECISION from another LPDP. It is also used by the PEP to communicate to the LPDP its failure in carrying out the LPDP's decision.
- *DPMP_RETRIEVE_STATUS*: a unicast message including a request for monitoring information. It is sent from the monitor to either the local PEP or a specific monitor.
- *DPMP_REPORT_STATUS*: a unicast message containing reported monitoring information. It can be a response for a DPMP_RETRIEVE_STATUS message or triggered by a specific event.

Each DPMP message consists of a header followed by a number of typed body objects. The header includes a common header and a variable optional part specific for some particular messages. We note that DISCOVER and OFFER messages don't contain neither options nor body. We note also that any transport protocol can be used with DPMP. We have defined appropriate timers and confirmation messages in order to handle message losses. In particular, we propose to use UDP since it is a lightweight protocol.

3.2.2 Policy Distribution

In the scope of this paper, we describe in details and evaluate the policy distribution mechanism. The main objective of this mechanism is to distribute proactive policies to non-configured nodes with a low communication overhead. We need to reduce the number of messages transmitted, received and processed at each node.

We call a configured node a node that has implemented proactive policies. Initially, all nodes are not configured. The network manager has to introduce a set of proactive policies through a policy management tool in at least one node.

Nodes can join or leave the ad hoc network at any time. Each new node starts a policy discovery procedure. The mechanism is simple. A non-configured LPDP (NC-LPDP) requests for proactive policies.

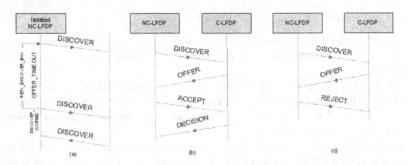

Fig. 3 Policy Discovery Process

As shown in Figure 3.a, a NC-LPDP first broadcasts a DISCOVER message to its neighbouring nodes and waits for the receipt of an OFFER message until the DIS-COVER_TIMEOUT timer expires. If it doesn't receive any response, it re-sends the DISCOVER message. This process can be repeated up to RETX_DISCOVER_MAX retransmissions. When the allowed retrials are exhausted, the node concludes that there is no configured node in the neighbourhood. It is due to an isolation state or a network partition event. We call this period of isolation "isolation period". The node waits for a DISCOVER_WAITING period and then repeats the policy discovery procedure.

As depicted in Figure 3.b, if a configured LPDP (C-LPDP) receives a DIS-COVER message, it responds with an OFFER message. Upon receiving an OF-FER message, the NC-LPDP checks the message. If the offer is refused, a REJECT message is sent back to the C-LPDP with the corresponding error code and the NC-LPDP waits for the receipt of another OFFER message. Otherwise, the NC-LPDP responds with an ACCEPT message. Upon receiving an ACCEPT message, the C-LPDP sends a DECISION message back to the NC-LPDP. This message embeds related proactive policies. DECISION messages may be lost. The NC-LPDP waits for a DECISION_WAIT_MAX. If the timer expires without receiving the DECI-SION message, it re-sends another ACCEPT message and waits for a response. If the retrial fails, the NC-LPDP re-broadcasts a new DISCOVER message to its neighborhood. If a NC-LPDP receives a DECISION message, it processes policy objects, installs policies and updates its state to a configured LPDP. Then, it continues to listen to DPMP messages.

It is important to note that the NC-LPDP can receive multiple OFFER messages from its neighbors (if it has more than one configured neighbor). The NC-LPDP chooses the first one. Thus, the OFFER message doesn't contain policy information in order to reduce the signaling overhead. In fact, it is evident that the size of an OFFER message (consisting of the common header), is smaller than the DECISION size (that depends on the number of policies). For example, the size of the LPDP common header is 24 bytes while the size of policies may reach a few kilobytes.

4 simulations and Results

In this section, we evaluate the performance of the proposed policy distribution mechanism.

4.1 Simulation Environment

We implemented the described policy distribution mechanism and evaluated its performance using the network simulator NS-2. We have considered different scenarios. In all these simulation scenarios, we have used the random-waypoint mobility model. The minimum node speed parameter was set to around 95% of the maximum speed. The pause time was fixed to 10 seconds. We have used AODV as routing protocol, although any other routing protocol can be deployed. Different chosen constants and timers values were set as follows: 1 second to DISCOVER_TIMEOUT, 5 seconds to DISCOVER_WAITING and 10 to RETX_DISCOVER_MAX. Simulation started with one configured node randomly chosen. The arrival of the nodes is assumed to be a poisson-process. The arriving node could appear anywhere within the simulation area. We run each simulation scenario until all nodes were configured. we experimented with a large number of topologies. 30 runs of each simulation scenario were performed with varying random simulation seeds. Each scenario represents a random initial placement of arriving nodes. The 95% confidence interval is computed for all simulation results.

In order to evaluate the performance of our DPMP distribution mechanism, we have considered the following metrics:

- *Latency*: It is the time taken by the protocol DPMP from the instant a non-configured node enters the network and sends a DISCOVER message until it receives a DECISION message. So, for a node that joins the network at time t1 and obtains policy decisions at time t2, its related latency is (t2-t1). The DPMP latency is averaged over all nodes in the network.
- *Message overhead*: it represents different types of DPMP messages required for the policy distribution process, namely DISCOVER, OFFER, ACCEPT and DE-CISION messages. We consider the average amount of bytes generated by these messages.

4.2 Simulation Results

In the first set of simulations, we examine the impact of varying the network size, the mean node arrival rate and node speed on latency. The transmission range of each node is set to 100m. The nodes arrival is assumed to be a poisson-process.

In order to assess in more details the impact of varying network topology in the mean latency, we have varied node population from 50 to 250 nodes and we considered two network density 150 and 300 nodes/km^2. Figure 4 plots the mean latency as a function of node population. The node speed was fixed to 5 m/s. The mean poisson arrival nodes was set to 0.2 node/s. As shown, starting from 100 nodes, the mean latency increases slightly when the network size increases. Moreover, we can observe that the mean latency decreases when the network density increases. The more the network density increases, the more the probability to have rapidly a configured node in the neighborhood increases.

Then, we varied the mean poisson arrival rate from 0.1 to 1 node arrivals/s. We considered three node speeds: 2m/s, 5m/s and 10m/s. Figure 5 plots the mean latency as a function of the mean poisson arrival of nodes for 100 node-system population and 300 nodes/km^2 network density.

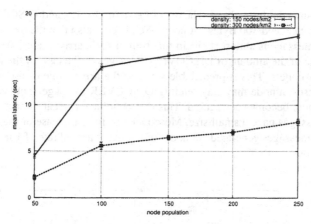

Fig. 4 Mean latency with varying node population and density; node speed = 5m/s

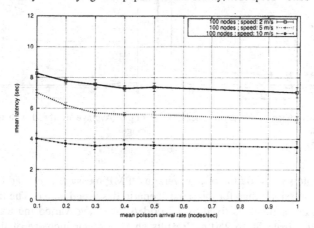

Fig. 5 Mean latency with varying mean node arrival rate

As depicted in Figure 5, the mean latency decreases slightly when the mean poisson arrival rate increases. Results show that the mean latency doesn't exceed 8.5 seconds. Moreover, we observe a decrease of the mean latency with the node speed increase.

In the second set of simulations, we evaluate the overhead generated by the DPMP protocol during distributing policies to all ad hoc nodes. We have fixed the network density to 150 nodes/km^2 for a population of 100 nodes. Nodes move with a speed of 5m/s and we have fixed policies size to 1024 Bytes. Considering the LPDP common header and the option of each message, the sizes of DPMP messages were set as follows: 49 Bytes to DISCOVER and OFFER messages, 51 Bytes to AC-CEPT message and 1076 Bytes to DECISION message. The effect of increasing the mean poisson arrival rate from 0.1 to 1 nodes/s on message overhead is depicted in Figure 6. Results show that the distribution policy process of the DPMP protocol does not produce high overhead. The overall size of OFFER and DISCOVER messages does not exceed 300 Bytes per node. We observe also that the overall size of a single type message is almost stable in function of node arrival rates. We observe a little increase of the amount of DISCOVER messages in the case of the mean poisson arrival 1 node/s. This is predictable since as the arrival rate of non-configured nodes increases, a node may stay sending DISCOVER messages until at least one of its neighbors becomes configured. This does not have a great impact since DISCOVER messages have a small size. Moreover, the little increase of the amount of DECISION messages generated per node for the mean arrival rate of 1 node/s is due to message loss.

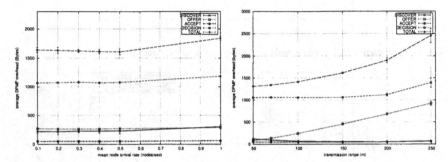

Fig. 6 Mean overhead with varying mean node arrival rate

Fig. 7 Average overhead with transmission range

Figure 7 plots the variation of the average DPMP message overhead in function of node transmission range for the same scenario described above. The mean poisson arrival rate of nodes is fixed to 0.2 node/s. We have varied the transmission range of nodes from 50 to 250 m. Results show a linear increase of the amount of OFFER messages with the transmission range increase. In fact, as transmission range increases, as the connectivity of nodes increases, the probability to have more configured nodes in the neighborhood increases. The amount of additional DPMP messages is varied from 180 and 1300 bytes per node. In brief, we can conclude that the DPMP policy distribution mechanism generates a limited additional overhead per node. In the majority of cases, policies information are exchanged one time per node as confirmed in Figure 8.

We have measured the average DPMP overhead when we varied policies sizes from 1024 to 7168 bytes. We have fixed the transmission range to 100 m. Results show a linear increase of the amount of DECISION messages generated per node with the increase of policies size. Amounts of DISCOVER, OFFER and ACCEPT messages generated per node are practically stable.

Finally, we can conclude that the increase of the DPMP overhead generated per node depends on policies sizes rather than on network topology. Moreover, the average number of DECISION messages exchanged per node is around 1 to 1.3 messages in all the undertaken simulations. We note also that in a real scenario, policies size may reach tens of KBytes.

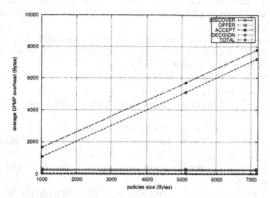

Fig. 8 Average overhead with varying policies size

5 Conclusions and Future work

In this paper, we present a fully-distributed PBNM system for MANETs. Policy information is distributed without central control. Our solution provides autonomy, self-configuration and limited human intervention. We have proposed and described a new protocol for policy distribution that addresses requirements for minimizing overhead and providing a reliable policy distribution. We have analyzed protocol performance through several simulation scenarios. Simulation results show that the increase in the mean of poisson-arrival node rates hasn't got a great effect neither on latency nor on DPMP message overhead. We verified also that varying node speed, network density and transmission range hasn't got a great impact on system performance. This clearly demonstrates the benefits of our distributed approach. In our future research activities, we will complete the implementation and validation of our designed DPMP protocol. We will also compare the performance of our fully-distributed policy-based management system to other policy-based solutions conceived for MANETs.

References

1. Perkins and Hughes: Factors Affecting the Performance of Ad Hoc Networks. (2002). In: Proceedings of the IEEE International Conference on Communications, Vol. 4, April 2002, pp. 2048- 2052.

2. Chakrabarti and Mishra: QoS issues in ad hoc wireless networks, *IEEE Communications Magazine*, February 2001.
3. Mirhakkak, Schult and D. Thomson: Dynamic Quality-of-Service for Mobile Ad Hoc Networks. (2000). In: IEEE MobiHoc, Boston, Massachusets, USA, August 2000.
4. Horn. Autonomic Computing:IBMs perspective on the State of Information Technology. (2001). IBM Corporation
5. Schmid, Sifalakis and Hutchison: Towards Autonomic Networks. (2006). In: proceedings of 3rd Annual Conference on Autonomic Networking, Autonomic Communication Workshop (IFIP AN/WAC), Paris, France, September 25-29.
6. Parashar and Hariri: Autonomic computing: An overview. UPP 2004. (2005). In: Springer Verlag, 3566:247259, January 2005.
7. Westerinen and al.: Terminology for Policy-Based Management. (2001). In: IETF RFC 3198, November 2001.
8. Munaretto, Agoulmine, M. Fonseca: Policy-based Management of Ad Hoc Entreprise Networks. (2002). In: HP Openview University Association 9th Annual Workshop. 2002.
9. Phanse and DaSilva: Protocol Support for Policy-Based Management of Mobile Ad Hoc Networks, Network Operations and Management Symposium, 2004. NOMS 2004. IEEE/IFIP, Vol. 1, 2004, pp. 3-16.
10. Chan and al: COPS usage for Policy Provisioning (COPS-PR). (2001). In: IETF REF 3048, March 2001.
11. Durham and al.: The COPS (Common Open Policy Service) Protocol. (2000). In: IETF RFC 2748, January 2000.
12. Chadha, Cheng, Cheng, Chiang, Ghetie, Levin and Tanna: Policy-Based Mobile Ad Hoc Network Management for Drama, *MILCOM Journal*, Vol 3, 2004, pp. 1317-1323
13. Chadha, Cheng, Chiang, Levin, Li, and Poylisher. DRAMA: A Distributed Policy-based Management System. (2005). In: Proceedings of the Third International Conference on Mobile Systems, Applications, and Services, June 6-8, 2005, Seattle, WA.
14. Ponnappan, Yang, Pillai.R: A Policy Based QoS Management System for the IntServ/DiffServ Based Internet. (2002). In: Third International Workshop on Policies for Distributed Systems and Networks (POLICY.02), 2002, pp. 159-169.
15. Verma, Calo and Amiri: Policy Based Management of Content Distribution Networks, *IEEE Network Magazine*, vol.16, March 2002, pp. 34-39.
16. Eddie Law: Scalable Design of a Policy-Based Management System and its Performance, *IEEE Communications Magazine*, vol.3, Issue 6, June 2003, pp. 72- 79.
17. Yavatkar, Pendarakis, Guerin: A Framework for Policy Based Admission Control. (2000). In: IETF RFC 2753, January 2000.
18. Hadjiantonis, Malatras, Pavlou: A context-aware policy-based framework for the management of MANETs. (2006). In: Proceedings of the seventh IEEE International Workshop on Policies for Distributed Systems and Networks (POLICY'06), June 2006, pp. 23 - 34.

Performance Evaluation of a Protocol for Fair P2P Auctions over MANETs

Ines Doghri and Hella Kaffel-Ben Ayed

Abstract In this paper, we explore the deployment of P2P auctions over MANETs. We define a P2P auction process and identify the need to have a fair registration and a fair bidding. We propose a distributed communication architecture and a protocol to support this kind of auctions. We perform a formal specification and verification of the BSAP protocol using PROMELA/SPIN and evaluate its performance.

1 Introduction

With the deployment of wireless communication and mobile computing, new ways for people to interact with each other and their surrounding environment are emerging. Mobile ad hoc networks (MANETs) do not need any infrastructure or management entity. They are characterised by their completely autonomous, dynamic, auto-organised and ubiquitous nature. The most attractive economic benefit is the low cost of this communicating infrastructure and of its management.

At the same time, peer-to-peer (P2P) systems constitute nowadays an increasingly important part of the online world. Ad hoc networks present similarities with P2P systems in terms of decentralization, equality and autonomy. This will help the raise of new P2P applications over MANETs such as mobile commerce. We propose here a novel concept: P2P auctions over MANETs.

In this paper, we first present the motivation and business scenario of this work. Then, we propose an architecture and a communication protocol to support P2P auctions over MANETS. The formal specification and verification of this protocol using PROMELA and SPIN are presented. Performance evaluation results are discussed. Afterwards, we discuss related work. Finally, we present the concluding remarks and the ongoing work.

Ines Doghri*, Hella Kaffel-Ben Ayed**
National School of Computer Science, CRISTAL Laboratory, University of Manouba, Tunisia,
e-mail: *ines.doghri@gmail.com, **Hella.kaffel@fst.rnu.tn

Please use the following format when citing this chapter:

Doghri, I., H. Kaffel-Ben Ayed, 2008, in IFIP International Federation for Information Processing, Volume 265, Advances in Ad Hoc Networking, eds. Cuenca, P., Guerrero C., Puigjaner, R., Serra, B., (Boston: Springer), pp. 85-96.

2 Motivation and problematic

During the last years, auctions became the major phenomenon of electronic commerce and are widely used to sell a variety of commodities, such as treasury bills, mineral rights, art works, etc. An auction is usually defined as a market institution with an explicit set of rules determining resource allocation and prices on the basis of bids from the market participants [1]. The commonly seen auctions types include English auction, Dutch auction and Vickrey auction [2]. New mobile and wireless networks types emerged, offering novel and interesting capabilities. They offer new ways of interactions. Users are nowadays equipped with sophisticated wireless terminals in order to be always connected and therefore to consult their e-mails, to work remotely with their companies, or to make e-commerce transactions. The ETSI (European Telecommunications Standards Institute) has defined the mobile commerce as: "The efficient delivery of electronic commerce capabilities, directly in the consumer's hand anywhere, anytime, via wireless technology" [10].
In the present study, we foresee ad hoc networks as a support for m-commerce and particularly for auctions. An auction process could be created anywhere as soon as a group of at least three persons equipped with wireless terminals agree to participate in the auction. One of them announces goods for sale or for purchase. The others would play the role of competing bidders that would submit bids. We could imagine various scenarios of spontaneous markets created temporarily for an auction event; such as markets set up in a harbour for the sale of stocks of fish or within the framework of a farm or in airport for the sales of last minute plane tickets. Nomadic exhibitions may also raise spontaneous P2P auction events. This way of deploying auctions may also be considered as an extension of auction events occurring over an infrastructure network, permitting this way to MANET users to participate to such markets. These scenarios imply multiple advantages and motivations such as ubiquity, convenience, availability, affordability and opportunity. However, the deployment of auction over MANETs raises various problems (security, trust, robustness, fairness, etc) resulting from the nature of these networks.

3 WAHS: a full distributed auction architecture

3.1 The architecture

Most Internet based auctions model usually rely on a central auction server (the auctioneer). This latter performs various functionalities and can implement multiple auction-related policies. The model of P2P auction over ad hoc networks [4] bears a resemblance to P2P networking model of ad hoc networks. Hence, we propose new communication architecture, called WAHS (Wireless Auction Handling System), to support P2P auctions over mobile ad hoc networks. It is based on the distribution of the auction site to fit the ad hoc context, but also to ensure a high level of security. Several studies removed the auctioneer from their auction models [8], [6] and [9]. All these works proved that omitting the auctioneer is due to autonomy considerations. Furthermore, in our context, decentralization prevents the auction inhibition in the case where the auctioneer becomes non-connected to the network.

We define one functional component that supports all the auctioneer functionalities', named BSAP (Buyer/Seller Agent Peer). It is associated with an auction initiator as well as with each bidder participating to the auction. One protocol, i.e. BSA Peer protocol (BSAP-protocol), is defined to support interactions between the functional components (the peers) of WAHS. P2P auctions over MANETs present similarities with the real time auctions. The following assumptions can be made about this type of markets: (i) These auctions would require the physical presence of bidders or their mobile devices since the beginning of the auction, (ii) The probability of new arrivals during the process is low, (iii) the mobility of mobile nodes is low (about 1m/sec), (iv) the nodes moving zone depends on the place where the market is set up (port, farm, airport, market, etc.) and (v) auctions are limited in duration.

3.2 The BSAP protocol specification

3.2.1 The P2P auction process

For the sake of simplicity we consider English auctions as a case study in the rest of the paper. However, the proposed architecture and protocol can be used to model any kind of open cry auction protocol. We devide the P2P auction process into three stages:

Stage 1. The Initialization phase

1- Auction advertisement: The initiator, a peer connected to the ad hoc networks who has a good to sell, initiates the auction application by broadcasting an "auction-advertise" message in order to inform all nodes about the auction event to be set up.

2- Auction access: Each interested node sends a "register-bidder" message to the initiator as soon as he receives the "auction-advertise" message. This latter becomes a registered participant of this auction.

3- Auction creation: After collecting all "register-bidder" messages, the initiator sets its primary list of members. He sends to all registered peers an "auction-create" message (in multicast) containing the list of participants (Access Control List). The ACL will allow further access control to the auction. The choice of multicast is in the purpose to satisfy the need for communication of group and to do not reveal the information of bidding to unrecorded nodes.

Stage 2. The Bidding phase

4- Submission: The first round begins for each bidder as soon as he receives the "auction-create" message. It sends its bid in a "submit-bid" message to all the members of the group and collects the others bids. Before accepting a bid, every bidder verifies if the sender is in the list; if not, it rejects its bid. Each peer computes the best bid and decides if it is going to outbid in the next round.

5- Auction quit: A bidder can leave at any time an auction by sending an "auction_exit" message to all members within the ACL.

6- New Auction access during the bidding phase: If a node J within the ad hoc network wants to access an ongoing auction, it starts a neighbour discovery process using the expanded ring search (ERS) technique [13]. Auction REQ message is used for this purpose. When a member of the auction I receives an Auction REQ message from node J, it sends back an Auction REP message to J, so that node J will record the address of the auction initiator and the node J will stop the neighbour discovery process. After that, node J contacts the initiator to join the auction process. If the initiator sends back to node J his acceptance, then J does registration. After doing all the necessary update, the initiator sends an auction_create message to all the list members.(cf. Fig. 1)

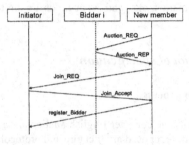

Fig. 1 Joining an auction process

Stage 3. Closing phase

At the end of the auction life, every bidder who believes that he submitted the highest bid during the very last round, sends a "winner_notif" message to the initiator. This avoid a possible inconsistency when many winners exist with different prices resulting to loss "submit_bid" messages due to wireless communication or congestion, etc. The initiator collects all "winner_notif" messages and compares the prices to identify the best bid. The transaction settlement occurs between the initiator and the winner.

3.2.2 The BSAP formal Specification & Verification

a. Modeling a broadcast system under SPIN

We used the PROMELA language to specify the BSAP protocol and SPIN to verify it. These tools are usually used to specify point to point communication. When two nodes want to communicate they use one predetermined channel which makes the connection between them [11]. Therefore, we implemented some add-ins under PROMELA to adapt SPIN to the modeling and the checking of protocols operating over Ad-hoc network. To model the CSMA/CA (Collision Avoidance) mode of transmission, we defined only one channel of communication which is indexed according to the number of nodes (this is also called matrix of the channels in [11]). Here is an example:

#define n 3 /*nodes number*/

mtype=auction_advertise,register_bidder,auction_create, submit_bid,winner_notif;/*BSAP messages*/

Chan q[n] = [1] of mtype,byte;/*indexed channel for broadcast*/

b. BSAP protocol Formal specification " automata "

We describe the different states of the BSAP bidder using the automata illustrated in the figure 2. In this figure, all circles represent the different states and transitions represent the events in/out from a state to another.

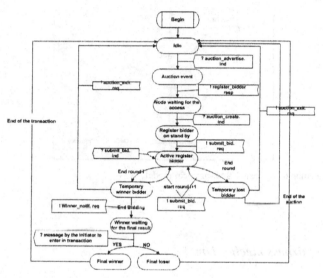

Fig. 2 The bidder automata

c. BSAP protocol verification

For the verification of the BSAP, we used the simulation facility of the validation tool SPIN to support early fault detection. Especially the message sequence chart (MSC) facility was very supportive in examining the communication pattern of our design. An important number of simulations has been made before finding a model which suits the requirements. A simulation of the basic BSAP Model is described on figure 3. Each line represents a process: BSAP initiator, BSAP bidder 1, etc. Each box represents one step in the process. The number in the box corresponds to the simulation step. Arrows correspond to the message transfer, and numbers on these arrows correspond to the transmitted message value. Also, "!" means sending and

"?" means receiving as described in [11]. The verification parameters are checked with no errors (no invalid end-state, no deadlock and no loop).

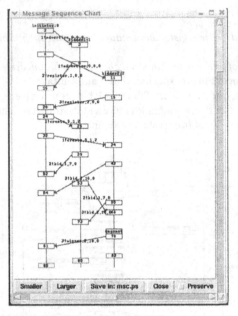

Fig. 3 Simulation of the basic BSAP-protocol model

3.3 The fairness mechanism

Fairness is a big challenge for auctions. It means that all participants should be treated equally [8]. It concerns essentially the bidding process and means that no bidder should have more information than any other to determine their bid, all submitted bids during a round should be evaluated during the same round and the bidder sending the highest bid should win the auction [12]. When auctions are deployed over ad hoc networks, intermediary bidders can receive bids and react before the other bidders and may finally win the auction. To prevent this, and provide a fair registration and a fair bidding, we assume that the initiator has to wait for a period of time, named Tregister, to collect registrations and each bidder has to wait for a period of time, named Tfair, to collect all bids. In the next section, we determine by simulation the estimations of Tfair and Tregister.

4 Performance evaluation

The goals of simulations are to: (i) compare the values of Tfair obtained by simulation with those obtained by one related work (eq. 3) and noted Tfair/[4], (ii) evaluate Tfair and (iii) estimate the communication overhead.

4.1 The simulation environment

The simulations were performed using the network simulator NS-2 with CMU extensions to support MANETs. We used the random waypoint mobility model since it considered as the best model for MANETs [14]. The link layer was implemented using IEEE 802.11 Distributed Coordination Function (DCF) and Medium Access Control Protocol (MAC). Taking into account the assumptions on the context of our application as in section 2, we choose a mobility scenario characterized by: the speed of the nodes in the network is 1 meters/second and the pause time is 5 seconds. We used AODV as a routing protocol since it is available over NS2; although any other routing protocol can be used. In order to have the 95 percent confidence interval for the mean of each gathered static, we run 30 simulations for each scenario.

4.2 The metrics

- To determine Tregister: we define a metric named "Register-out". Tregister value is the value of optimal register timeout when "Register-out" (eq. 1) reaches zero. This metric is calculated as follows:

$$Register - out = \frac{register - Nb - out}{RegNb} \qquad (1)$$

With:
Register − out=Rate of registrations out register timeout.
Register − Nb − out=number of register_bidder messages received out register timeout.
RegNb=total number of all registrations received by the initiator.

- To determine Tfair: we define a metric named "Bids-out-rnd". Tfair value corresponds to the optimal round timeout when "Bids-out-rnd" (eq. 2) is null. This metric value is computed in the following manner:

$$Bids - out - rnd = \frac{\sum_{j=1..Size-ACL} bids - out - rnd / bidder_j}{Size - ACL} \qquad (2)$$

With:

$bids - out - rnd/bidder=$ Rate of bids received per each bidder after the round timeout.

$Size - ACL =$ the number of registered members.

- To evaluate the overhead of our protocol by computing the number of unicast messages. This includes the various unicast messages required namely register_bidder, auction_create and submit bid. This indicates the communication overhead incurred by the protocol.

4.3 The simulation results

We first evaluated the BSAP-Protocol. To determine the optimal values of Tregister and Tfair, we varied two simulation timers: (i) Register timeout marking the end of the waiting time of the initiator during the initialization phase and (ii) the round timeout marking the end of a round duration during the bidding phase.

a. Tfair/BSAP obtained by simulation vs theoretical Tfair/[4]

In order to compare the fair round duration induced by our protocol with Tfair/[4], we used the scenarios shown in the table 1. These scenarios consider MANETS with static topologies, fixed nodes and a coverage area of 50 meters. The last line in this table corresponds to the Tfair/[4] for each scenario.

	Scenario 1	Scenario 2	Scenario 3
Network size	500m*500m	250m*250m	50m*50m
Maximal hops number	14	7	1
Tfair	12.6 s	6.3 s	0.9 s

Table 1 Simulation scenarios

Fig. 4 shows that the curve of Tfair/[4] diverges with that of Tfair/BSAP. We observe that Tfair/BSAP values increase by the rise of the number of hops but not linearly. The theoretical Tfair/[4] is then too large. Hence, we progress towards a dynamic Tfair. For that, the goal of the following simulations is to determine the factors affecting Tregister and Tfair.

b. Impact of varying node population on Tregister and Tfair

We varied the node population and analyzed by simulation the behaviour of the BSAP. This population is varied from 10 nodes to 100 nodes. The considered areas of the network were 183m x 183m, 258m x 258m, 408mx 408m, 483m x 483m and 578m x 578m for the 10, 20, 50, 70 and 100 node networks, respectively (ensuring the network density of around 300 nodes=km^2).

Fig. 5 , shows the rise of Tregister with the rise of nodes population. In order to

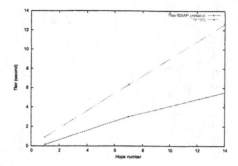

Fig. 4 Tfair vs hops number

have the maximum number of buyers, the initiator must wait for 3 seconds to allow up 10 bidders to join the auction and 20 seconds to have 100 bidders. In Fig. 6 , we see that all the curves are decreasing and the optimal round duration (Tfair) is varying with the number of nodes. In fact, the number of submit bid messages out of round reaches zero as follows: for 20 population node the mean Tfair is 6sec; for 50 population node the mean Tfair is 25sec; and for 70 population node the mean Tfair is 30 sec. For simulations in Fig. 6 , we used Tregister values from the Fig. 5 to have the maximum number of participants.

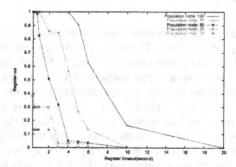

Fig. 5 Initialization phase: Register timeout versus Register-out Rate

c. Impact of varying node population on number of unicast messages

In Fig. 7, the total number of messages exchanged increases with the number of peer nodes. The Fig. 7 (a) shows that the number of create messages is the same as the number of register messages. That is logic because nodes who send their registration will receive the auction_create message from the initiator. But, when the number of peers increases to reach a high value as 100 nodes, the number of auction_create messages becomes lower than the number of register_bidder messages. This shows that there is some registration packets lost by the network. The use of

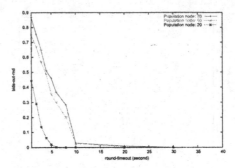

Fig. 6 Bidding phase: Round timeout versus Bids-out-rnd Rate

a reliable transport protocol would allow avoiding this loss. We can note from the Fig. 7 (b) that the curve has an exponential rise according to the increase of the node population. This result underlines our choice of the multicast communication mode in order to not overload the network by unicast messages. This is well adapted to satisfy the need of the many-to-many communication required by our BSAP protocol during the bidding process.

5 Related work

The work presented in [3] proposes the deployment of auctions over the mobile networks. The bidding information is disseminated in the network by the auctioneer and interested bidders submit their settings. Fairness is fulfilled by the setting of a "Timer Waiting". Bids are saved within the network layer of the auctioneer. When the timer expires, the auctioneer network layer delivers all the information received to the application for evaluation. The best bid is then sent to all participants. This approach presents many weaknesses such as: the periodic flooding of the current auction information in the network by the initiator that implies the messages redundancy. The trust in the auctioneer and the relaying of messages by intermediate nodes raises reliability and security problems. The presence of a central entity (i.e. the auctioneer) is not suitable in the context of ad hoc networks. At last, this approach introduces processing within the network layer.

In [5], the authors present a self-organizing distributed auction system using a mobile multihop ad-hoc network as a communication platform. In order to substantially increase the probability that negotiating peers successfully reach an agreement, communication is focused on a static geographic area, called the marketplace. To ensure a reliable communication channel between two devices, the proposed protocol assumes at least one copy of the agent exists. However, this solution may cause problems at the marketplace when agents make different agreements.

The work [4] aims at deploying a model of auction over an ad hoc network by pro-

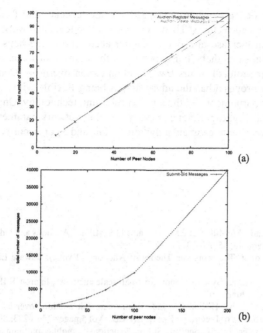

Fig. 7 Communication overhead for varying node population: Node population versus number of unicast messages both in (a) the initialization phase and (b) the bidding phase

viding fairness requirements. This model is based on the distribution of the auction site to fit the ad hoc context, but also to ensure a high level of security. Here, the authors proposed an estimation of Tfair:

$$T fair/[4] = 0.982656 * MaximalHopsNumber \qquad (3)$$

This solution design ensures the fairness but does not manage a dynamic number of participants, the nodes mobility. We note that to provide fairness, this approach requires the maximal hops number information. This latter information is provided by the network layer which creates a dependency of the approach on the network layer.

6 Conclusion & Future Work

In this paper, we proposed a distributed architecture and a protocol to support P2P auctions over MANETs. We focused on fairness and defined two time durations: Tregister and Tfair to provide a fair registration and a fair bidding. First, we implemented the broadcast system under SPIN model-checker and formally verified the BSAP protocol correctness. Then, comparison to one related work [4] show that Tfair has a slight increase in a linear manner according to the hops number. The simulation results show that Tfair depends on the number of nodes. Furthermore, we note that our protocol incurs low communication overhead. Compared to related works, our proposal has the advantage of being flexible with regards to both the MANETs' environment and the auction rules and technology. Ongoing work is on: 1) more simulation experiments by varying other network parameters, 2) assess the theoretical formula to estimate a dynamic Tfair and 3) on security of the BSAP protocol.

References

1. R.P.McAfee and J.McMillan, R.P.McAfee and J.McMillan . Auctions and bidding. Journal of Economic Literature, 25:699-738, 1987.
2. P.Klemperer,editor, The economic Theory of Auctions (2 vols.). Edward Elgar Publishing, 2000.
3. N.Lin , S.Shrivastava, "System support for small scale auctions", In proc. IFIP Med-Hoc-Net, Mahdia, Tunisia, June 2003.
4. A.Fourati, K.Al Agha, H.K. Ben Ayed "Secure and fair auctions over ad hoc networks", International Journal of Electronic Business(IJEB), Vol 5,pages:276 - 293, 2007.
5. H. Frey, D. Gorgen, J. K. Lehnert, P. Sturm, "Auctions in mobile multihop ad-hoc networks following the marketplace communication pattern",6th International Conference on Enterprise Information Systems ICEIS'04, Porto, Portugal, 2004.
6. B Rachlevsky-Reich, I Ben-Shaul, N T Chan, A Lo, and T Poggio, "GEM: A Global Electronic Market System" Information Systems Vol. 24, No. 6, pp. 495-518, 1999.
7. D.Hausheer, B.Stiller, "PeerMart : The Technology for a Distributed Auction-based Market for Peer-to-Peer Services", 2004. http://www.peermart.net/
8. Paul D. Ezhilchelvan and G. Morgan, "A Dependable Distributed Auction System: Architecture and an Implementation Framework", Fifth International Symposium on Autonomous Decentralized Systems (ISADS 2001), USA, March 26-28, 2001.
9. F. Brandt, "Secure and Private Auctions without Auctioneers", Technical Report FKI- 245-02, ISSN 0941-6358, Department of Computer sciences, technical university of Munich, February 2002.
10. ETSI "Mobile Commerce, Mobile Signature Service, Security Framework", Technical Report, France, (2003)
11. R.Gerth,   "A   concise   language   reference   for   promela", http://spinroot.com/spin/Man/Quick.html.
12. N. Asokan, "Fairness in Electronic Commerce", Technical report, IBM Research Division, March 1997.
13. C.E. Perkins, E.M. Royer, and S.R. Das, "Ad Hoc On Demand Distance Vector (AODV) Routing," Internet Draft, draft-ietf-manet-aodv-10.txt, March 2002 (Work in Progress).
14. T. Camp, J. Boleng et V. Davies, "A survey of mobility models for ad hoc network research", Wireless communications mobile computing (WCMC): special issue on mobile ad hoc networking Research, trends and Application, vol. 2, p483-502, 2002.

A Scalable Adaptation of the OLSR Protocol for Large Clustered Mobile Ad hoc Networks

Lucile Canourgues, Jerome Lephay, Laurent Soyer and Andre-Luc Beylot

Abstract Intense research activity is focused on solutions for the routing function in Mobile Ad hoc Networks (MANETs). The most recent efforts emphasize the scalability in large-scale networks, which arises as one of the major challenges to solve in the near future. This paper presents our solution for scalability of the Optimized Link State Routing (OLSR) protocol, the well known proactive routing protocol for ad hoc networks. Based on the Internet experience, which suggests that hierarchy is an interesting solution, our protocol assumes that nodes are grouped into clusters thanks to a clustering algorithm. We offer theoretical and simulation analyses of the control overhead generated by our approach, and we compare it to the Fisheye-OLSR and the C-OLSR protocols. Simulations show that our protocol outperforms these two solutions.

1 Introduction

Mobile Ad Hoc Networks (MANET) are special communication systems that can be deployed even when no network infrastructure exists or may be installed. They are of great interest for scenarios such as tactical military networks, law enforcement, disaster recovery or sensor networks. In a MANET, nodes are mobile and self-organized to establish multi-hop communications autonomously. Routing in such mobile with resource-constrained (bandwidth and energy) networks is one of

Lucile Canourgues
Rockwell Collins France and IRIT/ENSEEIHT and TeSA lab., 14-16 Port Saint Etienne, F-31000, Toulouse, France, e-mail: lcanourg@rockwellcollins.com

Jerome Lephay and Laurent Soyer
Rockwell Collins France, 6 avenue D. Daurat, BP 20008, F-31701 Blagnac Cedex, France e-mail: jlephay@rockwellcollins.com, lsoyer@rockwellcollins.com

Andre-Luc Beylot
IRIT/ENSEEIHT, 2 rue Camichel, F-31071 Toulouse, France e-mail: andre-luc.beylot@enseeiht.fr

Please use the following format when citing this chapter:

Canourgues, L., Lephay, J., Soyer, L., Beylot, A.-L., 2008, in IFIP International Federation for Information Processing, Volume 265, Advances in Ad Hoc Networking, eds. Cuenca, P., Guerrero C., Puigjaner, R., Serra, B., (Boston: Springer), pp. 97-108.

the most challenging issues. In this paper, we will focus on the Optimized Link State Routing (OLSR) [1] protocol, a proactive routing protocol standardized by the MANET WG [2].

OLSR [1] is a well-known link state proactive routing protocol widely employed in deployed MANET systems. Contrary to reactive routing protocols which discover routes on-demand at the time the application needs to communicate through some form of signaling (usually controlled broadcast technique), proactive protocols continually discover and maintain routes to all other nodes in the network. The control overhead associated with the proactive approachs is the main drawback of these solutions. OLSR uses the concept of MultiPoint Relays (MPRs) [3] to achieve an efficient flooding of the control messages in the network and thus to reduce control overhead. Nodes selected as MPRs by neighbor nodes periodically announce this information in their Topology Control (TC) messages. They inform thus the network nodes that they have reachability to the nodes which have selected them as MPR. In route computation, MPRs are used to form the minimal route from a given node to any destination in the network. Therefore, the MPR concept allows OLSR to reduce both the number of broadcast packet transmissions and the size of the link state update packets, leading to an efficient flooding of control message in the network.

Nevertheless, even though OLSR reduces the control overhead in dense and small networks, it still presents scalability issues. Indeed, when the network is scarse, all neighbors are chosen as MPRs and therefore the protocol degrades to a pure link state protocol. Moreover, the overhead of control messages is directly linked to the number of nodes, so it may become unaffordable in large networks with several hundreds of nodes. Finally, since each node must store a route to all other nodes in the network, the associated storage capacity requirement may become too burdensome when the size of the network increases, especially for MANET nodes for which memory resource is limited. These are the reasons why proactive protocols like OLSR are known to have poor scalability properties.

This paper is organized as follows. In section 2, we present the state-of-the-art regarding the solutions proposed to improve OLSR scalability. Then, in section 3, our solution is described. Section 4 provides theoretical and simulation analyses of the overhead generated by our approach compared to the FishEye OLSR and the C-OLSR approaches. Finally, we conclude this article in section 5.

2 Related work

As shown in [4], the control overhead in OLSR is mainly due to TC messages rather than Hello messages used for the neighborhood discovery. Consequently, propositions to improve OLSR scalability focus on reducing the amount of TC messages.

Fisheye-OLSR [5] integrates the fisheye technique into OLSR. The fisheye routing consists in adapting the frequency of the forwarding of topology information to the distance to the source. Thus, nearby nodes receive topology information more frequently than farther nodes. The routing information for a remote destination is only vague at first but becomes more and more accurate as the message goes closer to the destination. Analytical studies [6] show that this protocol improves the scalability of OLSR. Nevertheless, the problems of storage and overhead that make OLSR poorly scalable are not fully solved. Each node still has to store and compute a route to all potential destination nodes in the network. Moreover, TC messages are still broadcast on the whole network by all the MPRs, even if their frequency is reduced.

To overcome these issues, the solution is to limit each node view of the network by aggregating nodes. Indeed, aggregation enables the reduction of the algorithm complexity and the optimization of the resource (e.g. memory, medium ...) and simplifies the network management. In MANET, the aggregation of nodes is performed thanks to the clustering technique. Clustering allows to introduce levels of hierarchy in the network. Having levels of hierarchy enables the growth of the size of the each node's routing table to be only logarithmic instead of linear with respect to the number of nodes in the network. Based on a clustering protocol, several propositions to enhance the OLSR protocol have been made.

Hierarchical OLSR (HOLSR)[7] proposes a scalable improvement of OLSR based on clustering. Clusterheads are selected based on their higher communications capabilities (data rate, radio range frequency band, battery life ...). Topology information are sent only within the cluster and clusterheads exchange the address of the nodes belonging to their cluster through direct communications. To reach any other destination, data packets are firstly routed through the local clusterhead and then forwarded to the appropriate peer clusterhead. This may lead to suboptimal paths when, for example, the source and the destination are close but belong to different clusters. Moreover, the assumption of the existence of higher capabilities nodes is a strong assumption that may not be verified in tactical MANET.

OLSR tree[8] defines a clustering algorithm to introduce hierarchy in OLSR. The clustering algorithm is based on the connectivity of nodes. The network is divided into trees, where the root of the tree, the clusterhead, is the node having the maximum local connectivity. Once trees are created, a maintenance process is run. A hierarchical routing protocol based on OLSR is then employed. Routing within the tree scope is done with OLSR as if there were no tree. To route to other trees, OLSR is applied on the cluster topology thanks to "super messages" (Super TC, Super Hello, ...) exchanged by clusterheads. When a node needs to send data to a node outside its tree, it first sends the traffic to its root which then forwards the traffic to the destination node following the cluster path. OLSR tree proposed an interesting approach to improve OLSR scalability. Nevertheless, it is dependent on the clustering algorithm which itself is based on connectivity, i.e. a dynamic parameter in mobile networks. Consequently, cluster topology stability may be poor.

The C-OLSR protocol has been presented recently [9] and proposes a modification of OLSR which makes use of clustering to reduce the protocol overhead. Contrary to OLSR Tree, the protocol does not depend on a defined clustering protocol but assumes merely that a clustering algorithm is being executed in the ad hoc network. C-OLSR uses regular OLSR inside every cluster and TC messages forwarding is thus limited within the scope of a cluster. Then, the authors choose to leverage the same mechanisms of plain OLSR to the level of clusters. Therefore, they define new C-Hello and C-TC messages to emulate the behavior of an OLSR node by a cluster. C-MPR clusters are elected thanks to the C-Hello messages. The C-Hello messages must be forwarded over the entire neighbor clusters so that each node of a cluster may compute its own C-MPR set and the C-TC messages must also be forwarded over the entire clusters that are selected as C-MPR clusters.

As in OLSR Tree, applying OLSR at the cluster level imposes to exchange some sort of Hello (Super-Hello or C-Hello) and TC (Super-TC or C-TC) messages which may generate an important overhead. Moreover, in case of loss of one of these messages, the integrity of the routing function may be jeopardized. We propose a solution to adapt OLSR to a clusterhead environment where regular OLSR is applied inside every cluster for intra-cluster communications but where inter-cluster communications do not rely on a version of OLSR at the cluster level contrary to what is done in both OLSR Tree and C-OLSR.

3 Protocol Description

3.1 Overview

We propose a routing protocol based on OLSR which aims at improving the scalability features of the OLSR protocol in large-scale ad hoc networks. Our protocol makes use of clustering to greatly reduce the topology overhead and the routing table size. The routing protocol is fully independent from the clustering protocol used. The propagation of the topology control information is limited within the cluster. Each node annonces in its Hello messages the address of its clusterhead. For this purpose, we define a new Link Code. Contrary to other OLSR-based approaches which use clustering such as OLSR-Tree, OLSR is not applied on the clusterhead topology for out-of-cluster routing purposes. Indeed, rather than applying the complex OLSR message exchange and MPR selection on clusterheads, in our solution clusterheads only send special TC_Cluster messages over the network. Thanks to these TC_messages, each node knows the next hop node towards the clusterhead the destination depends on. We assume that a clustering protocol is employed within the ad hoc network. A K-clustering algorithm creating clusters with diameter larger than 2 hops is recommended. We also assume that every node is aware of its clusterhead address.

3.2 Hello messages

The first modification we performed on the OLSR protocol was that each node must include its clusterhead membership information, i.e. the address of its clusterhead, in its Hello message. Hello message format and link code format are defined in the RFC 3626.

With the aim to be compliant with the regular OLSR protocol (i.e. we want that our protocol can be used in networks where both the "regular" OLSR and our protocol co-exist), the Hello message format is not modified. A new Link Code is proposed. Consequently, in a Hello message advertising a clusterhead address, one of the link code blocks will be dedicated to the clusterhead address of the node sending the Hello. The new link code is as follows: the Neighbor Type is set to a new CH_NEIGH value and the Link Type field is set to the UNSPEC_Link value. The Neighbor Interface Address list is composed of one address, the clusterhead address. When a non-OLSR-cluster node receives such an Hello message, it discards the clusterhead related part since it does not understand the link code but the other blocks of the message advertising the neighborhood status are processed as usual.

Upon reception of a Hello message with a clusterhead address, the clusterhead address is saved in the neighbor set of the sending node. Therefore, a new field, the clusterhead_address field, has been added to the neighbor tuple which was previously made of three fields.

3.3 TC messages

A regular version of the OLSR protocol is used within each cluster. TC messages are never forwarded by a node that does not belong to the same cluster as the originator of the TC message. That way, TC message propagation is restricted to the cluster area. The MPR selection algorithm is performed without any consideration of the cluster for network consistency purposes. Therefore, each MPR sends periodic TC messages containing the list of its MPR selectors, i.e. the nodes which select it as MPR. When receiving a TC message, a node processes it following the algorithm described in RFC 3626 [1]. The forwarding decision is then based on the clusterhead of the sender, i.e. the node that has just forwarded the message (and not the originator). The TC forwarding algorithm is roughly the same as the default forwarding algorithm described in the [1] except the first step as illustated below.

> If the sender interface address of the message is not detected to be in the symmetric 1-hop neighborhood of the node, or **if the clusterhead address corresponding to the sender interface address is not the same as our clusterhead address**, the forwarding algorithm MUST silently stop here (and the message MUST NOT be forwarded).

There is no need to add the clusterhead address in the TC messages. Indeed, a node is able to know which is the clusterhead of the node having forwarded the message thanks to its neighbor set. Moreover, the clusterhead of the node that has forwarded the message is necessarily the same as the one that has previously forwarded the message to it, otherwise the message would not have been forwarded. Step by step, the clusterhead of the TC message originator is the same as the clusterhead of the sending node of a received TC message.

3.4 TC_Cluster Message

From the protocol described previously, a node is able to compute route to all the nodes in its cluster. Border nodes[1] are also able to compute routes to nodes belonging to neighbor clusters since they receive (but not forward) TC messages generated within these clusters. For the routes to nodes belonging to different clusters, our

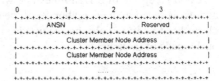

Fig. 1 TC_Cluster message format

approach is that each node should know the next hop toward the clusterhead the destination depends on. Then, once the data packet arrives in the cluster of the destination node, the intermediate node knows the exact route to the destination. To achieve such behavior, cluster topology information must be sent over the network. OLSR-Tree approach is to reproduce the OLSR protocol at the cluster level to create some "cluster paths". The approach we follow is different. We define a new TC_Cluster message that is sent by clusterheads over the network using the MPR flooding algorithm. This message does not contain the list of the MPR selectors of the clusterhead but rather the addresses of nodes belonging to its cluster. Since this message is flooded on the overall network, each node can maintain a node/cluster membership table and can therefore determine to which cluster a destination node belongs to. Nevertheless, knowing the clusterhead the destination node is related to is not enough to route a packet towards this destination node. Indeed, the path to the clusterhead or at least the next hop node on the path to the clusterhead is needed. This next hop information is retrieved when receiving the TC_Cluster message. Indeed, when a node receives a TC_Cluster message, it registers as its next hop to the clusterhead sending the message the node that has just forwarded the message, assuming that this is the first time this message is received. Since the message is flooded over the network, a node may receive several copies of a TC_Cluster message. Nevertheless, the first copy received is the only one considered for the next hop information since it has necessarily taken the faster, less congested path. The other copies are discarded.

---

[1] A border router is a node that is one hop away from a node that belongs to a different cluster i.e. a node that has a different clusterhead.

Figure 1 gives the format of the TC_Cluster message. The originator of a TC_Cluster message is the clusterhead, and the source address in the IP header is the candidate next-hop node toward the clusterhead. The number of hops to reach the clusterhead can also be computed through the TC_Cluster message thanks to the following formula: $TTL\_TC\_Cluster - TTL\_of\_the\_received\_message$, where TTL_TC_Cluster is a constant and is the TTL value the originator of a TC_Cluster message must set in the TTL field of the message and TTL_of_the_received_message is the TTL value indicated in the TTL field of the received TC_Cluster message. The TC_Cluster periodicity is lower than the TC periodicity assuming that the clustering protocol creates stable clusters.

3.5 Sending and Forwarding Data Packets

When a node has a data packet to send:

- if it knows the destination from its routing table (i.e. the node belongs to its cluster or the destination is a clusterhead), it sends the packet to the next hop indicated in its routing table
- if the destination is not in its routing table, it performs a look in the node/cluster membership table to know which cluster the node belongs to.

  - If the destination is not in the table, the packet is discarded
  - If the destination is in the table, the node looks into its routing table for the next hop to the clusterhead. The destination address of the node is not changed. When the next hop receives the data, the same process is performed.

4 Theoretical and Simulation Performance Analysis

In this section we want to evaluate the overhead generated by our protocol. Since our objective is mainly to reduce the control overhead caused by TC messages, we will only consider the TC messages control overhead. Firstly, we give theoretical analyses of the control overhead of our protocol and of the Fisheye-OLSR protocol in order to verify that employing a clustering approach allows to improve the overhead compared to the Fisheye technique. Then, we compare our approach to the C-OLSR and the Fisheye-OLSR protocols through a simulation study. In this simulation study, the MAC layer is considered as a perfect MAC since we are mainly interested in this paper in the evaluation of the control overhead of our protocol with respect to other OLSR scalable protocols. In future performance evaluation works, we will consider end-to-end performance such as the packet delivery ratio or the delay by implementing the protocol in a discrete event simulator that integrates a more realistic MAC layer and mobility such as OPNET or NS2.

4.1 Theoretical Analyis

4.1.1 Nework Model and Parameters

The network is represented by a Poisson Point Process over the plan denoted S with intensity λ. Let N be the number of nodes in the network. N follows a Poisson law with intensity $\lambda * S$. λ represents the mean number of nodes per unity of surface. It follows that the density of the network $M = \lambda$, which means that on average each node has M neighbors or that on a unit disk centered on a node, there are on average M nodes. Therefore, the number of nodes in the K-hop neighborhood of a node is equal to the number of nodes in a disk a radius K which is on average K^2M. Moreover, the radius of the network is $\sqrt{N/M}$. Let M_R be the average number of MPRs selected by a node with a neighborhood size M. It has been shown in [10] and [6] that $M_R \leq (9\pi^2M)^{1/3}$ and that $M_R \sim \beta M^{1/3}$ when $M \to \infty$ with $\beta \approx 5$.

The number of retransmissions of a TC message in the K-Hop neighborhood is equal to the number of MPRs in the K-Hop neighborhood, which is on average equal to the number of nodes in the K-Hop neighborhood times the probability for a node to be an MPR. Consequently, the number of retransmissions of a TC message in the K-Hop neighborhood of a node is on average : $M_R/M * K^2M = M_RK^2$. Then it follows that the number of nodes at exactly K hops of a node that may retransmit a TC message is on average : $M_R/M * (K^2 - (K-1)^2)M = M_R(K^2 - (K-1)^2)$.

4.1.2 Fisheye OLSR

In the Fisheye OLSR improvement, the period of the TC messages received from a node increases with the distance to the sending node. We can define a function F that gives the period of the TC messages based on the number of hops from the source, i.e. the TTL set in the messages. Let us consider the function $F : F(x) = \frac{4x}{3+x}$ as in [6] where x represents the TTL and $F(x)$ is the period of the TC message for the TTL x. The overhead generated by a TC message sent by an MPR in bits/s is :

$$\sum_{K=2}^{\sqrt{N/M}} \frac{1}{F(K)} (((K-1)^2 - (K-2)^2)M_R + 1) * TC_{size} \tag{1}$$

It should be noted that for a TTL of k, the message will be retransmitted $(k-1)$ times. TC_{size} is the size of a TC message in bits and is on average $(M_R + 5) * 8$ bits. Finally it follows that the overhead in bits/s due to the TC messages in the Fisheye OLSR protocol is on average:

$$(1) * \text{number of MPR in the network} = (1) * M_RN/M \tag{2}$$

4.1.3 Our approach

Let $TC_{Interval}$ be the period of the TC message. The default value is 5 seconds. Let C be the mean number of clusters in the network. It has be shown that for the Max-Min heuristic [11], an upper bound of the mean number of clusters can be found :

$$\mathbf{E}\left[\text{Clusterhead \# in S}\right] \leq \lambda \cdot v(S) \cdot \left(1 + \sum_{n=1}^{\infty} \frac{1}{n} \frac{E^n}{n!}\right) exp(-E)$$

with $E = \lambda \pi R^2$, where R is the propagation range of a node and $v(S)$ is the Lebesgue measure of S. This upper bound is computed for a radius of 1. It is shown that for radius greater than 1, the set of clusterheads is included in the one computed for radius 1. Therefore, this upper bound becomes less and less accurate as the radius increases.

In our approach, we have to distinguish the overhead generated by TC messages forwarding within each cluster from the overhead generated by the forwarding of the TC_Cluster messages. An upper bound of the mean number of nodes per cluster is equal to $r^2 M$ nodes, where r is the radius of the cluster. The overhead due to the forwarding of a TC message sent by an MPR within a cluster in bits/s is thus bounded by the following upper bound:

$$(1 + r^2 M_R) * TC_{size}/TC_{Interval} \tag{3}$$

Moreover, the mean overhead generated by the forwarding of a TC_Cluster message sent by a clusterhead in bits/s is :

$$(1 + NM_R/M) * TC\_Cluster_{size}/TC\_Cluster_{Interval} \tag{4}$$

Finally, the control overhead due to the TC and TC_Cluster message forwarding is bounded:

$$\mathbf{E}\left[\text{control message overhead}\right] \leq (4) * (NM_R/M) + (3) * C \tag{5}$$

4.1.4 Comparison of the theoretical bounds of the control overhead

In this section, we compare the theoretical overhead of the Fisheye OLSR and our proposal based on the expressions given in the previous sections. One should note that in the following results, the overhead due to the clustering algorithm has been added to the TC and TC_Cluster control overhead for our solution. As illustrated by figure 2, when the number of nodes increases, the overhead due to the TC messages with the Fisheye solution greatly increases whereas it increases slowly with our proposition. When the number of nodes is low (under 200 nodes), the overheads of the two approaches are close. This underlines a potential limit on the network size for the use of a clustering algorithm. Figure 3 presents the overhead of the TC messages in a network of 500 nodes as the density increases. It shows that the per-

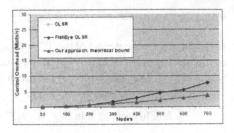

Fig. 2 TC overhead comparison between Fisheye OLSR and our protocol versus the number of nodes

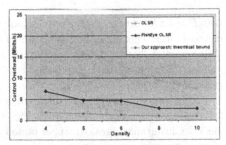

Fig. 3 TC overhead comparison between Fisheye OLSR and our protocol versus the density

formance of Fisheye OLSR improves as density increases just as the OLSR protocol itself does. This result is due to the fact that when density increases, the diameter of the network decreases, and the MPR algorithm is more efficient. Therefore, fewer retransmissions are needed to send TC messages to the network. However, our protocol still outperforms the Fisheye approach even in very dense networks. With our approach, the density has less impact on the control overhead.

4.2 Performance evaluation based on simulation

In this section, we compare the overhead of different approaches proposed to improve the scalability of OLSR. We will consider the fisheye OLSR solution and the C-OLSR solution to which we will compare our approach. These three protocols have been implemented thanks to the Scilab 4.1.2 [12] simulation tool. For the clustering, we implement the generalized max-min clustering algorithm [11]. Since we are mainly interested in the control overhead, we compare the control overhead caused by either the TC messages or their substitutes in each of these protocols:

- TC messages for the Fisheye-OLSR protocol
- TC messages forwarded within each cluster, C-Hello messages, C-TC messages and control message overhead due to the clustering protocol for the C-OLSR protocol
- TC messages forwarded within each cluster, TC_Cluster messages, and control message overhead due to the clustering protocol for our protocol.

Figure 4 presents a comparison between the upper theoretical bound and the simulated values of the overhead of the Fisheye OLSR and our solution. This results prove that the theoretical expressions really give upper bounds but it also shows that these bounds are rather far from the simulation values. Moreover, if the theoretical bound of our approach is higher than the theoretical bound of Fisheye-OLSR for small networks, the simulation shows that even with small networks, our approach performs better than Fisheye OLSR. Figure 5 presents a comparison of the control

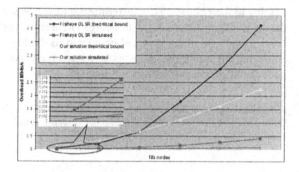

Fig. 4 Comparison of the theoretical and simulated values of the control overhead

overhead of Fisheye OLSR, C-OLSR and our solution as a function of the number of nodes. The results prove that employing a clustering algorithm allows to greatly improve the scalability of OLSR compared to the Fisheye solution. Moreover, we show that our solution presents better scalability compliance than the C-OLSR solution where OLSR is applied on top of the cluster topology. The difference between the overhead of C OLSR and our approach results only from the inter-cluster communications approach since both the clustering and the intra-cluster TC forwarding is similar in these two solutions. Therefore, the results prove that a solution that does not re-use the OLSR algorithm on top of the cluster topology presents better efficiency in term of control overhead than applying an adapted version of OLSR on the cluster topology.

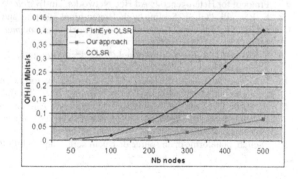

Fig. 5 Comparison of the control overhead of Fisheye OLSR, C-OLSR and our approach

5 Conclusion

This paper presents a scalable routing protocol for Mobile Ad hoc Networks that is based on and improves the well known proactive unicast routing protocol OLSR to make it scalable. The protocol assumes that nodes are gathered in clusters thanks to a clustering algorithm. The regular OLSR protocol is applied within the clusters and a new message type is defined to allow inter-cluster routing. These new messages, called TC_Cluster, are sent by the clusterheads and contain the list of the nodes belonging to their cluster. TC_Cluster messages are broadcast over the entire network thanks to the optimized MPR flooding. Theoretical and simulation analyses of the control overhead of our protocol compared to the Fisheye-OLSR and the C-OLSR show that our approach significantly reduces the control overhead as the number of nodes in the network increases.

Acknowledgements This work has been carried out under the financial support of Rockwell Collins and under the co-funding of the French research ministry and the European Social Fund.

References

1. T. Clausen and P. Jacquet, "Optimized Link State Routing Protocol (OLSR)." RFC 2636, October 2003.
2. J. Maker and I. Chakeres, "Mobile Ad-hoc Networks (Manet)." Charter, [on line] http://www.ietf.org/html.charters/manet-charter.html.
3. A.Qayyum, L. Viennot, and A. Laouiti, "Multipoint Relaying: An Efficient Technique for flooding in Mobile Wireless Networks." RR-3898, INRIA, Feb 2000.
4. A. Laouti, P. Mhlethaler, A. Najid, and E. Plakoo, "Simulation Results of the OLSR Routing Protocol for Wireless Network," in *Med-Hoc-Net workshop*, (Sardegna, Italy), 2002.
5. T. Clausen, "Combining Temporal and Spatial Partial Topology for MANET routing - Merging OLSR and FSR," in *IEEE WPMC'03*, (Yokosuka, Japan), 2003.
6. C. Adjih, E. Baccelli, T. Clausen, P. Jacquet, and G. Rodolakis, "Fish eye OLSR scaling properties," *Journal of communication and networks (JCN)*, vol. 6, no. 4, pp. 343–351, 2004.
7. Y. Ge, L. Lamont, and L. Villasenor, " Hierarchical OLSR - A Scalable Proactive Routing Protocol for Heterogeneous Ad Hoc Networks," in *WiMob'05*, Montreal, Canada 2005.
8. E. Baccelli, "OLSR Scaling with Hierarchical Routing and Dynamic Tree Clustering," in *IASTED International Conference on Networks and Communication Systems (NCS)*, (Chiang Mai, Thailand), March 2006.
9. F. Ros and P. Ruiz, "Cluster-based OLSR Extension to Reduce Control Overhead in Mobile Ad Hoc Networks," in *IWCMC'07*, August 2007.
10. P. Jacquet, A. Laouiti, P.Minet, and L. Viennot, "Performance evaluation of multipoint relaying in mobile ad hoc networks," in *Networking 2002*, (Pisa), 2002.
11. A. D. de Clauzade, M. Marot, and M. Becker, "An analysis of the generalised Max-Min d-cluster formation heuristic," in *Med-Hoc-Net 2007 Workshop*, (Ionian University, Corfu, Greece), June 2007.
12. "Scilab, plateforme open source de calcul scientifique." http://www.scilab.org.

Securing Multihop Vehicular Message Broadcast using Trust Sensors

Matthias Gerlach, Oleksandr Mylyy, Nestor Mariyasagayam, and
Massimiliano Lenardi

Abstract The ad hoc wireless exchange of position and velocity information
between vehicles enables a plethora of new applications that can increase the
safety and efficiency of driving. Efficient and reliable flooding mechanisms
for vehicular applications mandate correct and timely received positions, vehicular safety applications even more so. This work first assesses the impact
of different position faking attackers on the "goodput" of Multi-Hop Vehicular Beacon Broadcast (MHVB-B), a dissemination mechanism for vehicular
networks. Then we use a set of known and simple heuristics to improve the
detection of fake positions within MHVB-B data and briefly assess their impact on the goodput. At the core of this work, we define a framework for
integrating arbitrary trust sensors using Bayesian reasoning and describe a
way to determine their contribution to the overall assessment of message
trustworthiness, that we model as a conditional probability.

1 Introduction

Vehicular communication based on wireless short-range technology facilitates
a plethora of new applications at low cost for safety, traffic efficiency, and
infotainment using direct or multi-hop communication. Securing vehicular
communication does not only involve *preventive security measures* to ensure
access control (authorization) of nodes and ensure integrity, authenticity, and
confidentiality of messages. It also involves *detection and reaction methods*.
This is particularly true in large networks, where integrity and authenticity

Matthias Gerlach (e-mail: matthias.gerlach@fokus.fraunhofer.de) and Oleksandr Mylyy
are with Fraunhofer Institute for Open Communication Systems (FOKUS). Nestor
Mariyasagayam and Massimiliano Lenardi are with Hitachi Ltd. Sophia Antipolis Labs
(HSAL).

Please use the following format when citing this chapter:

Gerlach, M., Mylyy, O., Mariyasagayam, N., Lenardi, M., 2008, in IFIP International Federation for Information
Processing, Volume 265, Advances in Ad Hoc Networking, eds. Cuenca, P., Guerrero C., Puigjaner, R., Serra, B.,
(Boston: Springer), pp. 109-120.

do not guarantee the correctness of transmitted data due to insider attacks or faulty nodes.

For many vehicular applications, *mobility data beaconing* is necessary for cooperative message distribution (*routing*) or cooperative safety applications (*cooperative awareness*). Each node periodically sends out mobility data, i.e., position and velocity. The algorithms for mobility data beaconing have to introduce little overhead, and be scalable and robust in order to account for the properties of vehicular networks, i.e., short vehicle contact times, the network size, and the adverse radio environment. Consequently, important *quality of service parameters* for mobility data beaconing are timeliness of delivery (success rate) and how much of intended geographic area really has been covered. Mariyasagayam et al. present an algorithm for vehicular beaconing in pre-defined geo-regions by means of efficient flooding in [1] and an enhanced version in [2]. The algorithm, called MHVB-B, Multi-Hop Vehicular Beacon Broadcast, achieves a higher message dissemination success rate by selectively repeating messages based on distance from the originator. In this paper, we will discuss and assess the impact of position faking attacks on MHVB-B.

This paper is organized as follows. In Section 2 we discuss the objectives an attacker pursues with mobility data manipulation. Section 3 presents simulations we carried out on the impact of position faking nodes on MHVB-B and the impact of simple checks to assess incoming positions. In Section 4 we outline a novel trust framework and describe how arbitrary trust sensors can be integrated into the framework. Section 5 concludes this paper and outlines future work.

1.1 Related Work

With respect to security, it is commonly agreed that anonymous certificates and digital signatures should be part of a security solution for vehicular communication. IEEE 1609.2 [3], for example is a standard describing how to secure messages for vehicular communication using ECDSA as a mandatory asymmetric crypto-algorithm. Solutions based on certificates have also been proposed by Raya et al. [4] and Festag et al.[5], and Gerlach [6], for example. For the sake of this work, we assume certificates and signatures to prevent Sybil attacks. In [7], Golle et al. present a general approach to assess the validity of data in VANETs. Based on available sensor information, each node builds a model and attempts to find the simplest explanation for the received data with this model. The paper focuses on presenting a theoretic framework. Leinmüller et al. carried out simulations to evaluate the impact of position-faking nodes on geographic forwarding [8] and propose position verification algorithms in [9]. In particular, they found that using plausibility checks can detect the majority of false position reports.

2 Mobility Data Manipulation

Mobility data faking describes the process of changing a node's true position and velocity to fake values with the purpose of injecting those into the vehicular network. Current work identifies position faking or manipulation as a probable attack and describes ways to inject fake data into the network, e.g., by manipulation of sensor input to the on board unit. Aijaz et al. describe ways to manipulate the input to the on board unit [10, Figure 6], and hence the way to achieve the attack. Assuming the attacker has found a way to inject false movement information into the network, it should be discussed what kinds of change to mobility data can be detected – and what their potential impact may be.

Faking its identity, a node carries out a *Sybil* attack – potentially with different sets of mobility data. A Sybil attack can make the recipients believe that there is a traffic jam ahead, for example. For the sake of this work, we assume that Sybil attacks can be prevented using short lived certificates for vehicle authorization as discussed in Section 1.1. This reduces our discussion to faking position, speed and heading.

Faking the position of a node means that an offset is added to the position before it is sent out such that the fake position matches the objectives of the attacker. The attacker's objective can be to attack a certain node, or a certain mechanism, independent from the node. The same holds true for velocities, i.e., heading and speed. Consequently, we need to discuss the attacker's objectives in order to find out probable attacks with changed positions and velocities.

For vehicular settings, geo-addressing, i.e., rather addressing a geographic region than a certain node, is an important feature. Typically, there are two different phases for geo-addressed delivery of packets: *line-forwarding* and *area-forwarding*. The first is used to efficiently transport the message to the area of interest and the latter is used for disseminating the information within the target area. Position based routing mechanisms are often used for the line-forwarding. For area-forwarding, flooding is an example for a simple strategy. While attacks on greedy forwarding for line forwarding have been looked at by Leinmüller et al. (cf. Section 1), we will discuss the impact of position faking nodes at MHVB-B, i.e., an efficient area forwarding algorithm.

The objective of an attacker with respect to the networking mechanism will be the disruption of communication or the isolation of certain nodes. Looking at the above requirements, an attacker will attempt to spoil timeliness of delivery, and to decrease the number of nodes that can be reached within the destination region. The only way to achieve this is by faking movement information that prevent *all* potential forwarders sending their message to the next hop. Potential forwarders in MHVB-B are selected implicitly and in a distributed fashion as a function of distance to the sender. By overhearing the channel, MHVB-B nodes avoid duplicate retransmissions after receiving a packet from a node with a larger distance to the sender than itself. Consequently, a potentially viable attack on MHVB-B would be a forwarder that fakes its own position to be farther away from the source node (and calculates its back-off accordingly). Like this, receiving nodes in optimal position for retransmission would back-off and the packet may not reach all intended receivers in the defined region. Apart from this, the most relevant threat will be the dissemination of false positions for the use in applications, such that the attacker can cause accidents, gain an advantage (a free road) or otherwise use the system for harming people.

3 Simulation Results – Attacker Impact

For the analysis of possible attacks on mobility data we created a simple attacker framework in ns-2. We use it to test the influence of different attacks on MHVB-B. The malicious behavior of an attacker node can be realized through the assignment of an attack function, respective parameters, and attack timing to this node. The attack function parameters contain the type of attack that should be carried out. From the implementation side, the attacker code can easily be integrated into existing mobility aware nodes by inserting a *manipulate()-function* into a simulation agent's code before submitting positions for sending. Configuration of the attacker is done in a dedicated file using tcl according to the typical ns-2 configuration files.

Attacker Type	Used Parameters	Description
Normal node	attacker_functype	The node works as expected
OFFSET	Attacker *adds a predefined offset* to the real position	
	attacker_xpos_dist, attacker_ypos_dist	Value to define the value of the offset to be added
	attacker_random_xpos, attacker_random_ypos	Flag to define which direction shall be changed by attacker (x, y, or both). Value is changed within a predefined range

Table 1 Attacker framework configuration parameters for OFFSET attacker

For the purpose of this work we consider the offset type as the most commonly used attacker type. Table 1 depicts the major parameters for the attacker. If the offset value is calculated not in a random manner but according to the current goal, these attackers may be widely used for modeling different situations. The offset attacker may sensibly model a malicious node with a purpose.

3.1 Impact on MHVB-B

We run simulations for MHVB-B using our attacker framework with a variety of attackers. To estimate the effectiveness of the MHVB-B, the performance parameter success rate (sr) was defined for a node as the following ratio [1]:

$$sr = \frac{pkt\_number\_rcvd\_within\_threshold}{total\_rcvd\_pkt\_number}, where \tag{1}$$

$pkt\_number\_rcvd\_within\_threshold$ is the number of packets received by a node within the threshold=0.3s and is within the 400m radius of the originator, and $total\_rcvd\_pkt\_number$ is the total number of packets received by the same node during the entire simulation time. sr did not change significantly due to the definition of sr: if an intermediate attacker node drops received packets, the receiver node does not know that these packets were issued by the sender node and, as a result, does not change its $total\_rcvd\_pkt\_number$. By contrast, for simulating the impact of position faking nodes on MHVB-B, packets lost inside the network due to the different malicious actions, dropping packets etc. must additionally be taken into account by the performance analysis algorithm. Therefore, in order to make the attacker impact on MHVB-B visible, we define a new performance parameter, called *message goodput*. This parameter can be described as follows:

$$message\_goodput = \frac{good\_pkt\_number\_rcvd\_within\_threshold}{total\_rcvd\_pkt\_number} \tag{2}$$

where $good\_pkt\_number\_rcvd\_within\_threshold$ is the number of packets with correct, i.e., usable, movement information received by a node within the threshold=0.3 seconds and is within the 400m range of the originator, and $total\_rcvd\_pkt\_number$ is the total number of packets received by the same node during the entire simulation time. For our simulation, we counted correct and detected false positions as contribution to the good packet number. We argue that even some of the detected false positions may be used, depending on the given and assumed accuracy.

Figure 1 depicts the impact of position manipulation attacks on the goodput of MHVB-B for different attackers and attacker densities, and different movement scenarios as a function of distance between nodes. As first movement scenario we chose a single lane scenario with the length of 10 km and the node density of 30 node per km similar to the one described in [1]. For the second scenario, we took a realistic highway movement scenario with two lanes 15 km and the average node density of 7 nodes per km. Simulation time was 2 min for both cases. All attackers were offset attackers with different offset values. Together with the normal mode (without attacker in the network) we studied the attacker penetration of 20%, 40%, and 80% for each scenario. Figure 1 shows that goodput is degraded by the attacker by about

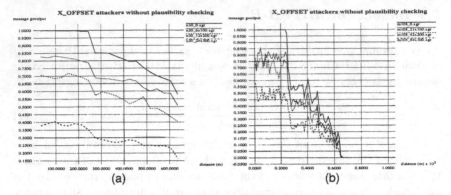

Fig. 1 Impact of different attackers on MHVB-B goodput without plausibility control. (a) single lane scenario (b) highway scenario

the amount of attackers in the network for each distance. We can observe a significant difference between the normal case and the offset attackers (with the offset value 300m and the penetration rate of 80%) over the entire simulation time with no significant difference between the two scenarios in terms of goodput degradation.

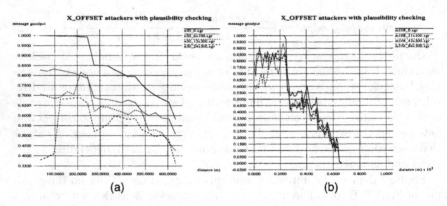

Fig. 2 Using plausibility mechanisms to improve goodput. (a) single lane scenario (b) highway scenario

Figure 2 presents the simulation results after applying simple plausibility control mechanism which comprised the plausibility checking using two well-known plausibility sensors – ART (acceptance range threshold) and MGT (mobility grade threshold) (cf. [9]). ART accepts positions only within a certain range; messages containing a position further away than, e.g., 500m are assumed to contain a false position. MGT assumes that the delta between two positions can only be such that a realistic velocity is not exceeded.

The impact of the plausibility checking can be derived from comparing this figure with Figure 1. We observe a significant improvement in message goodput for all cases. This fact, as well as the remaining difference in message goodput between the normal mode and the integrated attackers, is due to the relatively weak plausibility checks, which only detect significant position deviations and calls for the integration of more elaborate mechanisms. We are currently developing those for the use of our framework based on the Kalman filter.

4 Detecting and Handling False Mobility Data

The discussions and results in the previous sections identified the need for the assessment of movement information and appropriate measures of reaction and more elaborate checks. In this section, we will discuss a probabilistic framework detection of false movement data.

At the core of our discussion are the notions of trust and trustworthiness. While trust typically contains the element of a decision already – we decide to *trust* somebody or not – this is typically based on the evaluation of the *trustworthiness* of that person, its statements and behaviour. Along those lines, an application will decide to trust the given data, while our system attempts to assess the trustworthiness of this data beforehand. This distinction should be borne in mind for our trust sensors, which are really trustworthiness sensors.

4.1 Detection and Fusion – Trust Evaluation

Taking up the ideas of *security sensor fusion* of Gerlach et al. [11] and refining their work, we are currently implementing a framework for detecting and tagging movement information based on the input from different trust sensors. Incoming mobility data messages are assessed in the trust evaluation module that uses Bayesian inference for obtaining a statement about the trustworthiness of the given data using a value in the interval $[0,1]$ that can be interpreted as a probability. The trust decision is then taken by mobility data users. Both trust evaluation and decision methods may use context data to include more information about the environment for more accurate decisions.

Figure 3 depicts the input, output and data fusion process of our trust framework. A simple set of movement information comprises a node's position, speed, and heading. Acceleration would complete the picture, but we do not take it into account here. Note that a set of movement information is

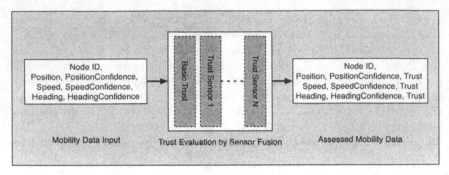

Fig. 3 Data flow in the sensor fusion framework

atomic, in the sense that it must be evaluated as a whole. For our trust evaluation system we assume that (1) accuracy information (confidence values)
is an integral part of the movement information, (2) trust sensor information
is fused using recursive application of Bayesian inference rule (the output
of the n-th sensor is the input to the $n + 1$-th reasoning step), and (3) we
can estimate the first prior probability as the basic trust of the system as
discussed in Section 4.2.1.

At the core of Bayesian inference – a well-known method of statistical
inference – is the inversion formula $P(C|sensor) = \frac{P(sensor|C)P(C)}{P(sensor)}$. In terms
of probability ratios, the formula can be written as (see also [12]):

$$\frac{P(C|sensor)}{P(\neg C|sensor)} = \frac{P(sensor|C)}{P(sensor|\neg C)} \frac{P(C)}{P(\neg C)} \qquad (3)$$

Taking positions as an example, the hypothesis C translates to "the position is correct". *sensor* is the notation to describe the knowledge and cor-
responding algorithms used in the sensor. The probability $P(C|sensor)$ de-
scribes the probability C is true given the sensor reading. This translates to
the *trustworthiness* of the position given the sensor reading. The ratios in
Equation 3 are typically described as *odds, likelihood ratio,* and *prior odds*.
The relevant input from a trust sensor is the likelihood ratio. Given the odds
after one sensor's likelihood ratio contribution, another's likelihood ratio can
be used to recursively update trustworthiness in Equation 3.

4.2 Trustworthiness Sensors

Every trust(worthiness) sensor provides the likelihood ratio $L(sensor|C)$ as
input to the fusion process:

$$L(sensor|C) = \frac{P(sensor|C)}{P(sensor|\neg C)} \tag{4}$$

Equation 4 requires us to estimate the probabilities for $P(sensor|C)$, i.e., the probability that our sensor confirms a correct message, and the probability that our sensor falsely confirms a wrong message $(P(sensor|\neg C))$. Sometimes we can directly estimate this ratio not even using probabilities, sometimes we need to use repeated trials (or a virtual experiment) to obtain these values. Note that it is not necessary that these two probabilities sum to unity.

4.2.1 Basic Trust Sensor – Prior Trust

The choice of the first prior probability, or equivalently the prior odds is crucial for using the Bayes formula in the recursive form. We propose to interpret the prior probability as the basic trust a node has in its environment. Basic trust models the general trustworthiness a node assigns to a statement before even assessing it, and is typically a function of a node's prior experiences.

For our communication based system this probability represents our belief that a message is correct when we receive one. Again given our Hypothesis C from above, this can be written as conditional probability $P(C|basic)$, where *basic* is the statement "we received a message". Assumed, due to system measurements, an in depth risk analysis, and appropriate security measures, we knew the average fraction of correct messages received is 99% then we could directly set this value as basic trust. For future definitions of basic trust our framework also allows the definition of individual, time, and position dependent basic trust.

4.2.2 Reception Range Threshold

Leinmüller et al. defined the acceptance range threshold (ART) sensor as a simple heuristic that only accepts positions from within the acceptance range [9]. The rationale behind ART is that it is impossible to receive a message from beyond the reception range due to the radio system constraints. Even though intuitively correct, it is difficult to model the power of trustworthiness statements and hence its contribution to the overall assessment to our sensor fusion system. Consequently, we extend the model of the acceptance range to what we call the *reception-range-sensor* to make it more accurate, and be able to include it into our sensor fusion framework.

Figure 4 depicts the underlying model for the reception range sensor, both how it can be visualized in real life (Figure 4-(a)), as well as a function of the reception probability over the distance (Figure 4-(b)). $P(d)$ could be an arbitrary function modelling the relation between reception probability and distance to the sender. Now defining d_{NodeB} as the claimed distance of Node

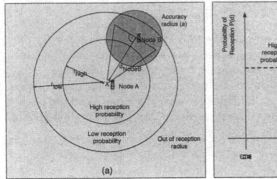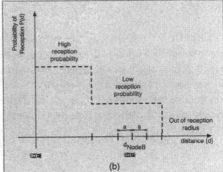

Fig. 4 Model of the reception probability sensor: (a) Overview (b) Probability of reception function over distance

B from the receiving node, a as the accuracy of this claim, we can calculate the likelihood ratio for this sensor as follows:

$$L_{dist} = \frac{\int\limits_{d_{NodeB}-a}^{d_{NodeB}+a} P(\delta)d\delta}{\int\limits_{0}^{\infty} P(\delta)d\delta - \int\limits_{d_{NodeB}-a}^{d_{NodeB}+a} P(\delta)d\delta} \tag{5}$$

Note that the transition from reality to the model depicted in Figure 4 does not account for the circular area around the position of Node B, to reduce complexity of the algorithm. Similarly, we do not take into account the accuracy of node A's position as we assume that it knows its position with a relatively high accuracy. Further, the above likelihood ratio only takes into account the distance from the receiver. Hence, it is not yet complete: the position can still be at any angle from the distance. Therefore, we need to add the probability that the given position is indeed within the direction it claims to be. The likelihood ratio can be calculated as:

$$L_{angle} = \frac{\Psi}{\pi} = \frac{\arctan \frac{a}{d_{NodeB}}}{\pi} \tag{6}$$

Ψ describes the angle spanned by the right angle triangle a (opposite leg) and d_{NodeB} (adjacent leg) as depicted in Figure 4-(a). As the distance and the angle are independent by the definition of polar coordinates, we can combine the two likelihood ratios to obtain the new likelihood ratio:

$$\frac{P(RRS|H)}{P(RRS|\neg H)} = L_{RRS} = L_{distance}L_{angle} \tag{7}$$

L_{RRS} is the overall likelihood of our reception range sensor counting the evidence RRS. We can now obtain $P(sensor|C)$ and $P(sensor|\neg C)$ by requiring the numerator N and denomitator D of Equation 7 to sum to unity.

4.3 Trust Decision – Handling False Data

In general, every application or networking mechanism defines its own way to deal with untrustworthy data. It can define the level below which it deems something too untrustworthy to act upon or it acts in the case of untrustworthy information – such as an intrusion detection system. In addition, this trust threshold may also depend on the situation the given node is in.

In the case of MHVB-B, different choices are possible. In first simulations carried out in this work, an MHVB-B node receiving false information dropped that particular message. As a result any (detected) false message was eliminated in the first hop. As repeaters may also cheat with their position and thus have an adverse impact on the reachable geographic region it may be prudent for intermediate nodes to check the position of the forwarder and – if this is not trustworthy – resend the packet. Even though this may result in a higher channel use, it would also make the protocol more resistant against false positions.

5 Conclusion and Future Work

In this paper, we evaluated the impact of position faking attackers on MHVB-B, an efficient dissemination protocol. After the initial results presented here, we conclude that the networking mechanism of MHVB-B seems to be fairly robust to position faking. For better visualization of the impact of position faking nodes, we created a new measure – goodput – that reflects the number of usable positions sent around in the network. We used well-known and simple plausibility mechanisms to improve the goodput and conclude that a more elaborate framework with more accurate trust sensors must be developed that we presented thereafter.

Future work will include to improve our attacker framework and carry out more simulations confirming the robustness of MHVB-B. Further we need to find a more accurate metric to reflect the impact of position faking to the networking mechanism. Last but not least, we will implement, evaluate and use our sensor-fusion framework to integrate more trust sensors, and develop more accurate trust sensors.

References

1. Mariyasagayam, N., Lenardi, M.: Broadcast algorithms for Active Safety Applications over Vehicular Ad-hoc Networks. In: Proceedings of 4th International Workshop on Intelligent Transportation (WIT), Hamburg, Germany (2007)
2. Mariyasagayam, N., Osafune, T., Lenardi, M.: Enhanced Multi-Hop Vehicular Broadcast (MHVB) for Active Safety Applications. In: Proceedings of 7th International Conference on ITS Telecommunications (ITST). (2007)
3. Institute of Electrical and Electronics Engineers: IEEE Trial-Use Standard for Wireless Access in Vehicular Environments - Security Services for Applications and Management Messages (2006)
4. Raya, M., Papadimitratos, P., Hubaux, J.P.: Securing Vehicular Communications. IEEE Wireless Communications Magazine, Special Issue on Inter-Vehicular Communications (2006)
5. Fonseca, E., Festag, A., Baldessari, R., Aguiar, R.: Support of Anonymity in VANETs - Putting Pseudonymity into Practice. In: Proceedings of IEEE Wireless Communications and Networking Conference (WCNC), Hong Kong (2007)
6. Gerlach, M., Rechner, H., Leinmüller, T.: Security Framework for Vehicular Applications. In Altintas, O., Chen, W., eds.: Proceedings of Third International Workshop on Vehicle-to-Vehicle Communications (V2VCOM), Istanbul, Turkey (2007)
7. Golle, P., Greene, D., Staddon, J.: Detecting and Correcting malicious data in VANETs. In: Proceedings of the first ACM workshop on Vehicular ad hoc networks (VANET). (2004) 29–37
8. Leinmüller, T., Schoch, E.: Greedy Routing in Highway Scenarios: The Impact of Position Faking Nodes. In: Proceedings of Workshop on Intelligent Transportation Systems (WIT 2006). (2006)
9. Leinmüller, T., Schoch, E., Kargl, F.: Position Verification Approaches for Vehicular Ad Hoc Networks. IEEE Wireless Communications Magazine (2006)
10. Aijaz, A., Bochow, B., Dötzer, F., Festag, A., Gerlach, M., Kroh, R., Leinmüller, T.: Attacks on Inter Vehicle Communication Systems - an Analysis. In: Proceedings of Second Workshop on Intelligent Transportation Systems (WIT). (2005)
11. Gerlach, M., Festag, A., Leinmüller, T., Goldacker, G., Harsch, C.: Security Architecture for Vehicular Communication. In: Proceedings of Fourth Workshop on Intelligent Transportation Systems (WIT), Hamburg, Germany (2007)
12. Pearl, J.: Probabilistic Reasoning - Networks of Plausible Inference. Morgan Kaufmann Publishers, Inc., San Mateo, California (1993)

Scalable Exchange of Packet Counters in OLSR

Ignacy Gawędzki and Khaldoun Al Agha

Abstract The HELLO messages of the OLSR protocol can be used as a way to exchange packet counters for each advertised link between the originating node and its neighbors. These counters are aimed to enable nodes receiving the HELLO messages to check that the property of flow conservation is verified on the originating node. The addition of this information incurs a significant overhead that could prevent the node from being able to advertise all its links in one HELLO message. Although plain OLSR has been designed to deal with partial information in its control messages, enabling the verification of the flow conservation property is not trivial. In this paper, we present a way to perform partial advertisement of packet counters and complete verification of the property of flow conservation that remains scalable. Simulation results show that in practical conditions, the use of the method incurs a limited overhead that makes it very acceptable.

1 Introduction

The technique presented by Gawędzki and Al Agha [1] (referenced as *the method* in the following) aims to detect data packet loss in mobile ad hoc networks by making each node verify the principle of flow conservation at each of its neighbors. To achieve that, every node advertises a series of differential packet counters for every link between itself and one of its neighbors. Upon reception of a counter advertisement from a neighbor, a node must be able to perform two kinds of checks: a node balance check for the originating node and a link balance check for each of the advertised links. The problem

Ignacy Gawędzki, e-mail: i@lri.fr
Khaldoun Al Agha, e-mail: **alagha@lri.fr**
Laboratoire de Recherche en Informatique
Université Paris-Sud 11, CNRS, Orsay, France

Please use the following format when citing this chapter:

Gawędzki, I., Al Agha K., 2008, in IFIP International Federation for Information Processing, Volume 265, Advances in Ad Hoc Networking, eds. Cuenca, P., Guerrero C., Puigjaner, R., Serra, B., (Boston: Springer), pp. 121-132.

here is that to be able to perform a node balance check, the counters for every link from that node are required. Moreover, all these counters have to be taking account of the same time interval, otherwise the node balance is impossible to check. As long as all the counters for all the links of the originating node are advertised at once in each periodic control message, the node balance check can be performed. Unfortunately, given the limited capacity of control messages in most practical applications, an increasing network density directly implies more and more links between a node and its neighbors, hence the impossibility, at some point, to pack all the counters in one advertisement.

The OLSR protocol [2] uses exchange of HELLO control messages to enable nodes to detect their neighbors and maintain an up-to-date set of links and neighbors. In the case where there are too many links to be advertised in one HELLO message, the protocol allows only part of the links to be advertised, provided that all the links are advertised often enough for the corresponding information not to expire at its neighbors. Depending on the different timing parameters (HELLO emission interval, default validity time, etc), a node may simply generate partial HELLO messages or additionally decrease the generation interval, to ensure no link will be advertised less often than the default validity interval.

The method does not, as such, support partial advertisements, so it needs to be adapted to be fully applied on the OLSR protocol. In the following section, a summary of the method and its requirements are provided. The adapted method is presented in section 3 and the correct way to make authentication of control messages possible in section 4. The impact of the adapted method on the performance of the network is studied in section 5 and lastly a conclusion is drawn in section 6.

2 Checking Flow Conservation

The method involves the maintaining by a node of six packet counters for every link between itself and its neighbors. The counter values are to be advertised periodically in control messages bearing a sequence number and the counters themselves are to be reset to zero right after their values have been advertised. Thus let us note $V_j^i(n)$ the set of counter values of the directed links (i, j) and (j, i) (which we will both refer to as undirected link $\{i, j\}$ in the following) transmitted by node i in its advertisement with sequence number n. Let us note $T_i(n)$ the instant in time at which i sends its advertisement number n. The sequence counter of i, noted $S_i(t)$ is the sequence number of the latest transmitted advertisement by i as of instant t. In fact, the sequence counter is incremented right before each advertisement is transmitted with the new value. Therefore, the following properties always hold:

$$\forall t, \quad \forall i, \quad \begin{cases} \mathsf{T}_i\left(\mathsf{S}_i(t)\right) \leq t < \mathsf{T}_i\left(\mathsf{S}_i(t)+1\right) \\ \mathsf{S}_i\left(\mathsf{T}_i\left(\mathsf{S}_i(t)\right)\right) = \mathsf{S}_i(t) \end{cases} . \tag{1}$$

Let $L_j^i(n)$ be what we will be calling the *link advertisement* and defined as follows:

$$\forall i,j, \quad \forall n \in \mathbb{N}, \quad L_j^i(n) = \left(n, V_j^i(n), R_j^i(n)\right) . \tag{2}$$

Here, $V_j^i(n)$ is the set of counter values for link $\{i,j\}$ taken over the interval of time $[\mathsf{T}_i(n-1), \mathsf{T}_i(n))$ and $R_j^i(n)$ is the set of reverse link advertisements, i.e. the set defined as follows:

$$\forall i,j, \quad \forall n \in \mathbb{N}, \quad R_j^i(n) = \bigcup_{m \in \mathcal{S}_j^i(n)} \left\{V_i^j(m)\right\} , \tag{3}$$

where $\mathcal{S}_j^i(n)$ is defined as follows:

$$\forall i,j, \quad \forall n \in \mathbb{N}, \quad \mathcal{S}_j^i(n) = \{m : \mathsf{T}_i(n-1) \leq \mathsf{T}_j(m) < \mathsf{T}_i(n)\} . \tag{4}$$

So for each link, a node collects the sets of counter values regarding that link that it receives from its other endpoint. The set of collected counter values is then put in its own advertisements of links, in addition to its own counter values.

Finally, let $A^i(n)$ be the set of link advertisements with sequence number n generated by i:

$$\forall i, \quad \forall n \in \mathbb{N}, \quad A^i(n) = \bigcup_j \left\{L_j^i(n)\right\} . \tag{5}$$

When some other node receives a set of link advertisements from another node, it has that node's counters plus all its neighbors' counters for each link between that node and its neighbors. Let P be the upper bound on the time interval between two successive advertisements of any existing link between a node and a neighbor.

To perform the verification of the property of conservation of flow at the originating node, a node receiving the set of link advertisements has to calculate a *node balance* for the originating node and a *link balance* for each link between that node and its neighbors. The calculation of the link balances for a link $\{i,j\}$ based on i's nth advertisement, noted $\widetilde{B}^{\times i}_{ij}(n)$ and $\widetilde{B}^{\times i}_{ji}(n)$, require only $L_j^i(n)$, whereas the $V_j^i(n)$ for every i's neighbor j are needed to calculate i's node balance, noted $\mathcal{B}_i(n)$. Fig. 1 illustrates the operation of this method in a situation where all the link advertisements do fit inside a control packet.

For instance advertisement number n contains the amount of all the traffic that flowed on the links for all the four neighbors j_0 to j_3, since i's $(n-1)$th

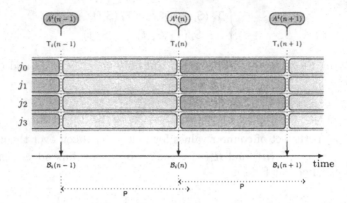

Fig. 1 Total advertisements at regular intervals. All the link advertisements fit inside each control packet.

advertisement set was sent. As soon as that advertisement is received by the neighbors of i, all the link balances $\widetilde{\mathcal{B}}^{x}{}^{i}_{ij}(n)$ and $\widetilde{\mathcal{B}}^{x}{}^{i}_{ji}(n)$ can be computed in addition to i's node balance $\mathcal{B}_i(n)$.

3 Partial Advertisements

In this section, we first state the problem at hand, next study possible approaches and finally present our solution.

3.1 Partial HELLO Messages in OLSR

The HELLO messages in the OLSR protocol are exchanged periodically between direct (i.e. one hop away) neighbors in order to allow nodes to acquire their local neighborhood and detect symmetric links. As this protocol was designed to be effective in dense networks, it is allowing the advertisement of only part of the links in its HELLO messages in case all of them do not fit at once. The way to achieve that is to declare a validity period for the information contained in each HELLO message that is sufficiently long not to expire before the next time that same information is advertised. Consequently, the HELLO generation period has to be properly modulated and the links about which information is to be put in next HELLO message have to be properly chosen, preferably among the ones that are waiting to be advertised the longest.

As it is the case for the acquiring of local neighborhood using partial HELLO messages, it should also still be possible to verify flow conservation in the case of partial link advertisements. Unfortunately, if sets of counters for only part of the links are provided in each control message, as illustrated on Fig. 2, where only two link advertisements fit into a single control message, the computation of node balance is impossible. Here, as soon as advertisement set number n is received by the neighbors of i, the link balances of only two out of four can be computed (for links $\{i, j_0\}$ and $\{i, j_1\}$) and i's node balance $\mathcal{B}_i(n)$ cannot be computed, since it would require a set of $V_j^i(n)$ for all the js accounting the traffic on the same interval of time. In fact, with this naive approach, i's node balance is never computed at all.

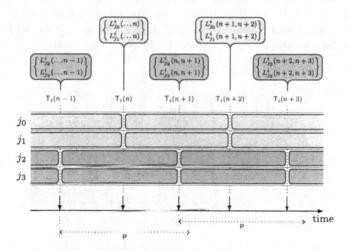

Fig. 2 Naive partial advertisements at regular intervals. Not all the link advertisements fit inside each control packet, hence the impossibility to compute the node balance. Here notations like $L_j^i(n, \ldots, m)$ are a shorthand for $L_j^i(n) + \cdots + L_j^i(m)$.

A straightforward approach to solve the problem would be to simply transmit at instant $\mathsf{T}_i(n)$ a burst of as many control messages as necessary to advertise all the links and thus allow other nodes to receive all the necessary $V_j^i(n)$ they need to compute $\mathcal{B}_i(n)$. But this approach is not acceptable in practice, just for the same reason a burst of HELLO messages is not desirable to advertise all the links: the control messages should have as little impact on the medium as possible. Therefore, we have sought more clever ways to enable partial advertisements while still enabling nodes to calculate both link and node balances.

3.2 Longer Node Balance Interval Method

In section 2, it is assumed that all link advertisements have the same sequence number that is incremented each time an advertisement set is sent. This is necessary to ensure that all the local counters account for data traffic that flowed during the same interval of time. So instead of taking the values of the counters to be advertised right before the advertisement containing them is sent, they could be simply retrieved all at once at regular intervals and sent in advertisements at some later instants. Once all the link advertisements have been sent, new counter values can be retrieved. The process is illustrated on Fig. 3 where again only two link advertisements fit into a single control message. In fact, whether the interval of counter values retrieval is lengthened (and so the bound P as well) or instead the interval of transmission of control messages is shortened makes no practical difference, apart from the fact that node and link balances may be calculated more or less often.

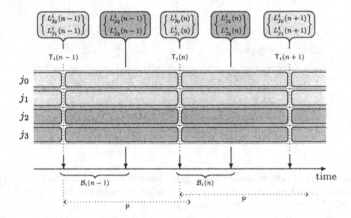

Fig. 3 Partial advertisements at regular intervals. Not all the link advertisements fit inside each control packet, but counter values are retrieved all at once, thus allowing the calculation of the node balance.

Here, it appears that nodes need to gather i's advertisements two by two, in order to recover the necessary information to compute i's node balance. So for instance the calculation of $\mathcal{B}_i(n)$ is possible only at some later instant between $T_i(n)$ and $T_i(n+1)$.

There are downsides to that approach, though. One of them is that it delays the calculation of balances. For node balance, the calculation is delayed until all the required link advertisements are received, whereas for link balances, it is delayed until the very link advertisements are sent.

3.3 Double Counter Values Method

There is an alternative to the approach of section 3.2 which has the advantage of not delaying the calculation of link advertisements at the cost of an increased overhead. The idea is that of maintaining, for each counter, a auxiliary variable: at some properly chosen times, the current values of the counters are assigned to their respective auxiliary variables and the counters are reset to zero; the advertisements contain thus the values stored in the auxiliary variables and the current values of the counters. This process is illustrated in Fig. 4 where we suppose that only one link advertisement (i.e. two counter values) fits into a single control message.

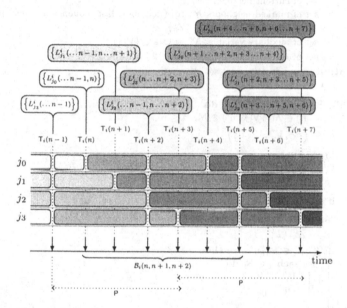

Fig. 4 Double partial advertisements. Not all the link advertisements fit inside each control packet, but double values allow the calculation of the node balance. Here, the notation $L_j^i(n \ldots m, p \ldots q)$ stands for $(L_j^i(n) + \cdots + L_j^i(m), L_j^i(p) + \cdots + L_j^i(q))$, whereas $\mathcal{B}_i(n, \ldots, m)$ stands for $\mathcal{B}_i(n) + \cdots + \mathcal{B}_i(m)$.

The two advertised counter values are to be simply summed for the calculation of the link balance, in order to reconstruct the required value. As for the node balance, another combination has to take place, in order to perform the node balance calculation over the interval of time separating two simultaneous assignments to auxiliary variables. For example, on Fig. 4, those assignments happen at $\mathsf{T}_i(n-1)$, $\mathsf{T}_i(n+2)$ and $\mathsf{T}_i(n+5)$. Consequently, at $\mathsf{T}_i(n+5)$, nodes that have gathered advertisements with sequence numbers from n to $n+5$ are able to compute $\mathcal{B}_i(n, n+1, n+2) = \mathcal{B}_i(n) + \mathcal{B}_i(n+1) + \mathcal{B}_i(n+2)$.

Formally, we have to redefine $L_j^i(n)$ as follows:

$$\forall i, j, \quad \forall n \in \mathbb{N}, \quad L_j^i(n) = \big(n, V_j'^i(n), V_j^i(n), R_j^i(n)\big) ,\qquad (6)$$

where $V_j'^i(n)$ is the tuple of values of auxiliary variables associated with the counters of which values are the tuple $V_j^i(n)$.

The details of the algorithm used to generate and manage the auxiliary variables is given in Fig. 5. Note that when a new neighbor j is to be advertised, a pair $(j, -\infty)$ is added to $\mathcal{M}_i$.

Input: current node i
current sequence number n_C
sequence number of last switch n_S
set of current neighbors $\mathcal{N}_i$
set of marked neighbors $\mathcal{M}_i$ (of (neighbor, last sequence number) pairs)
set of counters $\mathcal{V}^i = \cup_{j \in \mathcal{N}_i} \{V_j^i\}$
set of auxiliary variables $\mathcal{V}'^i = \cup_{j \in \mathcal{N}_i} \{V_j'^i\}$
set of reverse link advertisements $\mathcal{R}^i = \cup_{j \in \mathcal{N}_i} \{R_j^i\}$
Output: new advertisement set A^i

1 $A^i \leftarrow \emptyset$
2 **while** $\exists (j, n) \in \mathcal{M}_i : n < n_C$ **do**
3 $\quad$ let $(j, n) \in \mathcal{M}_i : \forall (j', n') \in \mathcal{M}_i, n \leq n'$
4 $\quad$ $L_j^i = \big(n_C, V_j'^i, V_j^i, R_j^i\big)$
5 $\quad$ $V_j'^i \leftarrow 0_V$
6 $\quad$ $V_j^i \leftarrow 0_V$
7 $\quad$ $R_j^i \leftarrow 0_R$
8 $\quad$ **if** $\text{size}(A^i) + \text{size}\big(L_j^i\big) > maximum\ size$ **then return**
9 $\quad$ $\mathcal{M}_i \leftarrow (\mathcal{M}_i \setminus \{(j, n)\}) \cup \{(j, n_C)\}$
10 $\quad$ $A^i \leftarrow A^i \cup L_j^i$
11 $\quad$ **if** $\forall (j, n) \in \mathcal{M}_i, n \geq n_S$ **then**
12 $\quad\quad$ **foreach** $j \in \mathcal{N}_i$ **do**
13 $\quad\quad\quad$ $V_j'^i \leftarrow V_j^i$
14 $\quad\quad\quad$ $V_j^i \leftarrow 0_V$
15 $\quad\quad$ $n_S \leftarrow n_C$

Fig. 5 Generating advertisements. The values 0_V and 0_R are simply sets of counter values all set to zero.

The big advantage of this method is that link balances are calculated as usual, with fresh values of counters retrieved an instant before and no additional delay. The delay induced in node balance calculation is not so much an inconvenience as it would be in the case of link balances. Indeed, as pointed out about the method, a non-zero link balance tells nothing by itself and successive values of link balances have to be accumulated in order to perform the check, whereas a non-zero node balance implies lost data traffic at that node directly. Therefore, it seems preferable to have a delay induced on node balance rather than on link balances.

In the trivial case where all advertisements fit inside the control message, the node and link balances could all be computed for each successive sequence numbers. With double counter values, for a given sequence number, only some link balances can be computed and each one of them is spanning several sequence numbers, whereas only a sum of several successive node balances can be retrieved.

4 Authentication of Messages

The method relies, among other assumptions, on the ability of nodes to authenticate the source of information contained in control messages. Therefore, the necessary infrastructure is assumed to be deployed that enables each node to verify the authenticity and integrity of any digitally signed piece of information. Since some information contained in HELLO messages is of second-hand origin, a simple signing of the whole message is not enough to verify all of its content. The details of how to protect the content of plain OLSR information in HELLO messages, though, is outside the scope of this paper.

In the present section, we are dealing with the details of the necessary elements for the verification of the additional information needed by the double counter values method of section 3.3.

Obviously, the authenticity and integrity of all first-hand information is verified by a common signature for the whole message. The second-hand information here are the sets of reverse link advertisements contained in each link advertisement. Any node receiving i's nth advertisement set $A^i(n)$ has to be able to verify, for every link to a neighbor j, the link advertisement $L_j^i(n)$ which in turn contains, among other things, the reverse link advertisement set $R_j^i(n)$ of second-hand origin.

To enable a node receiving $A^i(n)$ to verify every $R_j^i(n)$ it contains, the latter have to be signed by j. In other words, instead of $R_j^i(n)$, node i should put $\bar{R}_j^i(n)$, the signed version of $R_j^i(n)$ (defined below). This means in turn that i has to be provided the signature by j itself. The trick here is to require each node i to put $\bar{L}_j^i(n)$, the signed version of $L_j^i(n)$, instead of its unsigned counterpart in its advertisement set:

$$\forall i,j, \quad \forall n \in \mathbb{N}, \quad \bar{L}_j^i(n) = \left(n, V_j'^i(n), V_j^i(n), S^i\left(V_j''^i(n)\right), \bar{R}_j^i(n)\right) , \quad (7)$$

where $V_j''^i(n)$ is the sum, component by component, of $V_j^i(n)$ and $V_j^i(n)$. Finally, the set of signed reverse link advertisements is defined as follows:

$$\forall i,j, \quad \forall n \in \mathbb{N}, \quad \bar{R}_j^i(n) = \bigcup_{m \in \mathcal{S}_j^i(n)} \left\{\left(V_i''^j(m), S^j\left(V_i''^j(m)\right)\right)\right\} , \quad (8)$$

where S^j is the function used by j to generate a signature.

Since the separate tuples of values of auxiliary variables and counters are not needed for reverse link advertisements, they are summed component by component by the receiving node, while the necessary signature is provided directly by the originating node.

5 Performance Impact

To evaluate the performance impact of the double values method, we have run a series of simulations using the OPNET v12.0 software.

5.1 Simulation Model

The model is composed of mobile nodes moving according to the Random Ad hoc Mobility model [3], on a square area. Each node moves with a constant heading and velocity during an exponentially chosen interval of time. At the end of every interval, a new heading and a new velocity are uniformly chosen for the next period. The borders of the area in which the mobiles move are elastic, i.e. mobiles bounce off when they hit them. As the MAC and physical layers, an IEEE 802.11-style MAC with DS PHY timings [4] has been used. Nodes implement the OLSR protocol augmented with packet counters and the double counter values method from section 3.3. The relevant parameters are summarized in Table 1.

Table 1 Simulation Parameters

Area Surface	1000×1000 m^2	CS Power Thr.	-85 dBm (≈ 1200 m)
Velocity Range	$[0, 1]$ m/s	Rx Min. SNR	3 dB
Heading Range	$[-\pi, \pi)$	Rx Power Thr.	-70 dBm (≈ 213 m)
Mobility Interarrival	60 s	HELLO Interval	< 2 s
Tx Power	50 mW	TC Interval	5 s
Tx Frequency	2.4 GHz	Refresh Interval	2 s
Tx Bit Rate	11 Mbps	Maximum Jitter	0.5 s

Since a HELLO message can be lost, so can the advertisement set included in it. For the method to work with OLSR, all successive advertisements have to be received by the nodes performing the verifications. Consequently, we have implemented retransmission of lost advertisements, which details are omitted here for brevity.

5.2 Simulation Results

To evaluate the impact of the diffusion of counters on the capacity of the network, we have measured the total idle time of the medium in the MAC layer, averaged on all the mobiles. We define the idle time as the instants at which a node is considering the medium as not busy and is itself neither waiting for an inter-frame space (IFS) nor backing off. We deduce from that definition that the ratio of idle time of the medium is a good enough approximation of the ratio of available capacity of the medium at some node. The total simulated time for each run was 5 minutes.

The simulation runs are divided in three main batches, with successively 50, 75 and 100 nodes. In each batch, we have compared three main scenarios: plain OLSR with normal HELLO messages; OLSR with HELLO messages containing counters in the double value format; OLSR with HELLO messages containing counters in the double value format and with activated advertisement loss detection and retransmission. Finally, in each scenario, we have measured the idle time ratio with a varying maximum message payload size between 200 and 1500 bytes.

The results for the batch with 50, 75 and 100 nodes are shown in Fig. 6. The general picture is that plain OLSR has a very stable impact in that maximum message size range, while without retransmission, OLSR with counters has smaller impact than with retransmission. The reason why plain OLSR is so stable here is mostly due to the fact that in all runs, the entries for all the neighbors fit at once in each HELLO message, thus lowering the control overhead to a strict minimum. On the other hand, the visible impact on OLSR with counters is due to the fact that the added counter values are a significant overhead, thus preventing all the entries to fit inside a single HELLO message. In addition, retransmission of lost advertisements has an even larger impact, due to the additional overhead, though the difference of impact is obviously constant.

The general tendency for OLSR with counters is for impact on idle time to grow with decreasing maximum message size. This is an illustration of the fact that although approximately the same amount of information has to be diffused, the fact that it uses more independent transmissions increases the total overhead. Since there are more messages transmitted, more nodes contend for the medium more often, hence the lower average idle time ratio. Sending one big message can be considered the same as sending many smaller messages with no waiting in between.

Nevertheless, these results show that the impact of using counters on the average idle time is sufficiently close to the impact of plain OLSR, provided that HELLO message capacity is sufficiently large for the node density (i.e. average number of links to advertise). It appears that for batches with 50 and 75 nodes, message capacities of at least 250 bytes are enough, while for 100 nodes, message capacity below 450 is clearly unacceptable. The strong and irregular impact for 100 nodes below 450 bytes is due to the fact that

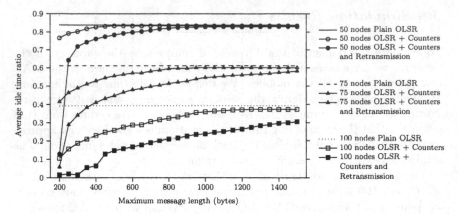

Fig. 6 Ratio of medium idle time, 50, 75 and 100 nodes.

the medium is saturated and contention for the medium is at its highest level (most of the nodes are either transmitting or waiting to transmit).

In practical cases, message capacity is more somewhere around 1400 bytes, so these results are encouraging.

6 Conclusion

We have presented a way of advertising counter values in OLSR for the application of the method of verification of flow conservation [1]. This approach was aimed to be scalable with the increasing number of counters to diffuse and the results show that in performs well in practical scenarios, compared to plain OLSR protocol without diffusion of counter values.

References

1. Ignacy Gawędzki and Khaldoun Al Agha. Proactive resilience to dropping nodes in mobile ad hoc networks. In *AINTEC*, pages 139–158, 2006.
2. T. Clausen and P. Jacquet. Optimized link state routing (OLSR) protocol. RFC 3626, IETF, October 2003.
3. A. MCDonald and T. Znati. A mobility-based framework for adaptive clustering in wireless ad hoc networks, 1999.
4. IEEE. *IEEE Std 802.11-1999, Part 11: Wireless LAN Medium Access Control (MAC) and Physical Layer (PHY) Specifications*, 1999.

Intrusion Detection in Mobile Ad Hoc Networks Using Classification Algorithms

Aikaterini Mitrokotsa, Manolis Tsagkaris and Christos Douligeris

Abstract In this paper we present the design and evaluation of intrusion detection models for MANETs using supervised classification algorithms. Specifically, we evaluate the performance of the MultiLayer Perceptron (MLP), the Linear classifier, the Gaussian Mixture Model (GMM), the Naïve Bayes classifier and the Support Vector Machine (SVM). The performance of the classification algorithms is evaluated under different traffic conditions and mobility patterns for the Black Hole, Forging, Packet Dropping, and Flooding attacks. The results indicate that Support Vector Machines exhibit high accuracy for almost all simulated attacks and that Packet Dropping is the hardest attack to detect.

1 Introduction

The adoption of Mobile Ad hoc networks (MANETs) has increased in recent years mainly due to their important advantages and their broad applicability. MANETs can be defined as dynamic peer-to-peer networks that consist of a collection of mobile nodes. The nodes employ multi-hop information transfer without requiring an existing infrastructure. Although MANETs are characterized by great flexibility and are employed in a broad range of applications, they also present many inherent vulnerabilities that increase their security risks. Due to their dynamic and cooperative nature, MANETs demand efficient and effective security mechanisms in order to be safeguarded. Intrusion prevention can be used as a first line of defense in order to reduce possible intrusions but undoubtedly, it cannot eliminate them. Intrusion de-

Aikaterini Mitrokotsa
Department of Computer Science, Vrije Universiteit, De Boelelaan 1081a, 1081HV Amsterdam Netherlands, e-mail: katerina@few.vu.nl

Manolis Tsagkaris, Christos Douligeris
Department of Informatics, University of Piraeus, Karaoli and Dimitriou 80, 18534 Piraeus, Greece, e-mail: m_tsag@yahoo.com, cdoulig@unipi.gr

Please use the following format when citing this chapter:

Mitrokotsa, A., Tsagkaris, M., Douligeris, C., 2008, in IFIP International Federation for Information Processing, Volume 265, Advances in Ad Hoc Networking, eds. Cuenca, P., Guerrero C., Puigjaner, R., Serra, B., (Boston: Springer), pp. 133-144.

tection using classification algorithms can help us to effectively discriminate "normal" from "abnormal" behaviour and thus, detect possible intrusions. Therefore, intrusion detection, serving as a second line of defense, is an indispensable part of reliable communication in MANETs.

Intrusion Detection has a long history of research in wired network defense but it is still in its infancy in the area of wireless ad hoc networks. There is though, a small number of proposed Intrusion Detection Systems (IDS) for wireless ad hoc networks. Zhang and Lee [14] proposed the first (high-level) IDS approach specific for ad hoc networks. They proposed a distributed and cooperative anomaly-based IDS, which provides an efficient guide for the design of IDS in wireless ad hoc networks. They focused on an anomaly detection approach based on routing updates on the Media Access Control (MAC) layer and on the mobile application layer.

Huang and Lee [6] extended their previous work by proposing a cluster-based IDS, in order to combat the resource constraints that MANETs face. They use a set of statistical features that can be derived from routing tables and they apply the classification decision tree induction algorithm C 4.5 in order to detect "normal" vs. "abnormal" behavior. The proposed system is able to identify the source of the attack, if the identified attack occurs within one-hop.

Deng et al. [2] proposed a hierarchically distributed and a completely distributed intrusion detection approach. The intrusion detection approach used in both of these architectures focuses on the network layer and it is based on a Support Vector Machines (SVM) classification algorithm. They use a set of parameters derived from the network layer and suggest that a hierarchically distributed approach may be a more promising solution versus a completely distributed intrusion detection approach. Liu et al. [8] proposed a completely distributed anomaly detection approach. They investigated the use of the MAC layer in order to profile normal behavior of mobile nodes and then apply cross-feature analysis [5] on feature vectors constructed from the training data.

Although some use of classification algorithms was present in all of the aforementioned papers, almost none contained comparisons between methods, apart from [14]. Thus, there is a lack of evidence to support the use of one algorithm compared to others, when it comes to intrusion detection in MANETs. Furthermore, there is virtually no data on the performance of such algorithm under different traffic conditions (i.e. mobility, number of malicious nodes), and how such meta-algorithmic parameters such as the sampling interval should be selected. The selection of the sampling interval is particularly important, as there could be a trade-off between good classification performance and quick response.

The main novelty of this paper relative to the aforementioned work, lies in the following. Firstly, we are performing a comparison between multiple, well-known, classification models, using labeled training data. Secondly, this comparison is done in a principled experiment, where the hyperparameters that must be tuned for each classification model are selected using a specific procedure, which is the same for all models. In this way we are sure of a fair comparison, as when employed in the field, algorithms would have to be tuned before seeing any actual test data. Finally, we examine how the performance of each algorithm changes for various values of network mobility, sampling interval and the number of malicious nodes. In our previous work [9], we have used a neural network in order to classify normal traffic and selective packet dropping attack. Our goal is to explore whether there exists a classification algorithm that demonstrates superior performance in detecting a given attack category for all, or most traffic conditions. Furthermore, we examine the importance of the sampling interval time of the statistical features and consequently how quickly the intrusion detection can be performed.

More specifically, we present a performance comparison of five efficient and commonly used classification algorithms (MultiLayer Perceptron (MLP), Linear classifier, Gaussian Mixture Model (GMM), Naïve Bayes classifier and Support Vector Machines (SVM)) applied to intrusion detection in MANETs. We use features from the network layer and evaluate the performance of the classification algorithms for the detection of the *Black hole*, *Forging*, *Packet Dropping* and *Flooding* attacks.

Following this introduction, the paper is organized as follows. Section 2 describes the quality metrics used for the classification comparison as well as the classification models employed. Section 3 describes the experiments that have been performed, the experimental setup and the results. Section 4 concludes the paper and discusses some future work.

2 Intrusion Detection Using Classification

We employ classification algorithms in order to perform intrusion detection in MANETs. Compared to other methods, classification algorithms have the advantage that they are largely automated and that they can be quite accurate. They have extended applications including intrusion detection in wired networks [7], great literature coverage and extended experimental use that denote their efficiency.

2.1 Intrusion Detection Model

The IDS architecture we adopt is composed of multiple local IDS agents, that are responsible for detecting possible intrusions locally. The collection of all the independent IDS agents forms the IDS system for the MANET. Each local IDS agent is composed of the following components:

Data Collector: is responsible for selecting local audit data and activity logs.

Intrusion Detection Engine: is responsible for detecting local intrusions using local audit data. The local intrusion detection is performed using a classification algorithm. Firstly, it performs the appropriate transformations on the selected labeled audit data. Then, it computes the classifier using training data and finally applies the classifier to test local audit data in order to classify it as "normal" or "abnormal".

Response Engine: If an intrusion is detected by the Detection Engine then the Response Engine is activated. The Response Engine is responsible for sending a local and a global alarm in order to notify the nodes of the mobile ad hoc network about the incident of intrusion.

2.2 Algorithmic Comparisons and Quality Metrics

When comparisons are made between algorithms, it is important to use the same measure of quality. For a given classification algorithm $f : \mathscr{X} \to \mathscr{Y}$, where $\mathscr{X}$ is the observation space and $\mathscr{Y}$ is the set of classes, a common measure of quality is the classification error C measured over an independent test set D,

$$\hat{E}(C|D) = \frac{1}{|D|} \sum_{d \in D} C(f(x_d), y_d), \tag{1}$$

where x_d is the observation of example d and y_d is its class and $C(y', y) = 0$ when $y = y'$ and 1 otherwise. However, it is important to note that in most of the literature, the *Detection Rate* (*DR*) and the *False Alarm* (*FA*) rate are used instead:

$$DR = \frac{TP}{TP + FN}, \qquad FA = \frac{FP}{TN + FP} \tag{2}$$

where TP, TN, FP, FN, denote the number of true (TP & TN) and false (FP & FN) positives and negatives respectively. The goal of an effective intrusion detection approach is to reduce to the largest extent possible the *False Alarm* rate (*FA*) and at the same time to increase the *Detection Rate* (*DR*).

2.3 Classification Models

In this section we describe the classification models we have used in order to perform intrusion detection i.e., the MultiLayer Perceptron (MLP), the Linear model, the Gaussian Mixture model (GMM), the Naïve Bayes model and the SVM model. All these models require labelled training data for their creation.

A specific instance of an MLP can be viewed simply as a function $g : \mathscr{X} \to \mathscr{Y}$, where g can be further defined as a composition of other functions $z_i : \mathscr{X} \to \mathscr{Z}$. In most cases of interest, this decomposition can be written as $g(x) = Kw'z(x)$ with $x \in X$, w being a parameter vector, while K is a particular kernel and the function $z(x) = [z_1(x), z_2(x), ...]$ is referred to as the *hidden layer*. For each of those, we have $z_i(x) = K_i(v_i'x)$ where each v_i is a parameter vector, $V = [v_1, v_2, ...]$ is the parameter matrix of the hidden layer and finally K_i is an arbitrary kernel. For this particular application we wish to use an MLP m, as a model for the conditional class probability given the observations, i.e.

$$P(Y = y|X = x, M = m), \qquad y = g(x). \tag{3}$$

The case where there is no hidden layer is equivalent to $z_i = x_i$, which corresponds to the *Linear model*, the second model into consideration.

The GMM, the third model under consideration, will be used to model the conditional observation density for each class, i.e. $P(X = x|Y = y, M = m)$.

This can be achieved simply by using a separate set of mixtures U_y for modeling the observation density of each class y. Then, for a given class y the density at each point x is calculated by marginalizing over the mixture components $u \in U_y$, for the class, dropping the dependency on m for simplicity:

$$P(X = x|Y = y) = \sum_u P(X = x|U = u)P(U = u|Y = y). \tag{4}$$

Note that the likelihood function $P(X = x|U = u)$ will have a Gaussian form, with parameters the covariance matrix Σ_u and the mean vector μ_u. The term $P(U = u|Y = y)$ will be represented by another parameter, the component weight. Finally, we must separately estimate $P(Y=y)$ from the data, thus obtaining the conditional probability given the observations:

$$P(Y = y|X = x) = \frac{1}{Z}P(X = x|Y = y)P(Y = y), \tag{5}$$

where $Z = \sum_{y \in Y} P(X = x|Y = y)P(Y = y)$ does not depend on y and where we have again dropped the dependency on m.

The fourth model under consideration is the Naïve Bayes model which can be derived from the Gaussian Mixture Model (GMM) when there is only one Gaussian mixture.

The last model we evaluated in order to perform intrusion detection in MANETs is the Support Vector Machine (SVM) [1] model, which uses Lagrangian methods to minimise a regularized function of the empirical classification error. The SVM algorithm finds a linear hyperplane separation with a maximal margin in this hyperspace. The points that are lying on the margin are called support vectors. The main parameter of the algorithm is c, which represents the trade-off between the size of the margin and the number of violated constraints, and the kernel $K(x_i, x_j)$. In this work we will utilize SVMs with a gaussian kernel of the form $K(x_i, x_j) = \frac{1}{\sqrt{2\pi}\sigma} \exp(-\|x_i - x_j\|^2/\sigma^2)$.

3 Experiments

In order to examine the performance of the classification algorithms, we conducted a series of experiments under varying conditions. In our experiments we performed comparisons in terms of the classification cost defined in equation (1) using ten different models: MLP, Linear, GMM with diagonal covariance matrices, Naïve Bayes

(GMM with a single Gaussian) and SVM models for binary and multiclass classification. In all cases we use the same set of features, as explained in the following section. In binary classification all attacks are lumped together so the task is just to identify the presence of an attack. The multiclass task requires the correct identification of each attack type. We investigated which sampling interval for statistical features is more appropriate, which algorithm presents the best performance in terms of *Detection Rate (DR)* and *False Alarm (FA)* rate and which algorithm is better for the detection of specific attacks. Furthermore, we investigated how the performance of the classification algorithms change when we vary the number of malicious nodes in the network and when we vary the mobility of the network.

3.1 Simulation Environment

In order to evaluate our approach we simulated a mobile ad hoc network (MANET) and we conducted a series of experiments. For our experiments we have made the assumption that the network has no preexisting infrastructure and that the employed ad hoc routing protocol is the Ad hoc On Demand Distance Vector (AODV). We implemented the simulator within the GloMoSim [4] library. Our simulation models a network of 50 hosts placed randomly within an 850 x 850 m^2 area. Each node has a radio propagation range of 250 meters and the channel capacity was 2 Mbps. The nodes in the simulation move according to the 'random way point' model. At the start of the simulation, each node waits for a pause time, then randomly selects and moves towards a destination with a speed uniformly lying between zero and the maximum speed. On reaching this destination it pauses again and repeats the above procedure till the end of the simulation. The minimum and maximum speed is set to 0 and 20 m/s, respectively, and pause times at 0, 200, 400, 700 sec. The simulation time of the experiments was 700 sec, thus a pause time of 0 sec corresponds to the continuous motion of the node and a pause time of 700 sec corresponds to the time that the node is stationary.

Each node is simulated to generate Constant Bit Rate (CBR) network traffic. The size of the packets sent by each node varies from 128 to 1024 bytes. We have studied the performance of the classification algorithms for various sampling intervals (5, 10, 15, 30 sec) in order to study how quickly these algorithms can perform intrusion detection. The sampling interval dictates both the interval for which the statistical features are calculated, and the period between each classification decision. We expect that longer intervals may provide more information, but with the cost of slower detection. We have also evaluated the performance of the classification algorithms for 5, 15 and 25 malicious nodes. In each case the number of all nodes in the network is set to 50.

In our experiments, we have simulated four different types of attacks:

- **Flooding attack:** We have simulated a flooding attack [13] for multiple paths in the network layer, where each malicious node sends forged RREQ (Route REQuest) packets randomly to all nodes of the network every 100 msec.

- **Forging attack:** We have simulated a forging attack [12] for RERR (RouteER-Ror) packets, where each malicious node modifies and broadcasts (to a selected victim) a RERR packet every 100 msec leading to repeated link failures.
- **Packet Dropping attack:** We have simulated a selective packet dropping [3] attack, where each malicious node drops all RERR packets leading legitimate nodes to forward packets in broken links.
- **Black Hole attack:** In a black hole attack [10], a malicious node advertises spurious routing information, thus receiving packets without forwarding them but dropping them. In the black hole attack we have simulated the scenario where each time a malicious-black hole node receives a RREQ packet it sends a RREP (RouteREPly) packet to the destination without checking if the node has a path towards the selected destination. Thus, the black hole node is always the first node that responds to a RREQ packet and it drops the received RREQ packets. Furthermore, the malicious-black hole node drops all RREP and data packets it receives if the packets are destined for other nodes.

A very important decision to be made is the selection of feature vectors that will be used in the classification. The selected features should be able to represent the network activity and increase the contrast between "normal" and "abnormal" network activity. We have selected the following features from the network layer:

- *RREQ Sent:* indicates the number of RREQ packets that each node sends.
- *RREQ Received:* indicates the number of RREQ packets that each node receives.
- *RREP Sent:* indicates the number of RREP packets that each node receives.
- *RError Sent:* indicates the number of RError (Route Error) packets that each node receives.
- *RError Received:* indicates the number of RError packets that each node sends.
- *Number of Neighbors:* indicates the number of one-hop neighbors that each node has.
- *PCR (Percentage of the Change in Route entries):* indicates the percentage of the changed routed entries in the routing table of each node. PCR is given by $(|S_2 - S_1| + |S_1 - S_2|)/|S_1|)$, where $(S_2 - S_1)$ indicates the newly increased routing entries and $(S_1 - S_2)$ indicates the deleted routing entries during the time interval $(t_2 - t_1)$.
- *PCH (Percentage of the Change in number of Hop):* indicates the percentage of the changes of the sum of hops of all routing entries for each node. PCH [11] is given by $(H_2 - H_1)/H_1$, where $(H_2 - H_1)$ indicates the changes of the sum of hops of all routing entries during the time interval $(t_2 - t_1)$.

For each sampling interval time (5, 10, 15, 30 sec) we have created one training dataset, where each training instance contains summary statistics of network activity for the specified interval using all the above features and in addition, the type of attack performed during this interval. This enables us to use supervised learning techniques for clasification. Each training dataset was created by running different simulations with duration 700 sec for different network mobility (pause time equal to 0, 200, 400, 700 sec) and varying numbers of malicious nodes. The derived datasets from each of these simulations were merged and one training dataset was produced for each sampling interval. A similar procedure was followed in order to produce the testing datasets.

3.2 Algorithmic Technical Details

In order to select the best parameters for each algorithm we performed a 10-fold cross validation [15] on the training dataset, which were created with random sampling. For each of the 10 folds, we selected 1/10th of the dataset for evaluation and the remaining for training. We then used the parameters selected to train a new model using all of the training set for each algorithm, which was the model that was evaluated.

For the MLP we tuned three parameters, i.e. the *learning rate (η)* and the *number of iterations (T)* used in the stochastic gradient descent optimization as well as the *number of hidden units (nh)*. Keeping *nh* equal to 0 we selected the appropriate η among values that range between 0.0001 and 0.1 with step 0.1 and the appropriate *T* selecting among 10, 100, 500 and 1000. Having selected the appropriate η and the appropriate *T*, we examined various values in order to select the appropriate *nh*. We selected the best among 10, 20, 40, 60, 8s0, 100, 120, 140, 160, 320. Additionally, we used the MLP model with no hidden units as a Linear model.

For the GMM we also tuned three parameters, i.e. the *threshold (θ)*, the *number of iterations (T)* and the *number of Gaussian Mixtures (ng)*. Keeping stable *ng* (equal to 20) we selected the appropriate θ among values that range between 0.0001 and 0.0001 with step 0.1 and the appropriate *T* among 25, 100, 500 and 1000. For the selection of the appropriate *ng*, after selecting the appropriate θ and the appropriate *T*, we examined various values for the *ng* and the selected best among 10, 20, 40, 60, 80, 100, 120, 140, 160, 320. Additionally, we used the GMM model with one Mixture component as a Naïve Bayes model.

For the SVM we tuned two parameters, i.e. the standard deviation (σ) for the gaussian kernel and the regularisation parameter *c* which represents the trade-off between the size of the margin and the number of misclassified examples. For the selection of the appropriate combination of σ and *c*, we examined various values for the σ (1, 10, 100, 1000) and the *c* (1, 10, 100, 1000) and selected the best.

3.3 Experimental Results

First, we examined which is the most appropriate sampling interval time of the used statistical features. We used the models produced by the training datasets with the appropriate parameters (Sect. 4.2). Figure 1 depicts the average as well as the minimum and the maximum classification error of the testing datasets. While 15 sec appears to be the best sampling interval in the test dataset on average, this does not hold for all cases. It will probably be best to use different intervals for different attacks and classification algorithms, but this is beyond the scope of the current work.

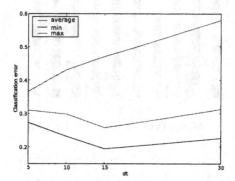

Fig. 1 Classification error versus sampling interval (dt)

Figure 2a depicts the average *Detecton Rate* (DR) and the *False Alarm* (FA) rate for all classification algorithms both for binary and multiclass classification. The best *Detection Rate* (DR) is achieved for the MLP classifier for multiclass classification and is equal to 78.95%, while the corresponding *False Alarm* (FA) rate is equal to 12.92%. The second best classifier with a high *Detection Rate* (DR) equal to 77% is achieved with the SVM classifier for multiclass classification. The corresponding *False Alarm* (FA) rate is quite lower compared to the one achieved with the MLP classifier and is equal to 0.97%. The classifier that presents the poorest performance is the Naïve Bayes classifier with *Detection Rate* (DR) equal to 41.88% and *False Alarm* (FA) rate equal to 0.47%.

Figure 2b depicts the *Detection Rate* (DR) for each type of attacks (Black hole, Forging, Packet Dropping, Flooding), for all classification models. It is obvious that for all classifiers the best *Detection Rate* (DR) is achieved for the *Flooding* attack, while the most difficult attack to detect is the *Packet Dropping* attack. The best *Detection Rate* (DR) for the *Black hole* and the *Flooding* attack is achieved with the *Linear* classifier for multiclass classification and is equal to 87.75% and 96.06% correspondingly. The best *Detection Rate* (DR) equal to 76.86% and 73.88% correspondingly for the *Packet Dropping* and *Forging* attack is achieved again with the *Linear* classifier but for binary classification.

Figure 3 depicts the average, minimum and maximum *classification error* for all classification algorithms for binary and multiclass classification versus the number of malicious nodes (Fig. 4a and Fig. 5a) that exist in the network and the mobility (pause time) (Fig.4b, Fig. 5b) of the network. In order to investigate the performance of the classification algorithms versus the number of malicious nodes the testing datasets were generated by keeping the mobility of the network stable (pause time

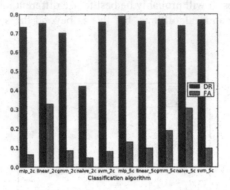

(a) Average Detection Rate and False Alarm

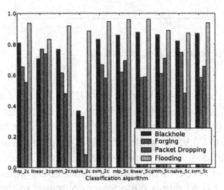

(b) Detection Rate of each type of attacks

Fig. 2 Comparison of all Classification algorithms

equal to 200 sec) and by changing the number of malicious nodes that exist in the network (5, 15, 25). Similarly, in order to investigate the performance of the classification algorithms versus the mobility of the network, we have kept stable the number of malicious nodes in the network (equal to 15) and changed the mobility of the network (pause time equal to 0, 200, 400, 700 sec). It is clear that in both (Fig. 3a and Fig. 3c) the binary and the multiclass classification, the higher the number of malicious nodes in the network, the easier it is to detect possible intrusions. Furthermore, it is clear that in both cases (Fig. 3b, Fig. 3d) it is easier to classify "normal" against "abnormal" network traffic in networks with medium mobility (pause time equal to 200 or 400 sec) compared to stationary networks (pause time equal to 700 sec).

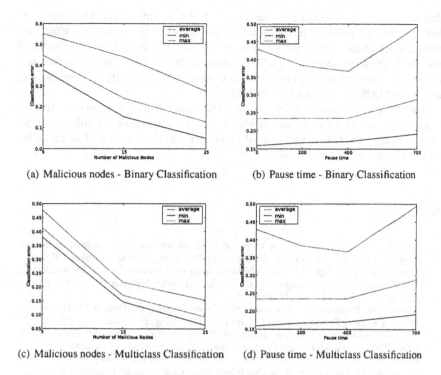

(a) Malicious nodes - Binary Classification   (b) Pause time - Binary Classification

(c) Malicious nodes - Multiclass Classification   (d) Pause time - Multiclass Classification

Fig. 3 Classification error versus malicious nodes and pause time for binary and multiclass classification

4 Conclusions

In this paper we presented a performance comparison of five efficient and commonly used classification algorithms (MultiLayer Perceptron (MLP), Linear classifier, Gaussian Mixture Model (GMM), Naïve Bayes classifier and Support Vector Machines (SVM)) applied to intrusion detection in MANETs. We have used features from the network layer and evaluated the performance of these algorithms for the detection of four serious attacks in MANETs, the *Black hole, Forging, Packet Dropping* and *Flooding* attack. We investigated which is the most appropriate sampling interval time and concluded that the sampling interval of 15 sec is on average the most efficient, based on the performance of the testing datasets, when the k-fold cross validation of the training datasets is performed randomly.

Furthermore, we concluded that the most efficient classifier for detecting all four types of attacks simultaneously is the SVM classifier for multiclass classification although the MLP classifier presents a satisfying *Detection Rate* (DR) and also a quite high *False Alarm* (FA) rate. The easiest attack to be detected is the *Flooding* attack, while the most difficult attack to detect is the *Packet Dropping* attack, something that was also implied in our previous work [9]. We also investigated how the number of malicious nodes in the network and the mobility of the network affects the performance of the classification algorithms in detecting intrusions. We concluded that the highest the number of malicious node in the network the easiest to detect intrusions. Furthermore, the classification algorithms present effective detection of attacks in MANETs with medium mobility.

For future work, we plan to investigate if the tuning of classification models using non-random k-fold but sequential may give us better performance. Furthermore, we plan to examine if the combination of classifiers and the creation of an ensemble classifier can give us better results.

References

1. Burges C.J.C.: A Tutorial on Support Vector Machines for Pattern Recognition. In: Knowledge Discovery and Data Mining, Vol. 2, pp. 121-167, Springer-Verlag, London, UK (1998).
2. Deng H., Zeng Q., Agrawal D.P.: SVM-based Intrusion Detection System for Wireless Ad Hoc Networks. In: Proceedings of the IEEE Vehicular Technology Conference (VTC03), pp. 2147-2151. Orlando, Florida, USA (2003).
3. Djenouri D., Mahmoudi O., Bouamama M., Llewellyn-Jones D., Merabti M.: On Securing MANET Routing Protocol Against Control Packet Dropping. In: Proceedings of IEEE International Conference on Pervasive Services (ICPS' 07), pp. 100-108, Istanbul, Turkey (2007).
4. GloMoSim: Global Information Systems Simulation Library, Version 2.0 (2000).
5. Huang Y., Fan, W., Lee W., Yu P.: Cross-Feature analysis for Detecting Ad-Hoc Routing Anomalies. In: Proceedings of the 23rd International Conference on Distributed Computing Systems, pp. 478. Rhode Island, USA (2003).
6. Huang Y., Lee W.: A Cooperative Intrusion Detection System for Ad Hoc Networks. In: Proceedings of the 1st ACM Workshop on Security of Ad Hoc and Sensor Networks (SASN03), pp. 135-147. Fairfax, VA, USA (2003).
7. Lee W., Stolfo S.J., Mok K.W.: A Data Mining Framework for Building Intrusion Detection Models. In: Proceedings of the IEEE Symposium on Security and Privacy, pp. 120-132, Oakland, CA, (1999).
8. Liu Y., Li Y., Man H.: MAC Layer Anomaly Detection in Ad Hoc Networks. In: Proceedings of 6th IEEE Information Assurance Workshop. West Point, New York, USA (2005).
9. Mitrokotsa A., Komninos N., Douligeris C.: Intrusion Detection with Neural Networks and Watermarking Techniques for MANET. In: Proceedings of IEEE International Conference on Pervasive Services 2007 (ICPS07), pp. 118-127, Istanbul, Turkey (2007).
10. Shurman M.Al, Yoo S.M., Park S.: Black Hole Attack in Wireless Ad Hoc Networks. In: Proceedings of ACM 42nd Southeast Conference (ACMSE 04),pp. 96-97, Alabama (2004).
11. Sun B.: Intrusion Detection in Mobile Ad Hoc Networks. Doctor of Philosophy, Computer Science, Texas A&M University (2004).
12. Ning, P.; Sun, K.: How to Misuse AODV: a Case Study of Insider Attacks Against Mobile Ad-hoc Routing Protocols. In: Proceedings of the 2003 IEEE Workshop on Information Assurance, pp.60-67, NY (2003).
13. Yi P., Hou Y.F., Zhong Y., Zhang S., Dai Z.: Flooding Attack and Defence in Ad hoc Networks. In: Systems Engineering and Electronics, Vol. 17, No. 2, pp. 410-416 (2006).
14. Zhang Y., Lee W., Huang Y.: Intrusion Detection Techniques for Mobile Wireless Networks. In: Wireless Networks Vol. 9, No. 5, pp. 545-556. (2003).
15. Kohavi, R.: A study of cross-validation and bootstrap for accuracy estimation and model selection. In: Proceedings of the Fourteenth International Joint Conference on Artificial Intelligence, Vol. 2, pp. 1137-1145 (1995).

Security for Context-Aware ad-hoc Networking Applications

Yeda Venturini, Vlad Coroama, Tereza C.M.B. Carvalho, Mats Naslund, and
Makan Pourzandi

Abstract With the rapid spreading of ubiquitous computing applications, the importance of security concepts coping with their needs is also growing. While the possible application areas are so vast that one all-purpose security middleware fitting all the different needs seems impossible to realize, it is undoubtedly meaningful to have security frameworks covering the needs of as many applications as possible. In this paper, we thus discuss a security middleware for context-aware ad-hoc networking applications in home and work environments. The article focuses on two novel issues: it shows that the solution is particularly well-suited for context-aware applications, an often-encountered type of applications within home and work environments; and it discusses the encountered, non-trivial trade-offs between ad-hoc networking, context-awareness, and strong security.

1 Introduction

More than 15 years ago, in his seminal article "The Computer for the 21st Century" [13], Mark Weiser has been the first to foresee the spreading of sensing, computing, and communication technologies into everyday things, an evolution which he called "ubiquitous computing." The numerous technological progresses and societal changes that happened ever since, make his vision nowadays seem more realistic then ever before. On technological front, as Mattern [8] argues, we have witnessed the ongoing miniaturization of electronics; rapid progresses in wireless communication technologies such as WiFi, Bluetooth, or Near Field Communication (NFC);

Yeda Venturini · Vlad Coroama · Tereza C.M.B. Carvalho
USP – University of São Paulo, Brazil, e-mail: {yeda,vcoroama,carvalho}@larc.usp.br

Mats Naslund · Makan Pourzandi
Ericsson Research, e-mail: {mats.naslund,makan.pourzandi}@ericsson.com

Please use the following format when citing this chapter:

Venturini, Y., Coroama, V., Carvalho, T. C. M. B., Naslund, M., Pourzandi, M., 2008, in IFIP International Federation for Information Processing, Volume 265, Advances in Ad Hoc Networking, eds. Cuenca, P., Guerrero C., Puigjaner, R., Serra, B., (Boston: Springer), pp. 145-156.

the diversification and miniaturization of sensors; the emergence of identification technologies such as RFID tags and of indoor and outdoor positioning technologies.

Together with these technological advances, a large amount of applications for ubiquitous computing technologies has emerged inside academia and industry. Albeit not all, many of the envisioned mobile and ubiquitous computing applications involve the ad-hoc networking of devices that have been enhanced with computing and communication technologies in a similar manner to Weiser's vision. They encompass many fields, such as healthcare, commercial, military, home and work environments, and – for now – usually only exist as prototypes or as scenarios for the near future. Nevertheless, by looking at the existing scenarios and prototypes, it quickly becomes clear that virtually all of them will need to provide security and privacy mechanisms. However, the existing prototypes typically either do not provide any security mechanisms at all, or they do so as a proprietary, one-time solution. We have thus proposed such a generic and flexible security middleware. In the beginning, our project has been limited to the networking of devices belonging to one owner only [12]. Recognizing the added value obtained by networking devices of different owners, we have more recently extended the project to allow for the networking of such devices as well [9].

After presenting our middleware as a solution for ad-hoc networking applications in home and work environments, the present article addresses two novel issues: Firstly, it shows that our solution is particularly well-suited for context-aware applications. Secondly, since not all ad-hoc networking applications are context-aware (and, in fact, most are not), it discusses the trade-offs that exist for a security solution aiming at both ad-hoc networking and context-awareness. The remainder of the paper is thus organized as follows: Section 2 presents the application scenarios targeted by our work. Out of the various security requirements in ad-hoc networking, section 3 shows which security services are relevant for these applications. Section 4 introduces the concept of context-awareness, and shows how it has to be supported by the proposed solution. Finally, section 5 summarizes the architecture of our solution, highlighting the trade-offs between ad-hoc networking, context-awareness, and strong security.

2 Sharing of Services inside Familiar and Work Environments

If Weiser's vision is to become true – and, as argued, many technological trends point into this direction – more and more "smart" personal devices will belong to one person, silently bringing services to their owner. Since tiny, wirelessly interconnected computers can be embedded into and enhance almost any everyday object [8], the range of possible applications and services brought by such devices is virtually endless. The possible scenarios reach from the military warfare – where myriads of tiny, dust-sized particles that can sense movements would be spread inside the enemy territory[1] – to such mundane everyday household devices like coffee cups [4] or toothbrushes [6]. It is clear then that it would be a futile undertaking to try designing a security middleware that would be ideally suited for all possible kinds of applications. As Hubaux et. al put it, "clearly, security requirements depend very much on the kind of mission for which the mobile ad-hoc network has been conceived, and the environment in which it has to operate" [5]. We thus present in this section the application scenarios that our middleware has been built for.

Within the ubiquitous computing research community, there has been a long tradition of scenarios and prototypes involving several devices belonging to the same person, which cooperate to bring services to their owner. Such services can reach from the simple synchronization of documents between the several information appliances of the user, to more ambitious visions and prototypes, closer to the vision of ubiquitous computing technology embedded into all sorts of everyday objects. In a project from the Japanese Waseda university [6], for example, the smart user's toothbrush (equipped with accelerometers and an RFID tag for identification) communicates with the likewise smart bathroom mirror, which then displays information such as weather forecast for the adults brushing teeth in the morning, or plays interactive games with the children. Going further, several projects have argued for the augmentation of entire houses with sensing, computing, and wireless communication facilities, thus realizing so-called "smart homes." Some of the best-known examples are the Philips HomeLab[2] and GeorgiaTech's "Aware Home" [7]. The prototypically realized services of smart homes include: a service for finding "Frequently Lost Objects" (FLOs), such as keys, wallets, or remote controls through the use of an indoor positioning system and the tagging of FLOs; or a service that automatically starts the air conditioned or the house heating when one of the residents approaches home (by using the vehicle's positioning system which communicates with the house via the driver's mobile phone).

Most of the above-mentioned applications need an underlying security concept, providing various security services, such as authentication and confidentiality. The wireless synchronization of documents between several devices of one person, for example, needs both. Likewise, it would be a bad idea for a thief outside the home to be able to use the service for finding lost objects to locate all the wallets inside the house, or to open the garage's door upon approaching the home. Nevertheless, most of the projects presented are prototypes, and typically either don't deploy any security at all, or use an ad-hoc proprietary security solution, which can have no impact on further research. Recognizing the need for a general-purpose, flexible security layer for such applications, we have proposed and implemented the concept of "Personal Security Domains" (PSDs) [12]. PSDs are a security middleware that can be used by such applications of cooperating smart home artefacts. Given their high abundance, we have focused the security middleware for ubiquitous computing applications inside the home environment and have from the beginning excluded military (and, to some extent, commercial) as target applications of the PSDs.

---

[1] See robotics.eecs.berkeley.edu/~pister/SmartDust/.

[2] See www.research.philips.com/technologies/misc/homelab/

Nonetheless, devices belonging to one person and bringing services only to their owner, do not exploit the full potential that ubiquitous computing has to offer in home and familiar environments. As a recent study [2] shows, several of the technological devices existing nowadays in homes are shared among family members rather than being exclusively used – the authors talk about "shared ownership" versus "individual ownership." The survey refers to the usage patterns of different technologies inside households. While some of the technologies were individually owned (i.e., mobile phones and music players), others were shared among the residents. Computers and TV sets, for example, were usually used by more persons, although often their number exceeded the number of home residents. Furthermore, computers were not only shared as physical devices. The profiling allowed by the operating system to logically separate the different users was usually not used in this home setting. This leads to the question whether the sharing of future ubiquitous computing devices would not also induce a new quality to the services brought to a group of people – in family or friends settings, but also in work environments. And indeed – numerous ubiquitous computing projects emphasize such sharing and common use of devices and services provided by these. A smart room, for example, could autonomously derive a meeting going on (by noticing a gathering of smart coffee cups [4]). It could then modify its own behavior, or that of other entities (for example, turning the mobile phones of participants to silent mode [4]). A business traveler entering the office building of the company she is visiting, can be provided temporary access rights to parts of its computing infrastructure, such as the right to use projectors for slides, or printers for handouts. The sharing of documents or contacts among the devices of work colleagues can be as meaningful as sharing them with friends. However, a fine-granular content management system is obviously needed for such an application – the owner must be able to decide which data to share with any of these groups. Being able to grant access to a smart home for friends also seems a meaningful feature; as well as letting them operate the aircon. Similarly, one could grant temporary access to cleaning stuff or repairmen, without the need of meeting them or handing them an (easy to duplicate) physical key.

Obviously, all of these scenarios also need security concepts in order to control the access to data and services, and/or to ensure the privacy of communications. We have thus broaden our concept of PSDs to MPSDs ("Multiple Personal Security Domains"), as presented in [9] and summarized in section 5. An MPSD is realized by the (temporary) joining together of two or more PSDs (belonging to as many owners) with the aim of sharing some of the services offered by these.

3 Security for Shared Family and Work ad-hoc Networks

From the early stages of the project, the question of which security services are relevant inside shared family and work ad-hoc networks of personal devices – and should thus be offered by our middleware to its client applications – has thus been raised. In their seminal paper "Securing Ad Hoc Networks" [14], Zhou at al. define following security requirements for ad-hoc networks: *availability, confidentiality, integrity, authentication, non-repudiation*, and *authorization*. While these requirements are general to any type of network, the authors identify three challenges that make them harder to achieve in an ad-hoc wireless network: *the use of wireless links*, the non-negligible *probability that nodes will be compromised* due their typically poor physical protection, and the *high network dynamics* with nodes frequently leaving and joining the network [14]. This facilitates, among others, following types of attacks: jamming attacks on the physical layer, disrupting the network protocol on network layer, and eavesdropping. Hubaux at al. [5], taking a slightly different approach, first differentiate between vulnerabilities of the basic and of the security mechanisms. Vulnerabilities of the basic mechanisms are similar to Zhou's approach, including eavesdropping, active interference and routing protocol attacks. As for the security mechanism, Hubaux considers the establishment of keys as the most critical and complex issue. The initialization phase, and the level of trust between the entities involved in it, are examples of issues that need to be answered for a good solution. Since Zhou at al. [14] also focus their proposed solution on how to secure routing and how to establish a secure key management service in an ad-hoc networking environment, both articles are concerned with key management as the main challenge in an ad-hoc network. Authentication, confidentiality, and integrity can all be achieved through a secure and robust key management.

As argued above, the security requirements depend on the network purpose and the environment in which it has to operate. Looking at the security requirements defined by Zhou [14] and Hubaux [5], it is easily noted that not all have the same importance within our target home and work environment scenarios. Denial-of-service attacks, for example, are more or less likely, depending on the layer the attack would occur on. Due to the typical small spread of the network, as well as the heterogenous physical transport protocols that will be used by most applications (e.g., WiFi, Bluetooth, GSM, etc.), we believe an attack on the physical layer to be unlikely, and will not pursue it further. A denial-of-service attack on the network layer would consist of the disruption of the routing protocol. This is a more likely attack in the target scenarios, and – as section 5 will show – one that is being considered by our solution which eliminates routing through the use of service discovery and then direct peer-to-peer communication. Finally, as Zhou et. al put it: "the adversary could bring down higher-level services like the key management layer" [14]. This is a more likely threat, that our solution has to account for.

Confidentiality and *authentication* are two security requirements at the very core of the target scenarios. In virtually all scenarios, the user's device needs to be sure of the authenticity of the other devices it is exchanging information with. While confidentiality is not as general a requirement as authentication, it is highly relevant to some of the scenarios, such as the document synchronization of possibly sensitive information. These two security requirements can be accomplished – as the countering of denial-of-service attacks on high layers – with a strong key management mechanism. *Non-repudiation*, on the other hand, is not of importance to our scenarios. Since they do not involve commercial applications (in which the sending or receiving of messages possibly needs to be proven in court), our middleware can ignore non-repudiation mechanisms. Likewise, a lack of message *integrity* due to benign failures like bad connectivity, does not constitute a large problem in any of the scenarios. Even more, it is a problem that usually gets taken care of (if possible) on the lower layers.

Summarizing, due to the nature of the scenarios and from the considerations above, our middleware has to focus on providing the client applications with strong authentication and confidentiality mechanisms. It also needs to counter denial-of-service attacks on the routing mechanisms and on the services on higher layers.

4 Context-Aware ad-hoc Networking Applications

More often than not, ad-hoc networking applications are one-purpose only, and consist of a large amount of small nodes working together towards that task. Especially sensor networks applications fall under this category, such as the already mentioned military battlefield monitoring through "smart dust" particles, or the detection of oil spills or forest fires through a network of wireless sensors [1]. Such applications are characterized by a large amount of relatively small nodes, each with a limited amount of computing power, usually a limited amount of energy (since they are typically battery-operated), that are distributed into an often hostile environment (e.g., the enemy territory, or a forest with all the problems caused to the nodes by weather and wildlife). Three more factors make the algorithms for this kind of ad-hoc networks additionally challenging: the wireless communication ranges of the nodes are typically quite short, the network topology is a-priori unknown (since the nodes get typically distributed into the environment with a random pattern, e.g., by being thrown from an airplane), and the probability of any individual node to fail is relatively high due to the rough environment they operate in. For all these reasons, in such applications there's a large emphasis on the routing protocols, and on the security mechanisms, which have to function despite the failure of single nodes.

By contrast, the applications our security middleware is being built for, operate under much friendlier constraints. The nodes envisioned are either electronic devices (e.g., PDAs, smart phones), or large and typically immobile devices, such as garage doors, air conditioned devices, or vehicles. They thus either inherently possess strong computing capabilities, or plenty of space for these to be built in. Energy supply is not an issue either – such devices are either already connected to the power grid (aircon, garage door), or can generate a virtually unlimited amount of energy by burning fuel (vehicles), or have strong rechargeable batteries, that users are already used to charge on a regular basis (PDAs, phones). The supplemental power needed for their "smartness" and for the wireless communication thus represents no obstacle. Furthermore, the devices in our target scenarios are collocated in close physical proximity. The information does not have to be routed over large distances.

Obviously, these constraints don't pose for a security middleware the kind of challenges that arise from application domains such as those described above. However, there is an entirely different range of characteristics that makes other aspects of the design rather challenging. Firstly, as argued in the last section, the applications often need stronger authentication and confidentiality services as compared to such ad-hoc networking applications as presented above. Secondly, not only must the middleware allow for all sorts of different applications to be built on top of it; most envisioned devices will typically run an entire collection of heterogenous services in parallel, which all have to be supported by the framework. Thirdly, these services must be able to exhibit a refined and fine-granular model of rights and authorizations, as the examples of the repairman being granted temporary access to a house, or of the businesswoman being granted the rights to use part of the computing infrastructure of a different company show. This sort of granularity is never encountered in the typical sensor networks applications. Fourthly, and arguably most challenging, many of the applications using our middleware will be context-aware, a central concept to our solution, and thus presented in the current section.

Being able to sense their surroundings and often being mobile, an outstanding attribute of ubiquitous computing applications is their capability to adapt to changes in the environment. This feature is called *context-awareness*. The term has first been defined by Shilit as "software that adapts itself to the location of use, the collection of nearby people, hosts, and accessible devices, as well as to changes to such things over time" [11]. The definition has later shifted towards a more user-centric view, and has also become more general. The definition widely accepted nowadays has been provided by Dey and Abowd: "Context is any information that can be used to characterize the situation of an entity. An entity is a person, place, or object that is considered relevant to the interaction between a user and an application, including the user and the application themselves" [3]. Several other contributions, such as Schilit's [11], have listed the most important aspects of context: *user environment* (location, collection of people nearby, social situation), *physical environment* (lightning conditions or acceleration of a vehicle), *computing environment* (available processing power, communication protocols). Such definitions, although not as general and thus sometimes too constraining, help to identify the most common types of context. Dey and Abowd further differentiate between *primary* and *secondary* types of context: "Location, identity, time, and activity are the primary context types for characterizing the situation of a particular entity" [3]. All secondary types of context can be derived from these fundamental ones: the email address, for example, from the identity of an entity, or the people nearby from its location.

For the scenarios presented in section 2, following primary types of context are relevant: identity, location, time, and computing resources. The user's *identity* is relevant to virtually all envisioned applications. From it, the key security issue of *access rights* (both physical and logical access) is derived. From the user's *location*, several types of secondary context can be derived. Access rights can depend on the user's location as well, not only on her identity. In our example of the businesswoman visiting for a few days a foreign company, she is granted access to parts of the building's computing infrastructure. However, these rights could be restricted to only the times she resides inside the building (and some social control over the way she uses the infrastructure exists), and not when she is in the hotel, for example. Furthermore, location also implies *proximity*: which other personal devices are in the vicinity, and which devices belonging to others. Likewise, the *time* also determines access rights. A repairman could be granted a two-hour timeslot to enter the home without the residents being present, for example, or a cleaning aid could be granted access every Tuesday. The available *computing and communication resources* can be highly relevant for security-sensitive applications (and the middleware supporting them), especially for remotely-executed services. Depending on the kind of communication protocols available, such services could be executed or not.

5 Multiple Personal Security Domains and Context-Awareness

According to ISO/IEC 10181-1, a security domain is "a set of elements, a security policy, a security authority and a set of security relevant activities in which the set of elements are subject to the security policy, administered by the security authority, for the specified activities." This concept is applied in some commercial products like the Java Micro Edition architecture (J2ME), where the elements subject to the security policy are Java applications running on the device's Java Virtual Machine (JVM). Our implementation of the security domain concept is different from J2ME. The elements can be applications hosted or distributed in different mobile devices. The granularity of the security policies is much higher: It is possible to define rules for devices, applications, applications hosted on a specific device, or even for a particular operation of an application. We summarize here concepts and architecture of our middleware, more details can be find in [9] and [12].

In our terminology, a *Personal Security Domain* (PSD) is a group of fixed and/or mobile components, where each component can be authenticated, trusted and securely communicated with through a common security association, subject to a security policy. The PSD must have an owner, called *controller*, who creates the PSD with the components that he owns or is responsible for. PSD components can be geographically distributed. A *PSD partition* is a subdivision of a PSD formed by all PSD components that are at the same location and can thus communicate directly (layer 2 of the OSI model). PSDs can be joined together, forming a *Multiple PSD* (MPSD). The controller role for an MPSD can be either shared among the PSD controllers or one PSD controller alone takes this role. The MPSD controller creates the MPSD with the desired PSDs, while the security policy for PSD components is still defined by the respective PSD controller. While PSDs typically have long lifetimes, MPSDs are temporary security associations with a shorter lifespan.

Figure 1 shows the layer structure of the PSD system, consisting of the Security Enforcement Layer (SEL) and the Security Domain Layer (SDL). While the SDL implements the PSD control and management APIs, the SEL provides secure communication between entities of the (M)PSDs, ensures entities authentication, communication security (confidentiality and integrity), and the applications access control (authorization). It enforces dynamically the security policy for the (M)PSD. It is also responsible for the management of the entities' trust values, which are used in a trust based authorization model.

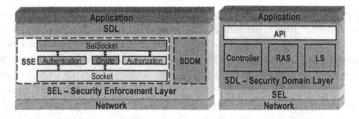

Fig. 1 Layers of the Security Domain Architecture.

The SEL has two basic components: the SelSocket Encapsulation (SSE) and the Security Domain Data Manager (SDDM). The SSE enforces the security based on the security data provided by the SDDM. The SDDM manages security data, provided by the Security Domain Layer (SDL), which will be presented shortly. To make its usage easier and more transparent for application developers, the Sel-Socket works similar to a standard socket. However, before releasing the connection for an application, the SelSocket authenticates the entities and verifies the authorization for communication. After authorization, the application can send messages that get encrypted by the SelSocket with the session key, which has been previously exchanged during authentication. The SelSocket enforces authentication and authorization based on the security data provided by the SDDM for the requesting application. The SEL has two special features that contribute for security in ad-hoc networks: domain authentication and trust-based authorization. The domain authentication is based on a (renewable) key shared among the entities of a PSD. This authentication is enforced before the mutual entity authentication. It aims at an early identification of the PSD entities in a densely populated medium, as in wireless communication. Additionally, the domain authentication provides the privacy needed by the entity authentication. Besides the fine-granularity for rules, the authorization service relies on a trust concept to face the possibility that some PSD entity has been compromised. Suspicious behavior of entities generates security events, which dynamically reduce the trust of that PSD entity. Authorization rules for applications, services, or devices with critical security requirements can be based on minimal trust, so that any misbehavior of some PSD entity causes its disallowance. These features contribute towards overall availability, through the early disconnection of non-PSD entities or of compromised ones, avoiding hence denial-of-service attacks, as well as eavesdropping attacks during entity authentication.

The Security Domains Layer (SDL), on the other hand, provides an API for PSD management and for the development of applications on top of the MPSD, as well as three basic services: *controller*, *lookup* and *remote access*. The PSD creation, entity joining or leaving, as well as security policy definition, are operations performed by the *controller service*. A PSD possesses a symmetric key and an auto-signed certificate (root certificate), which are known by any PSD entity. The PSD controller is thus the personal Certificate Authority (CA) for the respective PSD, issuing certificates for PSD entities during the joining process and revoking certificates for the leaving process. The symmetric key is shared among all PSD entities and used for domain authentication. This key is also used to generate a pseudo-random number [12] for multicast messages, so that only entities sharing the same key answer to the originator. For example, home devices will not answer to a location message if the requestor is not a home device. The *remote access service* (RAS) enables access to resources across partitions, which can be independent networks, thus dealing with conflicting addresses in different partitions and enforcing the security between them. The device that hosts the RAS and receives the remote connection requests needs to have a valid IP address. The *lookup service* (LS) allows devices to discover other devices and services available. The LS allows a service-based network formation, in which the user does not need to know in advance the available services. When a service starts, it searches for the LSs in its reach area and announces itself to all of them. For service use, the user searches for available LSs, requests a service, receives the available service list, and selects a service to use. The list of available services has all information required for service connection. We developed a novel service location protocol, with additional functionalities (as compared to SLP or JINI, for example), which are related to the available remote connections and security. Firstly, the LS answers only to entities from the PSDs it trusts. Secondly, it supports customized attributes for entities' registration, which can be primary context information with different interpretation depending of the device or the service type. Finally, it is possible to discover services in a remote partition through the RAS service.

Taken together, all these concepts offer the strong security needed by applications, while allowing at the same time the flexibility needed for their context-awareness. The authorization-based service discovery offered by the LSs (differentiating between services offered within the own PSD and services from affiliated MPSDs), for example, provides fine-granular contextual information about the local computing environment: the locally available own and foreign devices, their services, as well as the communication protocols available for accessing them. Through the transparent communication between RAS and LS, the application can also gain detailed information about physically remote environments and decide upon accessing services there. To test context-awareness inside MPSD, we have implemented a prototypical file and address book sharing application and tested it in a setting with seven MPSDs. The promising results, however, lie outside the scope of this paper.

Some ad-hoc networking projects go even further and allow for very subtle ways of taking into account the physical context surrounding the application. Robinson and Beigl [10], for example, in a solution similar to ours (but for a different class of applications, as will be shown shortly), let devices that are in close physical proximity form a so-called "Trust Context Space." They assume that, as in real-life people sharing the same physical boundaries have a certain level of trust, devices sharing the same sort of common space should also automatically share trust. They implemented a prototypical application where all devices within the same walls, independently, derive a common key from the sounds within the physical space they share.

While the beauty of this solution lies in its absolute lack of any explicit user intervention (such as pairing of devices), for our class of applications such a solution would not work for two reasons – one of fundamental, the other of pragmatic nature. The fundamental problem is the fine-granularity needed by our applications. Not all people in the same office should share the same secrets (e.g., the visiting businesswoman will only have restricted access), and not all of a device's secrets should be shared with everyone (e.g., the private contacts or calendar items should not be shared with work colleagues). This sort of semantic knowledge cannot be automatically derived by the middleware, but has to be explicitly defined by the owner of the device. The pragmatic problem lies in the imprecision of the sensors detecting environmental attributes such as sound. This limits the length of the key that can be derived, while keeping the error rate low enough for the solution to still be practical.

Due to both reasons, a solution such as Robinson's and Beigl's, while allowing for a very spontaneous ad-hoc networking, with no previous knowledge about other devices or any human intervention, can only be used by applications needing no more than a basic level of security. It actually seems that there is an inherent trade-off between ad-hoc networking and context-awareness, when looking at the security features. If a context-aware application should allow a very spontaneous ad-hoc networking, with no previous device pairing or knowledge about other device's existence, nor any human intervention, the security level that can be guaranteed is relatively low. If, as in our case, the security level must be relatively high, some compromises have to be done in terms of the spontaneity of the networking allowed. This trade-off has governed the design of our middleware.

6 Conclusions

In the present article, we have summed up the experiences from the project "Multiple Personal Security Domains," a security middleware focused on a specific class of ubiquitous and mobile computing applications. After having first argued why we have limited the class of targeted applications to ad-hoc networks of smart devices in home and work environments, we have shown how these applications differ from most other applications within the ad-hoc networks and especially the sensor networks research. We have then presented the specific needs of such applications: a strong security model for authentication and confidentiality, but also the means to fine-granularly distribute access rights (both physical and logical), which raises from the context-awareness of many of the target applications. We have shown how our middleware copes with both these major needs, and how it is thus well-suited for ad-hoc networking, context-aware applications in home and work scenarios.

We have further presented, from our experience in developing the middleware's architecture, the trade-off existing between ad-hoc networking, context-awareness, and fine-granularity of strong access rights. Numerous applications, such as several sensor networks applications, rely on a very pure form of ad-hoc networking, which comes along with various specific challenges for the networking and authentication algorithms. However, such applications do not require any form of context awareness, nor do they typically have to ensure the confidentiality of communication.

If, as in the case of our target applications, a high degree of fine-granularity is required, some compromises have to be made in terms of the spontaneity of the ad-hoc networking. We have solved this dilemma by allowing for a first step in which some of the devices define trust relationships among them, relationships that get then spread throughout the network and also autonomously influence the levels of trust when combining more such personal domain networks into a "multiple personal security domain." When, on the other hand, a high degree of security is needed, a compromise has to be made in terms of the context-awareness of the middleware itself. In our case, the middleware does not automatically generate keys from the environment, but relies on the strong keys provided by a certification authority. To put it bluntly, we have thereby sacrificed some of the possible context-awareness of the middleware itself, in order to provide the applications with a strong security, while at the same time allowing them to keep a high degree of context-awareness. We believe these insights to have an impact beyond our middleware solution, for further ad-hoc networking and context-awareness research in general.

References

1. Bohn, J., Coroama, V., Langheinrich, M., Mattern, F., Rohs, M.: Living in a world of smart everyday objects – social, economic, and ethical implications. HERA 10(5), 763–786 (2004)
2. Brush, A.J.B., Inkpe, K.M.: Yours, mine and ours? Sharing and use of technology in domestic environments. In: J. Krumm, G.D. Abowd, A. Seneviratne, T. Strang (eds.) Proc. of UbiComp 2007, LNCS, vol. 4717, pp. 109–126. Springer, Innsbruck, Austria (2007)
3. Dey, A.K., Abowd, G.D.: Towards a better understanding of context and context-awareness. In: Proc. of the CHI 2000 Workshop on Context-Awareness (2000)
4. Gellersen, H.W., Schmidt, A., Beigl, M.: Adding some smartness to devices and everyday things. In: Proc. of WMCSA, pp. 3–10. Los Alamitos, CA, USA (2000)
5. Hubaux, J.P., Buttyan, L., Capkun, S.: The quest for security in mobile ad hoc networks. In: N.H. Vaidya, M.S. Corson, S.R. Das (eds.) Proc. of MobiHOC'01, pp. 146–155 (2001)
6. Kawsar, F., Fujinami, K., Nakajima, T.: Augmenting everyday life with sentient artefacts. In: G. Bailly, J.L. Crowley (eds.) Proceedings of the 2005 joint Conference on Smart objects and Ambient Intelligence (sOc-EUSAI), pp. 141–146. ACM, Grenoble, France (2005)
7. Kidd, C.D., Orr, R., Abowd, G.D., Atkeson, C.G., Essa, I.A., MacIntyre, B., Mynatt, E., Starner, T.E., Newstetter, W.: The aware home. In: N. Streitz, J. Siegel, V. Hartkopf, S. Konomi (eds.) CoBuild'99, LNCS, vol. 1670, pp. 191–198. Springer, Pittsburgh, PA, USA (1999)
8. Mattern, F.: The vision and technical foundations of ubiquitous computing. Upgrade 2(5), 2–6 (2001)
9. Matushima, R., Venturini, Y.R., Sakuragui, R.R.M., Carvalho, T.C.M.B., Ruggiero, W.V., Naslund, M., Pourzandi, M.: Multiple personal security domains. In: S. Onoe, M. Guizani, H.H. Chen, M. Sawahashi (eds.) Proc. of IWCMC, pp. 361–366. Vancouver, Canada (2006)
10. Robinson, P., Beigl, M.: Trust context spaces. In: D. Hutter, G. Mller, W. Stephan, M. Ullmann (eds.) Proc. of Sec. in Pervasive Computing, LNCS, vol. 2802, pp. 157–172. Springer (2003)
11. Schilit, B., Adams, N., Want, R.: Context-aware computing applications. In: Proc. of WM-CSA, pp. 85–90. Santa Cruz, CA, US (1994)
12. Venturini, Y.R., Sakuragui, R.M., Matushima, R., Carvalho, T.C.M.B., Ruggiero, W.V., Naslund, M., Pourzandi, M.: Security enforcement layer for security domain. In: Proc. of I2TS'2005, pp. 19–26. Florianopolis, SC, Brazil (2005)
13. Weiser, M.: The computer for the 21st century. Scientific American 265(3), 66–75 (1991)
14. Zhou, L., Haas, Z.J.: Securing ad hoc networks. IEEE Network 13(6), 24–30 (1999)

No Ack in IEEE 802.11e Single-Hop Ad-Hoc VoIP Networks

Jaume Barceló, Boris Bellalta, Anna Sfairopoulou, Cristina Cano, Miquel Oliver

Abstract This paper analyzes the impact of the No Ack policy in VoIP ad-hoc single-hop IEEE 802.11e networks. The No Ack policy consists on suppressing the MAC layer acknowledgement packets. This option dramatically reduces the duration of MAC frames and thus increments the maximum number of VoIP flows that can coexist in the network. The negative side is an increased packet loss rate and the consequent drop of voice quality as perceived by the users. The article presents a model to quantify the benefits of suppressing acks and assess the viability of the No Ack policy. It follows an argumentation to identify which is the best codec to combine with acknowledgement suppression and in which conditions the usage of No Ack can be beneficial. Finally, it is suggested to modify the stations to switch to No Ack policy as the network approaches congestion.

1 Introduction

Both IEEE 802.11 [1] networks and voice-over-IP (VoIP) are mature technologies and have been widely adopted for personal and enterprise use. Calls in a single-hop ad-hoc network are less frequent, since they require the proximity of the caller and callee. Nevertheless, when the proximity requirement is satisfied, the calls can be established free and in infrastructure-less scenarios.

Even in areas equipped with infrastructure, the use of ad-hoc communications is beneficial. The use of infrastructure mode implies that each packet has to be relayed by the access point, and therefore it doubles the number of transmissions in the network. This is a waste of the scarce radio resources. Moreover, changing to infrastructure mode also increments the end-to-end delay. And finally, the access point usually represents the bottleneck of the infrastructure network having to receive and transmit flows from and to all the stations. This is illustrated by Fig. 1.

Barceló, Bellalta, Sfairopoulou, Cano and Oliver
Universitat Pompeu Fabra, Passeig de Circumval.lació 8 e-mail: jaume.barcelo@upf.edu

Please use the following format when citing this chapter:

Barceló, J., Bellalta, B., Sfairopoulou, A., Cano, C., Oliver, M., 2008, in IFIP International Federation for Information Processing, Volume 265, Advances in Ad Hoc Networking, eds. Cuenca, P., Guerrero C., Puigjaner, R., Serra, B., (Boston: Springer), pp. 157-166.

The station-to-station communication is possible in infrastructure scenarios using Direct Link Setup (DLS) thanks to the quality of service (QoS) amendment to the standard [2].

However, the combination of VoIP and IEEE 802.11 is highly inefficient . The number of calls that can coexist in a IEEE 802.11 VoIP network is an order of magnitude lower than what could be expected when comparing the rates of the network to the rates of the codecs. The reasons for such impairment have already been analyzed [13] and can be summarized as:

- The time wasted in contention (i.e. the channel is iddle and all the stations are backing off with packets ready to transmit).
- The physical preambles and the overhead placed by the different layers of the protocol stack.
- Each packet needs to be separately acknowledged.

The high overhead per transmitted packet seriously penalizes the transmission of small payload packets, which is in fact the case of VoIP packets. The problem can be alleviated in four different ways:

- Header compression, to reduce overhead. The 40-byte RTP/UDP/IP header can be compressed to 2-7 bytes [5, 4, 6, 11].
- Packet aggregation. Combine different packets to produce only one packet that contains all the data [13].
- Use only one ack packet to acknowledge a set of packets (Block-Ack)[12].
- Refrain from sending acknowledgement packets (No Ack).

While the first three solutions have been extensively studied, the fourth is still an open research issue. The possibility of not sending acknowledgements is available in the IEEE 802.11e [2] extension for quality of service. Intuitively, this option will decrease the packet delay and increase the number of simultaneous calls. However, it is expected that this solution will also increase the packet loss ratio which negatively affects the QoS.

This article presents a simple model to analyze a VoIP over IEEE 802.11 scenario and to assess which is the impact of using the IEEE 802.11e No Ack option.

After this introductory section, the rest of the paper is outlined as follows. Section 2 offers a brief description of the scenario and the protocols involved, details

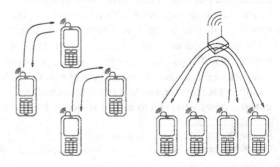

Fig. 1 This figure compares ad-hoc (left) to infrastructure-based (right) VoIP calls in a IEEE 802.11 network.

the causes of the inefficiency, and presents a model that can be solved numerically. Section 3 compares the collision probabilities and the maximum number of flows to those obtained when acks are suppressed. It also takes some perspective on the results and analyzes which are the real benefits of suppressing the acks. It details in which conditions it would be desirable to apply ack suppression, which are the more appropriate codecs, and give some implementation clues for a real-world deployment. Finally, Section 4 concludes the paper.

2 Description and Model of IEEE 802.11 Voice Networks

A VoIP [8] application digitalizes the voice, then uses a codec to compress it and outputs a fixed-rate bitstream (See Fig. 2). Popular codecs include G.711 (64 Kbps) and G.729 (8 Kbps). Each codec has its own properties, such as the offered bitrate, the computational complexity of codification/decodification and the offered Mean Opinion Score (MOS). MOS is a measure of the voice quality as perceived by the user [7].

The packetizer collects the data from the encoder and periodically generates a voice packet. The packetization interval has a deep impact in the overall network performance [3]. Increasing the packetization interval introduces additional delay but drastically reduces the number of packets traversing the network. A choice of codec and packetization interval fixes the length of the payload of each packet. As an example, a G.711 codec combined with a 20ms packetization interval means a payload of 160 bytes per packet. The transport layer and network layer consist on the addition of RTP, UDP, and IP headers, which add up to 40 bytes of overhead.

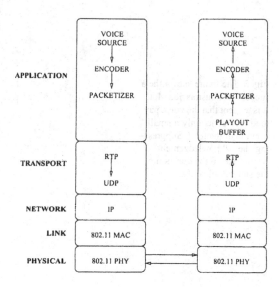

Fig. 2 The figure presents the complete protocol stack in implementing VoIP over IEEE 802.11.

Our proposal is to suppress acknowledgement packets at the link layer, which is an option contemplated in IEEE 802.11e amendment to the standard. In any case, the link layer also introduces its own headers. Finally the physical layer introduces preambles and headers that are transmitted at a fixed rate (physical rate), while the rest of the packet is transmitted at a speed that depends on channel conditions (data rate).

The time required to transmit a packet is:

$$T_{tx} = T_{plcp} + \frac{MAC + IP + UDP + RTP + VOICE}{DATA_{RATE}} \tag{1}$$

Where T_{pclp} is the duration of the transmission of the Physical Layer Convergence Protocol (PLCP) preamble and header at the physical bitrate. MAC, IP, UDP and RTP represent the length (in bits) of the respective headers. $VOICE$ is the length (in bits) of the payload. $DATA_{RATE}$ is the bitrate at which data is transmitted. The latter depends on channel conditions, but in this work it is assumed to be 11 Mbps for all the stations.

The duration of a successful transmission slot is computed as follows:

$$T_s = T_{tx} + SIFS + T_{pclp} + T_{ACK} + DIFS \tag{2}$$

where T_{ACK} is the duration of the acknowledgement packet. The duration of a collision slot is $T_c = T_{tx} + EIFS$, where $EIFS$ is the duration of the Extended Inter-Frame Space

Fig. 3 shows a complete successful slot. The shaded area correspond to the voice payload.

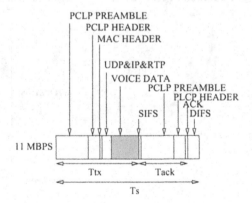

Fig. 3 The figure shows the a successful transmission slot. It is evident that the voice payload represents only a small fraction of the total. Suppressing the acknowledgement would reduce the duration of the slot significantly.

2.1 Performance Impairment

The time that is used to transmit actual voice data ($VOICE/DATA_{RATE}$) compared to the time it takes a successful transmission slot (T_s) can be taken as a measure of efficiency. Depending on the choice of codec, packetization interval and data rate, this efficiency will vary. Table 1 presents a summary in which the efficiency is computed for various combinations. The last column of the table shows the efficiency improvement for the hypothetical case in which the acks are suppressed.

Table 1 Efficiency (T_{tx}/T_s) with and without acknowledgements.

Case	With acks	Without acks	Improvement
G711, 20ms, 11Mbps	0.18637	0.28231	51%
G711, 10ms, 11Mbps	0.10276	0.16436	59%
G729, 20ms, 11Mbps	0.027836	0.046866	68%
G711, 20ms, 2Mbps	0.46037	0.54329	18%

To obtain the efficiency improvement detailed in the last column of Table 1, the usage of No Ack is required. When the No Ack policy is used by a station, there is no MAC-level recovery, and the transmission reliability is reduced. Hence the standard [2] recommends to use this policy only with some other additional protective mechanisms. However, since VoIP applications can accept a certain level of packet loss, in the following section we will study the consequences of using No Ack without such protective mechanisms.

2.2 Modelling 802.11 with acks

Assume that n mobile stations participate in an ad-hoc single-hop IEEE 802.11e network. Each station generates a VoIP flow, which is characterized by the periodical transmission of a short fixed-size packet. ρ is the load that a station offers to the network.

Assume also that the network is uncongested and the MAC queues do not fill up. Nevertheless, some packets may be discarded after reaching the maximum retransmission limit (R). Thus the actual load successfully transmitted by the network is:

$$r = \rho(1 - p_{cc}^{R+1}). \tag{3}$$

where p_{cc} is the probability that a collision occurs when the station attempts a submission.

The successful transmitted bitrate can also be calculated as the amount of data in a packet (l bits) multiplied by the successful transmission probability of station i ($p_i(s)$), and divided by the average duration of a slot.

$$r = \frac{p_i(s) \cdot l}{p(s)T_s + p(c)T_c + p(e)T_e}. \tag{4}$$

Where $p(s)$, $p(c)$ and $p(e)$ are the probabilities that any given slot is successful, collision and empty, respectively. Manipulating Eq. 4 and plugging in Eq. 3 we obtain:

$$p_i(s) = \frac{r \cdot (p(s)T_s + p(c)T_c + p(e)T_e)}{l}. \tag{5}$$

$$p_i(s) = \frac{\rho(1 - p^{R+1}) \cdot (p(s)T_s + p(c)T_c + p(e)T_e)}{l}. \tag{6}$$

The probability that station i successfully transmits in a given slot is the probability that i transmits while the other $n - 1$ stations remain silent. It can be expressed as a function of τ (the probability of a transmission attempt) and n the number of flows.

$$p_i(s) = \tau(1 - \tau)^{n-1}. \tag{7}$$

The probability that one and only one station transmits in a given slot is

$$p(s) = n \cdot \tau(1 - \tau)^{n-1}. \tag{8}$$

The probability that no station transmits is

$$p(e) = (1 - \tau)^n. \tag{9}$$

And the probability of a collision is

$$p(c) = 1 - p(s) - p(e). \tag{10}$$

The probability that a packet collides, conditioned to the probability that station i is attempting a transmission is:

$$p_{cc} = 1 - (1 - \tau)^{n-1}. \tag{11}$$

Eqs. 7 - 11 can be substituted into 6. The resultant equation has only one unknown variable (τ) and can be solved using numerical methods.

$$l \cdot \tau(1 - \tau)^{n-1} =$$
$$\rho((1 - (1 - (1 - \tau)^{n-1})^{R+1}) \cdot (n \cdot \tau(1 - \tau)^{(n-1)} \cdot T_s +$$
$$+ (1 - n \cdot \tau(1 - \tau)^{(n-1)} - (1 - \tau)^n)T_c + (1 - \tau)^n \cdot T_e). \tag{12}$$

Once the transmission probability τ is computed, it can be used to obtain the rest of performance metrics that depend on it. Eq. 12 is also useful to figure out the theoretical maximum number of active flows. If Eq. 12 converges, it means that the computed scenario is feasible. Otherwise, the number of flows is excessive and must be reduced.

The model described above can also be used in the case in which acks are suppressed. It is a special case in which $T_s = T_{tx} + DIFS$ and $R = 1$.

3 Performance Analysis

Using Eq. 11 from the previous section, the conditioned collision probability can be plotted (Fig. 4). In this example the codec is G.711, the packetization interval 20ms and the $DATA_{RATE}$ is 11MBps. NS2 [10] is used to validate the results.

The price to pay for increasing the capacity of the network in terms of feasible number of flows is an increased packet loss probability. A packet is lost if it suffers a collision each time that a transmission is attempted. The packet loss ratio is:

$$P_{loss} = P_{cc}^R. \tag{13}$$

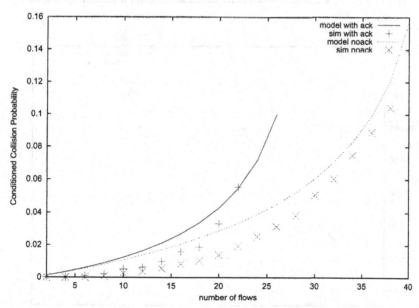

Fig. 4 It can be observed in the figure that the ack suppression leads to lower collision probability and increased number of concurrent flows.

If the acknowledgements are omitted, each packet is transmitted only once and therefore $P_{loss} = P_{cc}$. Figure 5 presents P_{loss} in a logarithmic plot.

The ultimate goal of the performance tuning of the IEEE 802.11e network is to admit the maximum number of calls with acceptable QoS. Fig. 4 shows that suppressing the acknowledgement packets significantly increases the number of VoIP flows that can coexist in the network, before reaching the congestion condition. The congestion is characterized by MAC queues building up and the packet loss due to queue overflow reaching values of 10% and higher [9]. Under this condition, the quality of all calls is unacceptable.

Given that the network is uncongested and no packets are lost due to MAC queue overflow, there are still two aspects that can threaten the quality of the calls: delay (and jitter) and packets loss due to collisions.

Delay and jitter negatively affect the MOS of the calls. Generally is considered that delays under 150ms are well suited for all user applications, and that up to 400ms are acceptable for international calls. The main contributors of the end-to-end delay are the encoding delay (about 10ms for G.729 and even less for G.711), the packetization delay (20ms in all the examples used throughout this article) and the jitter buffer (typically 60ms). The mean delay introduced by the (single-hop) network in non-congested conditions is well below 5ms [3]. Hence the total delay does not pose the MOS at risk.

The other threat for the MOS is the packet loss due to collisions. As can be observed in Fig. 5, the acknowledgement&retransmission mechanism drastically

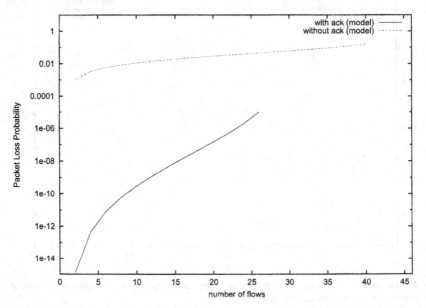

Fig. 5 This logarithmic plot shows that the packet loss probability is significantly higher when acknowledgements are suppressed.

reduces the packet loss due to collisions. Therefore, the packet loss caused by collisions is negligible when acks are used and the MOS remains unaffected. This is not the case when the acks are suppressed.

Without acks, there is no chance of retransmission and the probability of losing a packet is P_{cc}. G.711 and G.729 react very differently to the loss of packets. While G.711 is quite robust and can accept up to 5% of losses and still deliver acceptable quality, G.729 behaves badly for packet losses as low as 3%. This means that G.711 could accept up to 26 flows (13 calls), G.729 allows only 20 flows (10 calls). The alleged advantage of G.729, its lower rate, is overcomed by the excessive overhead mentioned in section 2.

3.1 Implementation Issues

Apparently, the new feature of No Ack introduced by IEEE 802.11e is of limited use, since it does not increment the number of acceptable quality calls. In our opinion, there is only one case in which it would make sense to suppress acks: when the network becomes congested. At this point, in which calls are dropped due to excessive delay and packet loss, switching to No Ack would allow the users to maintain low-quality calls.

To implement this switch in a distributed fashion, each station should constantly monitor its MAC queue. As soon as the queue builds up (a symptom of congestion), the stations should set the QoS control subfield of the packets to No Ack, until the queue returns to its previous empty state.

The applicability of this mechanism is reduced to collision-limited scenarios. If packet losses are due to low SNR and the stations react by suppressing acknowledgements, the underlying problem will remain. Even worse, the suppression of acknowledgements would prevent the data-rate fallback to a more robust modulation.

4 Conclusion

This paper analyzes the applicability of a new feature introduced to wireless LANs by the standard amendment IEEE 802.11e that consists on suppressing MAC layer acknowledgements. The scenario under study is a VoIP ad-hoc network. This kind of networks suffers from an accentuated inefficiency problem, mostly due to the requirement of separately acknowledging each MAC frame. Additionally, VoIP applications can tolerate a certain number of packet losses. Hence we deemed this networks appropriate to benefit from the suppression of the acks.

A model that permits the quantification of the benefit of suppressing the acks is presented. Using this model, the collision probability is computed for an increasing number of flows. The results shows that by suppressing the acks, the collision probability drops and the number of VoIP flows that can be simultaneously allocated in the network grows. These results are validated by means of simulation.

The negative part of suppressing the acks is an increased packet loss rate. This is the metric that actually limits the maximum number of calls when the No Ack policy is used. The codec of choice to combine with the suppression of acks is G.711, since it admits a greater packet loss than G.729. The maximum number of calls that can be achieved using the G.711 codec and suppressing the acknowledgements is the same as with acknowledgements.

However, when increasing the number of calls over that maximum – that we have computed to be 28 flows, 14 calls – the behaviour of the network depends on the policy applied. If acknowledgements are sent as usual, the network congests and calls are dropped. If we opt for a No Ack policy, the perceived quality of the call drops below a MOS of 3.5 and some users will complain about unsatisfactory quality. However, in the latter case, network congestion is prevented.

Finally, it is suggested a distributed mechanism to switch to No Ack policy when the network approaches congestion.

References

1. 802.11, I.S.: Wireless LAN Medium Access Control (MAC) and Physical Layer (PHY) Specifications. ANSI/IEEE Std 802.11 (1999 Edition (Revised 2003))
2. 802.11e, I.S.: Wireless LAN Medium Access Control (MAC) and Physical Layer (PHY) Specifications; Amendment: Medium Access Control(MAC) Quality of Service Enhancements. IEEE Std 802.11e (2005)
3. Barceló, J., Bellalta, B., Cano, C., Sfairopoulou, A.: VoIP Packet Delay in Single-Hop Ad-Hoc IEEE 802.11 Networks. Wireless On demand Network Systems and Services, 2008 IEEE/IFIP The Fifth Annual Conference on 1 (2008)
4. Casner, S., Jacobson, V.: Compressing IP/UDP/RTP Headers for Low-Speed Serial Links. RFC 2508 (Proposed Standard) (1999). URL http://www.ietf.org/rfc/rfc2508.txt
5. Degermark, M., Nordgren, B., Pink, S.: IP Header Compression. RFC 2507 (Proposed Standard) (1999). URL http://www.ietf.org/rfc/rfc2507.txt
6. Engan, M., Casner, S., Bormann, C.: IP Header Compression over PPP. RFC 2509 (Proposed Standard) (1999). URL http://www.ietf.org/rfc/rfc2509.txt. Obsoleted by RFC 3544
7. ETSI, T.: 101 329-6 Actual measurements of network and terminal characteristics and performance parameters in TIPHON networks and their influence on voice quality (2001)
8. Goode, B.: Voice over Internet protocol(VoIP). Proceedings of the IEEE **90**(9), 1495–1517 (2002)
9. Hole, D., Tobagi, F.: Capacity of an IEEE 802.11 b wireless LAN supporting VoIP. Communications, 2004 IEEE International Conference on 1 (2004)
10. The network simulator ns-2, v2.30. http://www.isi.edu/nsnam/ns
11. Pries, R., Maeder, A., Staehle, D.: Do we need Header Compression for VoIP in Wireless LANs? 12th EUNICE Open European Summer School 2006 pp. 77–82 (2006)
12. Tinnirello, I., Choi, S.: Efficiency analysis of burst transmissions with block ACK in contention-based 802.11 e WLANs. Communications, 2005. ICC 2005. 2005 IEEE International Conference on 5 (2005)
13. Yun, S., Kim, H., Lee, H., Kang, I.: 100+ VoIP Calls on 802.11 b: The Power of Combining Voice Frame Aggregation and Uplink-Downlink Bandwidth Control in Wireless LANs. Selected Areas in Communications, IEEE Journal on **25**(4), 689–698 (2007)

Constraining the network topology in IEEE 802.15.4

Anna Abbagnale, Emanuele Cipollone, Francesca Cuomo

Abstract The IEEE 802.15.4 standard defines a MAC *association procedure* that allows devices of a Wireless Personal Area Network (WPAN) to associate one each other in accordance to parent-child relationships. This standard can be adopted in Wireless Sensor Networks (WSNs) used to monitor environmental phenomena and to collect data in specific nodes named sinks. The ZigBee Alliance, with the Zig-Bee Specification, defines upper layers of a WSN architecture based on the IEEE 802.15.4. Tree shaped multi-sink networks can be formed by adopting in conjunction these two standards. A key aspect to be evaluated for these kind of networks is how their performance are affected by constraining some topological characteristics. In this paper, in accordance to the ZigBee Specification, we constraint the tree depth of a WSN and evaluate some performance metrics that have a remarkable relevance for WSNs. Moreover, we propose a new strategy to join an existing WPAN that allows a node to select a suitable coordinator to connect with. Performance results show the trade-off in the selection of the maximum tree depth. While benefits of having reduced tree depths can be measured during traffic delivery, due to a reduction of the energy consumption, a counter-party is the energy spent in the network formation that deeply depends on this topological parameter. Moreover, the maximum tree depth has also a great impact on the percentage of nodes that are able to join a network.

Key words: IEEE 802.15.4, ZigBee, Sensor Networks, Topology Formation.

1 Introduction

Wireless Sensor Networks (WSNs) are traditionally composed of a multiplicity of sensor nodes that sense physical or environmental phenomenona (e.g. atmospheric

Anna Abbagnale, Emanuele Cipollone, Francesca Cuomo
University of Rome "Sapienza", INFOCOM Dpt, via Eudossiana 18, 00184 Rome (Italy)

Please use the following format when citing this chapter:

Abbagnale, A., Cipollone, E., Cuomo, F., 2008, in IFIP International Federation for Information Processing, Volume 265, Advances in Ad Hoc Networking, eds. Cuenca, P., Guerrero C., Puigjaner, R., Serra, B., (Boston: Springer), pp. 167-178 pressure, temperature, sound, vibration, etc.) and generate samples of them, that have to be delivered, possibly through multi-hop paths, to a specific node (named sink) collecting the information [1, 2]. Generally, sensor nodes are battery powered, whereas sink is connected to an outlet.

The IEEE 802.15.4 standard [3] can be used as basic technology for the development of low energy and low cost WSNs. It defines physical and MAC (Medium Access Control) layers, while the upper layers of the protocol stack are specified by the Zig-Bee Alliance [4]. Recently, some papers have treated these standards by presenting potentialities [5] and performance [6, 7]. The paper of Baronti et al. [6] presents an overview of the energy efficiency, communication, data management and security solutions adopted by the standards and proposed in the recent literature.

The paper in [7] discusses results derived by simulating, in *ns-2* [8], the IEEE 802.15.4 to (1) compare the performance between 802.15.4 and 802.11; (2) study the association and tree formation; (3) investigate the orphaning and coordinator relocation; (4) exam unslotted CSMA-CA and slotted CSMA-CA behaviors; and (5) compare three different data transmissions, namely, direct, indirect and with guaranteed time slot (GTS).

Another key aspect that should be analyzed is how this technology behaves when the applications require the set-up of a network topology with attention to the energy efficiency and network connectivity. To set-up the network topology, the IEEE 802.15.4 defines a formation strategy (MAC *association procedure*) that forms WPANs coordinated by a node (the sink) named PAN coordinator. Nodes associ-ated to a single PAN coordinator are arranged in a tree in accordance to parent-child relationships. In an IEEE 802.15.4 WSN, it is possible to have Full Function De-vices (FFDs), that allow the association of other nodes to the network and Reduced Function Devices (RFDs), that do not permit the association of other nodes. The sink is always a FFD, intermediate nodes allowing data relay (router) are FFDs too, whereas the RFDs are the leaves of the tree. The level of a node in the tree is in-tended as the distance (in terms of number of hops) of the node from the sink. Node belonging to level d are named d-nodes, so nodes at level $d = 0$ are sinks, nodes at level $d = 1$ are directly connected to the sinks, nodes at level $d = 2$ are at a two-hop distance from the sink, etc.

In the same region it is possible to have more than one sink. In this case each sink is a PAN coordinator and the overall network topology results in a *forest* of disjoint trees. This is a multi-sink network. This type of network overcomes the following problems of single-sink (or single-tree) architectures:

• when the number of sensor nodes increases, the sink has to collect an amount of information that may exceed its data processing capability (*scalability problem*);
• if in a tree several nodes belong to high levels, the delivery of the samples to the sink involves a large number of nodes, so the network energy drastically reduces (*energy consumption problem*).

In the paper in [9] the topologies formed by means of the IEEE 802.15.4 MAC *association procedure* are investigated. Specific attention is dedicated to the char-acterization of network lifetime and event notification reliability for different sinks distribution and varying the range of the event detection. Multi-sink topology performance is compared with classical single sink ones. This topological analysis highlighted that some topologies are not energy efficient, since very high trees are formed; these results could be used to better design the IEEE 802.15.4 *association procedure*.

Besides the possibility to have multi-sinks, it is interesting to evaluate also the impact on the performance of the tree characteristics. In particular, a key parameter to be controlled is the *tree depth* defined as the maximum level that a node can have in the tree. The use of this parameter can affect the network performance, since it shapes the structure of the topologies resulting from the IEEE 802.15.4 *association procedure*. In this paper we aim at considering both the multi-sink capability and the constraint on the tree depth to evaluate the network topology performance. The work of [10] aims at proposing a model to optimize the network formation by constraining the tree depth. Here we perform a detailed analysis on constrained (in terms of depth) network topologies in order to support the network optimization.

The paper is organized as follows: Section 2 briefly describes the motivations of our work. Section 3 focuses on the *association procedure* defined in the IEEE 802.15.4 to form a connected network. In Section 4 we show and discuss the results of the simulation analysis. Finally, the overall conclusions of this analysis are provided in Section 5.

2 Motivations of our work

The possibility to have trees with controlled topological characteristics has been addressed by the ZigBee Alliance. In the ZigBee Specifications the following parameters are defined [4]:

- *nwkMaxDepth (Lm)*, the maximum depth in the network, that is the maximum number of levels of the tree;
- *nwkMaxChildren (Cm)*, the maximum number of children a parent may have;
- *nwkMaxRouters (Rm)*, the maximum number of children with the role of router a parent may have.

These parameters are determined by the ZigBee coordinator which corresponds to an IEEE 802.15.4 PAN coordinator. Using these parameters every node, able to be parent, calculates the addresses to be assigned to its children. The size of the addresses block depends on the level of the node in the tree.

The aim of this work is to evaluate pros and cons that the network formation may have when the parameter *Lm* is taken into account. This analysis can be used as a basis for works that analyze the performance of the ZigBee networks (e.g. the paper [11]), where the tree creation is achieved by implementing the ZigBee recommendations as for the tree parameters. Some recent works analyzed also the ZigBee network dimensioning as a function of the tree parameters [12]. Also in this case a deep analysis of the tree topologies characteristics is fundamental to dimension the network resources. In this paper we propose a new strategy that allows a node to join an existing WPAN and takes into account the constraint on the *Lm* parameter. We then analyze the impact of this parameter on the following metrics:

* *percentage of nodes connected to the network*;
* *percentage of energy consumption for network formation*;
* *percentage of energy consumption for packet delivery*.

The first metric has an impact on the coverage of the reference area and on the reliability of event detection. The other ones are important because energy saving is a fundamental goal for WSNs. It is important to notice that the energy consumption for network formation is often not considered in literature and the networks are analyzed from the time instant in which they are already formed.

3 IEEE 802.15.4 Topology Formation

An IEEE 802.15.4 WPAN [3] is composed of one PAN coordinator and a set of sensor nodes. The PAN coordinator is the primary controller of the network and it is responsible for initiating the network operations. The standard defines a set of procedures implemented by the PAN coordinator to initiate a new WPAN and by other nodes to join an existing WPAN. The PAN coordinator assigns a PAN ID (PAN identifier) to the network and selects a channel among those specified in the standard.

The procedure adopted by sensor nodes to join a WPAN is named *association procedure* and it establishes relationships between devices within a WPAN. The operations performed by a node to join a WPAN are: STEP 1) the node searches for the available WPANs, STEP 2) it selects a coordinator[1] belonging to the available WPANs and STEP 3) it starts a message exchange with the selected coordinator to associate with it.

The discovery of available WPANs (STEP 1) is performed by scanning the *beacon frames* broadcasted by the coordinators. Two beacon broadcasting modes are defined in the standard: beacon-enabled and nonbeacon-enabled.

In beacon-enabled mode, the associated nodes transmit beacon frames periodically, hence the information on the available WPANs can be derived by eavesdropping the wireless channels (*passive scan*). In nonbeacon-enabled mode, the beacon frames shall be explicitly requested by a node by means of a *beacon request command frame* (*active scan*).

After the channels scan, the sensor node selects the coordinator (and, therefore, implicity the WPAN) to connect to (STEP 2) and it sends an *association request* message to the chosen coordinator (STEP 3). The coordinator grants and denies the access to the network of the new node by replying with an *association response command frame*. It is important to notice that the criterion used to select the coordinator (STEP 2) is not defined in the standard but is implementor dependent.

---

[1] Coordinators are sinks or those nodes that can act as relay nodes.

The whole association procedure results in a set of parent-child relationships between nodes. These relationships define univocally a tree rooted at the PAN coordinator.

3.1 Proposed strategy for coordinator selection

In this subsection' we describe our implementation of the coordinator selection (STEP 2 of the association procedure) suitably designed to take into account the multi-sink feature and the constraint on the maximum number of levels of the trees (*Lm* parameter).

In Algorithm 1, we report the pseudo-code of the operations which are executed by a node trying to connect to a network. A generic node in the network is indicated as x. Nodes that are coordinators are indicated as C and the level within the tree where they belong is indicated as d_C. A generic node x begins the association procedure with the channels scan procedure (STEP 1) as described before and it is able to listen a number of coordinators equal to *numCoord*; so, a possible coordinator for the node x is indicated as $C^{(j)}$, with $j = 1, ..., numCoord$ and its level is $d_{C^{(j)}}$. With $LQI_{C^{(j)}}$ we indicate, in accordance with the IEEE 802.15.4 standard, the quality of the link between the coordinator $C^{(j)}$ and the node x.

Among the coordinators found by node x (lines 4 - 5), the selection of the coordinator (STEP 2) is performed by means of the following operations:

- node chooses the coordinator having the lowest level $d_{C^{(j)}}$ (lines from 14 to 17);
- if there are two or more coordinators belonging to the lowest level, among the *numCoord* coordinators, the node chooses the one with the highest value of the *LQI* parameter (lines from 23 to 26);
- if there are two or more coordinators belonging to the lowest level and having the same value of the *LQI* parameter, the node chooses randomly one of them (lines from 31 to 36).

In all the three cases, the chosen coordinator is really selected if it has a level less than the *nwkMaxDepth (Lm)* parameter.

4 Performance analysis

4.1 Simulation model

We consider a multi-sink scenario with N sensor nodes and S sinks, randomly deployed in a square of side L and area $A = L^2$. All nodes are motionless and FFDs (this means that they act as possible coordinators in each WPAN, allowing association to other nodes). The transmission range of each device is R. We hypothesize that the considered scenario is static, that is node/link failures cannot occur. However at

MAC level we assume that beacon frames and data packets can collide, since they are transmitted in accordance with the CSMA-CA protocol as defined in the IEEE 802.15.4 standard. The N nodes operate in nonbeacon-enabled mode, while the S sinks are configured in beacon-enabled mode. As for the propagation model, the *two-ray ground reflection* one [13] is used; it contemplates both the direct path and one ground reflection path. We suppose that sinks have infinite energy, because they are connected to an outlet, whereas the initial energy of the other nodes is set to $1J$. We assume that the energy spent during the transmission is equal to the one spent for the reception and this value is set to $0,39\ \mu J/bit$ [15]. The adopted routing protocol is HERA (HiErarchical Routing Algorithm) [14]: this is a hierarchical protocol, where data generated by sensors and directed to the sink are routed along the parent-child relationships, i.e., every node relays data to its parent.

We performed simulations using a modified version of the *ns-2* module originally provided by Zheng and Lee in [8]. In particular, we extended the original version of this simulator (that implements the *association procedure* provided by the IEEE 802.15.4 Standard), to simulate IEEE 802.15.4 multi-sink networks with a constraint on the maximum number of levels of the trees, represented by the *nwk-MaxDepth (Lm)* parameter. At the beginning of the simulation nodes try to join a network, therefore during this phase the percentage of nodes connected to a network increases up to reach a specific value. When this value steadies, we stop the *association procedure* for all nodes. From this time instant (named in the following t_{IN}) nodes connected to the network start to generate traffic. During each IEEE 802.15.4 superframe each sensor node transmits one packet (19 *bytes* at MAC level): the used traffic model is the Constant Bit Rate (CBR) one.

In Table 1 all the simulation parameters are summarized.

Table 1 Simulation assumptions and parameters

Parameter	Value	Parameter	Value
Number of sinks, S	$25, 30, 35, 40, 45, 50$	Initial energy of the sensor nodes	$1\ J$
Number of sensor nodes, N	1500	Transmission energy E_{TX}	$0,39\ \mu J/bit$
Side of the square area, L	$1000\ m$	Reception energy E_{RX}	$0,39\ \mu J/bit$
Radio transmission range, R	$150\ m$	Routing protocol	HERA [14]
Propagation model	*Two-ray ground*	Traffic model	CBR

4.2 Simulation metrics

In this Subsection we formally define the three metrics introduced in the Section 2.

The *percentage of nodes connected to the network* is the ratio between the number of sensor nodes connected to the network (N_c) at the end of the *association procedure* (that is at the time instant t_{IN} of Fig. 1) and the total number of sensor nodes (N). So, this metric is calculated as:

$$\text{Percentage of nodes connected to the network } (\%) \ = \ \frac{N_c}{N} \qquad (1)$$

The *percentage of energy consumption for network formation* is the percentage of energy that a node spends on average to join the network, compared with its initial energy. We indicate with $x^{(k)}$ a generic node, where $k = 0, 1, ..., N-1$. If $E^I_{x^{(k)}}$ is the initial energy of $x^{(k)}$ and $E^T_{x^{(k)}}$ is the residual energy of the same node at the time instant t_{IN}, the percentage of spent energy by $x^{(k)}$ ($E^{NF}_{x^{(k)}}$) is calculated as:

$$E^{NF}_{x^{(k)}} \ (\%) \ = \ \frac{E^I_{x^{(k)}} - E^T_{x^{(k)}}}{E^I_{x^{(k)}}}, \qquad k = 0, ..., N-1 \qquad (2)$$

The result of the equation 2 is averaged on all the N sensor nodes to obtain the *percentage of energy consumption for network formation*, E_{NF}.

The *percentage of energy consumption for packet delivery* is the percentage of energy that a node spends on average, during a superframe, to support a CBR traffic. During a superframe a generic node consumes energy to transmit its packet and to receive and relay packets transmitted by other nodes.
In Fig. 1 is represented the time axis, where:

- t_{IN} is the time instant in which we stop the *association procedure* and sensor nodes connected to the network start to transmit periodically their packets;
- $E^S_{x^{(k)}}$ is the energy that a generic node $x^{(k)}$ (with $k = 0, 1, ..., N_c - 1$) has in the time instant $t_{IN} + \delta_{IN}$ (where the first superframe starts after t_{IN});
- t_{FIN} is the time instant in which the network is declared dead (this happens when the first node exhausts its energy);
- $E^F_{x^{(k)}}$ is the energy that a generic node $x^{(k)}$ (with $k = 0, 1, ..., N_c - 1$) has in the time instant $t_{FIN} - \delta_{FIN}$ (where the last superframe ends before t_{FIN}).

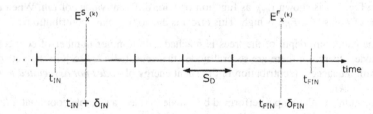

Fig. 1 Time axis partition in superframes.

If S_D is the *superframe duration*, the number of superframe M contained in the time interval $[t_{IN} + \delta_{IN}, t_{FIN} - \delta_{FIN}]$ is calculated as:

$$M \ = \ \frac{(t_{FIN} - \delta_{FIN}) - (t_{IN} + \delta_{IN})}{S_D} \qquad (3)$$

The energy spent by the node $x^{(k)}$ during a superframe ($E_{x^{(k)}}^{S_D}$) is, therefore, calculated as:

$$E_{x^{(k)}}^{S_D} = \frac{E_{x^{(k)}}^{S} - E_{x^{(k)}}^{F}}{M}, \quad k = 0, ..., N_c - 1 \tag{4}$$

To obtain the correspondent value in percentage, we divide the result of the equation 4 for the initial energy of the node $x^{(k)}$:

$$E_{x^{(k)}}^{S_D} (\%) = \frac{E_{x^{(k)}}^{S_D}}{E_{x^{(k)}}^{I}}, \quad k = 0, ..., N_c - 1 \tag{5}$$

The result of the equation 5 is averaged on all the N_c sensor nodes, to obtain the *percentage of energy consumption for packet delivery, E_{PD}*.

4.3 Simulation results

In Fig. 2 it is shown the percentage of nodes connected to the network as function of S for different values of Lm. It is important to notice that this percentage nodes increases with Lm. For low values of Lm, a reduced number of nodes succeeds in the association. This phenomenon is attenuated if S increases. However, when the value of Lm is low (e.g. $Lm = 3$) the percentage of nodes connected to the network remains low even if S is high. This is due to the fact that in this case some nodes perform several attempts to connect to the network, thus causing several MAC collisions and, hence, exhausting completely their energy before successfully joining the network. The difference in the percentage of nodes connected to the network for values of $Lm \geq 9$ is low. In general, when S increases, the percentage of connected nodes is high, since the nodes deployed in the reference area can distribute on a greater number of trees.

In Fig. 3 it is shown E_{NF} as function of S for different values of Lm. When the value of Lm is low, E_{NF} is high. This effect is due to two main contributions:

- the maximum depth of the trees is reached with a minor number of connected nodes, therefore there are several nodes that repeatedly try to join the network without success (contribution in the spent energy of *nodes not associated to the network*);
- the number of attempts performed by a node to select a suitable coordinator (and therefore to join successfully the network) increases, due to constraint on Lm (contribution in the spent energy of *nodes associated to the network*).

On the other hand, we can notice that when S varies, this performance metric remains nearly constant. This result could not seem intuitive, because we expect a decrease of E_{NF} when S increases. However, it is to be noticed that when S increases, also the number of transmitted beacons increases; as a consequence, MAC collisions and the energy spent to transmit and to receive beacons rise too.

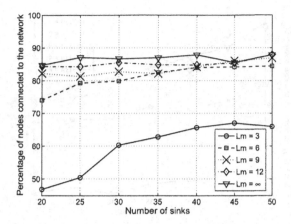

Fig. 2 Percentage of nodes connected to the network as function of number of sinks for different values of the *Lm* parameter.

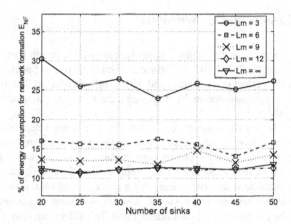

Fig. 3 Percentage of spent energy for network formation as function of number of sinks for different values of the *Lm* parameter.

In Fig. 4 it is shown E_{PD} as function of S for different values of *Lm*. In this case there is an opposite trend with respect to the Fig. 3. In fact when *Lm* is low, E_{PD} decreases, because the number of hops to reach the sink decreases too (in accordance to the used routing protocol). Moreover, if the value of *Lm* is high (e.g., $Lm \geq 6$), E_{PD} decreases when S increases. The reason is that the nodes can distribute on a greater number of trees and so some of them could have a maximum depth less than *Lm*, guaranteeing that data packets reach the sinks with a minor number of hops.

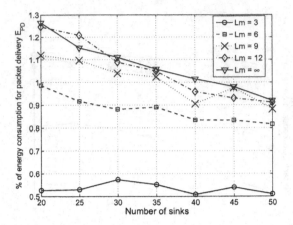

Fig. 4 Percentage of spent energy for packet delivery as function of number of sinks for different values of the *Lm* parameter.

5 Overall Results and Conclusions

In this paper, we analyzed tree shaped multi-sink networks, which form by adopting in conjunction the IEEE 802.15.4 standard and the ZigBee Specification. We evaluated how the performance of this kind of networks is affected, in terms of connectivity and energy consumption, by imposing a constraint on the maximum depth of the network (*Lm*).

Performance results show the trade-off that can arise in the selection of this parameter. While benefits of having reduced tree depths can be measured during traffic delivery, due to a reduction of the energy consumption, a counter-party is the energy spent in the network formation that deeply depends on this topological parameter. Moreover, the maximum tree depth has also a great impact on the percentage of nodes that are able to connect in a network. A very low number of connected nodes is achieved if the *Lm* parameter is maintained low. This effect can only partially be alleviated by increasing the number of sinks in the network.

The achieved results suggest that it is very important to choose a suitable value of *Lm*. It depends on characteristics of the WSN architecture (e.g., in terms of number of sinks) and on application requirements. For applications that need low routing delays and/or low energy consumption for packet delivery, it might be thought to choose low values of *Lm*, but only if this choice does not imply a significant loss of coverage. On the other hand for applications that need a high reliability in events notification to sink it seems more convenient to select an high *Lm*, since this allows to obtain high values of connectivity and a good coverage of the area to be monitored. Therefore a suitable value of this parameter has to be chosen in order to achieve the best trade-off among network performance of interest.

Acknowledgment

This work has been partially supported by the EC-funded Network of Excellence CRUISE, in the framework of the FP6.
A special thanks goes to Fabio Trifiró for the support in the simulations.

References

1. H. Karl, A. Willig, *"Protocols and Architectures for Wireless Sensor Networks"*, Wiley, 2005.
2. I. F. Akyildiz, W. Su, Y. Sankarasubramaniam, E. Cayirci, *"A Survey on Sensor Networks"*, IEEE Communications Magazine, Aug. 2002, pp. 102-114.
3. IEEE standard: Part 15.4: Wireless Medium Access Control (MAC) and Physical Layer (PHY) Specifications for Low-Rate Wireless Personal Area Networks (WPANs), IEEE, 2006.
4. ZigBee Specification, 2006, Zigbee Alliance, available at http://www.zigbee.org.
5. J. Gutierrez, E. Callaway, R. Barret, *"Low-Rate Wireless Personal Area Networks - Enabling Wireless Sensors with IEEE 802.15.4"*, IEEE Press, 2003.
6. P. Baronti, P. Pillaia, V.W.C. Chooka, S. Chessa, A. Gottab, Y. Fun Hua, *"Wireless sensor networks: A survey on the state of the art and the 802.15.4 and ZigBee standards"*, Elsevier Computer Communications 30, 2007, pp. 1655-1695.
7. J. Zheng, M. Lee, *"A Comprehensive Performance Study of IEEE 802.15.4"*, IEEE press 2004.
8. J. Zheng, M. Lee, *"NS2 Simulator for IEEE 802.15.4"*, http://ees2cy.engr.ccny.cuny.edu/zheng/pub/, 2004.
9. E. Cipollone, F. Cuomo, S. Della Luna, U. Monaco, F. Vacirca, *"Topology Characterization and Performance Analysis of IEEE 802.15.4 Multi-Sink Wireless Sensor Networks"*, Med-HocNet 2007, Corfu' (Greece), June 13-15 2007.
10. C. Buratti, F. Cuomo, S. Della Luna, U. Monaco, J. Orriss, R. Verdone, *"Optimum Tree-Based Topologies for Multi-Sink Wireless Sensor Networks Using IEEE 802.15.4"*, IEEE VTC 2007-Spring, pp. 22-25, Dublin (Ireland), April 2007.
11. F. Claudios, R Radeke, D. Marandin, *"Performance Study of Reconfiguration Algorithms in Cluster-Tree Topologies for Wireless Sensor Networks"*, PIMRC 2007, September 2007.
12. A. Koubaa, M. Alves, E. Tovar, *"Modeling and Worst-Case Dimensioning of Cluster-Tree Wireless Sensor Networks"*, RTSS'06, pp. 412-421, 2006.
13. *"The Network Simulator manual"*, http://www.isi.edu/nsnam/ns/ns-documentation, 2005.
14. F. Cuomo, S. Della Luna, U. Monaco, T. Melodia, *"Routing in ZigBee: Benefits from Exploiting the IEEE 802.15.4 Association Tree"*, ICC 2007, June 2007.
15. Moteiv Corporation Website, http://www.moteiv.com/community/Tmote_Sky_Downloads

---

Algorithm 1 SELECTION OF THE COORDINATOR

1: $minLevel = \infty$; /* level of the last selected coordinator */
2: $S_C = \emptyset$; /* selected coordinator */
3: $numCoord = 0$; /* number of coordinator found during the channels scan (STEP 1) */
4: /* STEP 1 - node x performs channels scan to find possible coordinators */
5: $numCoord$ = number of coordinators found;
6: store the LQI level of each found coordinator; /* LQI = Link Quality Identifier */
7: /* start STEP 2 */
8: **if** $numCoord$ is equal to 0 **then**
9:     /* node x did not find coordinators in STEP 1 */
10:     association procedure failed;
11:     go to line 1;
12: **else**
13:     **for** $j = 1$ *to* $numCoord$ **do**
14:       **if** $d_{C^{(j)}} < minLevel$ **then**
15:         **if** $d_{C^{(j)}} < Lm$ **then**
16:           $minLevel = d_{C^{(j)}}$;
17:           $S_C = C^{(j)}$; /* coordinator $C^{(j)}$ is selected */
18:         **else**
19:           $C^{(j)}$ is discarded;
20:           /* the coordinator $C^{(j)}$ is discarded since its level exceeds Lm */
21:         **end if**
22:       **else**
23:         **if** $d_{C^{(j)}}$ is equal to $minLevel$ **then**
24:           **if** $LQI_{S_C} < LQI_{C^{(j)}}$ **then**
25:             **if** $d_{C^{(j)}} < Lm$ **then**
26:               $S_C = C^{(j)}$; /* coordinator $C^{(j)}$ is selected */
27:             **else**
28:               $C^{(j)}$ is discarded;
29:             **end if**
30:           **else**
31:             **if** LQI_{S_C} is equal to $LQI_{C^{(j)}}$ **then**
32:               **if** $d_{C^{(j)}} < Lm$ **then**
33:                 a coordinator is randomly selected between S_C and $C^{(j)}$;
34:                 S_C = coordinator selected at line 33;
35:                 $minLevel = d_{S_C}$
36:                 /* d_{S_C} is the level of the coordinator selected at line 33 */
37:               **else**
38:                 $C^{(j)}$ is discarded;
39:                **end if**
40:             **end if**
41:           **end if**
42:         **end if**
43:       **end if**
44:     **end for**
45:     **if** S_C is equal to $\emptyset$ **then**
46:       association procedure failed;
47:       go to line 1;
48:       /* end STEP 2 */
49:     **else**
50:       send an *association request* message to S_C;
51:       ... /* STEP 3 - continue the association procedure defined by the IEEE 802.15.4 Standard */
52:       **if** *association procedure was successful* **then**
53:         x is connected to the network through S_C;
54:         exit from the algorithm;
55:       **else**
56:         go to line 1;
57:       **end if**
58:     **end if**
59: **end if**

Throughput and Delay Bounds for Cognitive Transmissions

F. Borgonovo, M. Cesana, L. Fratta

Abstract Cognitive networks are based on agile and opportunistic use of spectrum resources. This work focuses on those network scenarios where primary or licensed users coexist with secondary or unlicensed ones. Secondary users opportunistically access the shared resources whenever vacant, with the strict constraint of being invisible to primary users. We derive here analytical bounds on throughput and transmission delay of secondary users under different assumptions on secondary and primary users traffic statistics, and we comment on the use of the proposed models to dimension secondary transmissions.

1 Introduction

The world of wireless communications is nowadays facing a serious problem of spectrum shortage. Such problem is not only due to "real" limitations on the available bandwidth, but also (and mainly) to inefficient policies in spectrum management. Indeed, todays wireless networks are characterized by a fixed spectrum assignment policy, which often leads to waste large spectrum portions due to sporadic utilization by the licensed users [1]. This situation is driving the development of novel spectrum sharing paradigms, with huge interest of different actors: academia, standardization bodies, spectrum regulation bodies and manufacturers.

The enabling technology at the physical layer is constituted by Cognitive Radios devices with capabilities of sensing the spectrum and dynamically adapting their transmission parameters in an agile and opportunistic way [2, 3]. Such technology

The authors are with the:
Advanced Network Technologies Laboratory (ANT Lab),
Dipartimento di Elettronica e Informazione,
Politecnico di Milano,
Piazza L. da Vinci 32,
20133 Milan, Italy,
e-mail: {borgonov, cesana, fratta}@elet.polimi.it

Please use the following format when citing this chapter:

Borgonovo, F., Cesana, M., Fratta, L., 2008, in IFIP International Federation for Information Processing, Volume 265, Advances in Ad Hoc Networking, eds. Cuenca, P., Guerrero C., Puigjaner, R., Serra, B., (Boston: Springer), pp. 179-190.

at the physical layer is consequently driving the development of a new networking paradigm, as well, which is often referred to as Cognitive Networking.

We consider in this paper a general cognitive scenario, where the end users are distinguished into primary and secondary ones. Primary users or transmissions are allowed to use exclusively the licensed portions of the spectrum, whereas secondary transmissions may occasionally access the licensed spectrum in an opportunistic way, whenever it is vacated by the primary users. Secondary users are therefore equipped with Cognitive tunable Radios and may share the primary band with the licensed users with the strict constraint not to harm primary ones.

On the secondary users'side, this calls for effective mechanisms to dynamically detect spectrum usage, identifying which portions of the spectrum are free for use at each time, to quickly reconfigure the radio interface to chase "spectrum holes", and finally, to effectively coordinate with other secondary users, resolving collisions and/or scheduling transmissions.

The aforementioned functionalities are referred to as the *cognitive cycle* [4], which involves spectrum sensing and spectrum decision, to effectively detect the presence of primary users, spectrum sharing and spectrum access, to effectively coordinate with other secondary users accessing the shared resources. Generally speaking, the achievable performance of cognitive transmissions depends on the efficiency of the protocols handling the aforementioned phases of the cognitive cycle (sensing, decision, sharing and access).

In this work, we aim to provide bounds on the throughput and delay performance of secondary users in the aforementioned cognitive scenario, when assuming an idealized cognitive cycle. Namely, we leverage queuing theory to derive closed form expressions for the throughput and delay of secondary users in case of perfect sensing, and spectrum access; moreover, we comment on the impact of the traffic characteristics (packet dimensions, primary traffic load, traffic statistics, etc.) on the derived bounds.

The paper is organized as follows: in Section 2, we give an overview of the literature in the field of cognitive networks modelling. In Section 3, we derive throughput bounds for secondary transmissions, whereas in Section 4 we show how to use the derived throughput bounds to optimize the packet length of secondary transmissions. Delay bounds are derived in Section 5, whereas Section 6 concludes the paper by commenting on its contributions, and proposing directions for future work.

2 Related Work

Since Mitola's PhD dissertation in 2000 [2], the research in the field of cognitive networks has been extremely lively and rich. Broadly speaking, the research production can be classified depending on the specific cognitive cycle problem addressed. References [5, 6] focus on spectrum sensing issues. In [5], the authors propose a collaborative sensing approach which allows secondary users to share sensing information to increase the overall sensing reliability; on the other hand, Kim and Shin study in [6] proactive and reactive sensing mechanism and propose an algorithm to dynamically decide the optimal sensing approach.

The issues related to spectrum decision, access and management are addressed in [7, 8, 9]. In [7], the authors propose a distributed Medium Access Control (MAC) protocol able to handle spectrum sensing, decision and access at the same time. Decision theory is used to design and optimize the protocol parameters, with particular attention to spectrum prediction functionalities. In [8], Jia *et al.* design a MAC protocol which accounts for hardware constraints (single transceiver, sensing overhead), whereas Su and Zhang [9] leverage a cross-layering approach to implement a MAC based on cooperative sensing among secondary users.

The aforementioned pieces of work are targeted to the design and optimization either of physical layer sensing functionalities, or medium access control ones. In either cases, the focus is on single hop cognitive links. On the other side, also cognitive multi-hop wireless networks are recently attracting considerable attention [10]. In [11], Chowdhuri and Akyildiz extend the design of spectrum sensing and management techniques to the environment of wireless mesh cognitive networks, whereas references [12, 13, 14] address the problem of routing optimization in multi-hop cognitive environments.

In this paper, we are not concerned with the design of specific protocols for cognitive networks, but rather we aim at developing a modelling framework to evaluate the performance of cognitive scenarios, eventually providing guidelines for the optimization of the implemented protocols.

Generally speaking, the evaluation of cognitive networks is a new and intriguing field of research since many variables and parameters concur to its definition. In this field, reference [15] proposes a dirty paper coding technique to maximize the throughput of secondary users with selfish behavior. Jovicic and Viswanath address in [16] the selfless case where secondary users cooperate in relaying primary messages, and derive information-theoretic bounds on the achievable rates. An information theoretic approach is used also in [17] to find throughput bounds when cooperation among primary and secondary users is not possible.

Besides information theory, game theory is also a widely used analytical tool to characterize the cooperative/non-cooperative behavior of secondary users in dynamic environments (e.g., [18]). See [19] for a nice review of the field.

In general, the common approach to assess the capacity of cognitive transmissions resorts to information theory or game theory, and neglects (primary and secondary) traffic dynamics; on the other hand, we are able to capture traffic statistics by leveraging queuing theory in the throughput and delay analysis. Queuing theory is also applied to Cognitive Radio environments in [20], where the authors study the stability of the queues of two single-link users (one primary user and one secondary user), under different assumptions on cooperation and sensing reliability.

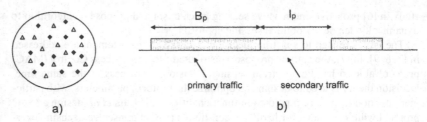

Fig. 1 *Cognitive network scenario with primary (triangles) and secondary (diamonds) users (a), a sample of the channel occupation out of primary and secondary transmissions (b).*

3 Throughput Bounds

We consider a network scenario where sets of primary and secondary users potentially share a common radio resource (see Figure 1.a), and secondary users completely avoid to generate interference on primary users by accessing unoccupied spectrum portions, only.

Since we are mainly interested in studying the impact on throughput and delay of cross-traffic interference (primary vs secondary), we start off from the following simplifying assumptions, which refer to an ideal system and are adopted to obtain bounds to the performance of a real system.

- primary/secondary users co-location; primary and secondary transmissions sharing the same radio resources make up a fully connected cluster, that is, each transmissions is received by all the users in the cluster (either primary or secondary ones);
- perfect intra-class scheduling; collisions among users of the same type are avoided;
- perfect sensing; secondary transmissions have perfect sensing capabilities of primary traffic, that is, no sensing errors (detections, false positives) occur;
- ideal collision detection: secondary ongoing transmissions leave the channel as soon as a primary one is detected without causing any interference to the primary incoming transmissions;

A first rough bound on the throughput can be obtained observing that the overall system (primary+secondary transmissions) can be modelled as an G/G/1 queue with prioritized users with preemption-resume of low priority users [21]. Let μ_p and μ_s be the average service frequency experienced by primary and secondary users, respectively; the average achievable throughput values of primary and secondary users (λ_p, λ_s) are given by:

$$\lambda_p \leq \mu_p \ , \ \lambda_s \leq \mu_s(1-\rho_p), \tag{1}$$

where $\rho_p = \frac{\lambda_p}{\mu_p}$.

Proof of first part of Eq. (1) is straightforward since the primary traffic is not affected by secondary one. To prove the second part, we leverage the concept of secondary users extended service time (or completion time according to the jargon of [22]), C_s, defined as the time it takes for a secondary packet to go through[1]. The calculation of the extended service time comes easily from the observation that each secondary transmission takes its own service time plus the service time of all the preempting primary transmissions entering during the extended service time itself, that is,

$$E[C_s] = E[X_s] + \frac{\lambda_p}{\mu_p} E[C_s], \qquad (2)$$

being X_s the random variable representing the secondary users transmission time. The average throughput of secondary users (λ_s) is upper bounded by the reciprocal of the extended service time ($E[C_s]$).

$$\lambda_s \leq 1/E[C_s] \qquad (3)$$

Substituting Eq. (3) in (2) and solving in λ_s we obtain the second part of Eq. (1).

The throughput bound provided by Eq. (1) is over-optimistic, since it is based on the simplifying assumption that the secondary users' packets preempted by primary users halt the service until channel is free, at which time the secondary transmission is continued from the time at which it was interrupted [2].

In real wireless communication systems, work conserving (preemption-resume) strategy is not feasible, since each transmitted packet must carry signalling information (e.g. bits for the Cyclic Redundancy Check, physical layer preambles, MAC addresses etc.); consequently, whenever a transmission is aborted, the corresponding packet must be entirely retransmitted, eventually repeating in the retransmission the very same signalling information carried by the original transmission.

If the resume assumption is dropped and preempted packets must be fully retransmitted, the analysis of the secondary users extended service time is more elaborated , since the transmission of secondary packets is no longer a work-conserving process. Let's suppose that the traffic (arrival and service processes) generated by primary users are statistically known. Figure 1.b shows a realization of the traffic process associated to primary transmissions, where r.v. B_p and I_p represent the busy period and the idle period of the primary traffic, respectively. Secondary traffic can only exploit the idle periods of primary sources to go through.

Assuming saturation condition for secondary transmissions, the secondary throughput is given by $\lambda_s^* = 1/E[C_s^*]$, where $E[C_s^*]$ is the average extended service time of a secondary user, which can be expressed as follows, according to the total probabilities theorem:

$$E[C_s^*] = \int_0^{+\infty} E[C_s^*/X_s = x] f_{X_s}(x) dx \qquad (4)$$

---

[1] including all the time wasted due to preemption of primary users

[2] work-conserving preemption strategy

The extended service time depends on whether the accessing secondary transmission fits into the corresponding idle period of the primary traffic. The preemption/non-preemption probabilities q and p of a secondary packet of duration x are given by:

$$p = P(I_p > X_s/X_s = x) = 1 - F_{I_p}(x)$$
$$q = 1 - p,$$
(5)

where $F_{I_p}()$ is the $c.d.f.$ of r.v. I_p. Moreover, the average duration of primary traffic idle period where preemption happens can be written as:

$$E[I_p/I_p \leq x] = \int_0^x t \frac{f_{I_p}(t)}{F_{I_p}(t)} dt.$$
(6)

In case the primary users idle period (I_p) is exponentially distributed, Eq. (6) leads to:

$$E[I_p/I_p \leq x] = \frac{1}{\lambda_p} - x \frac{p}{q}$$
(7)

The extended service time of Eq. (4) conditioned to $X_s = x$ can be written as:

$$E[C_s^*/X_s = x] =$$

$$= x + \sum_{i=1}^{+\infty}(i-1)E[B_p/I_p \leq x]pq^{i-1} +$$
$$+ \sum_{i=1}^{+\infty}(i-1)E[I_p/I_p \leq x]pq^{i-1}$$
(8)

$$= x + (E[B_p/I_p \leq x] + E[I_p/I_p \leq x])(\frac{1-p}{p})$$

The average extended service time and (consequently the throughput) of secondary transmissions is then obtained by substituting Eq. (6) into Eq. (8), and expressing the average duration of primary traffic busy period as $1/(\mu_p(1-\rho_p))$ in Eq. (4). The throughput for secondary users when secondary user service time is exponentially, deterministically and uniformly distributed with common average $1/\mu_s$ is given by:

$$\lambda_s^{exp} = (1-\rho_p)(\mu_s - \lambda_p) \qquad \lambda_s^{det} = \frac{\lambda_p(1-\rho_p)e^{-\lambda_p/\mu_s}}{1-e^{-\lambda_p/\mu_s}}$$
$$\lambda_s^{unif} = \frac{2\lambda_p^2(1-\rho_p)}{\mu_s e^{2\lambda_p/\mu_s} - 2\lambda_p - \mu_s}$$
(9)

Figure 2 shows the secondary users traffic versus the primary users traffic for different values of secondary users service time, in case of exponentially distributed secondary and primary users service time. From the results in Fig 2, one can observe that, as expected, the difference between the preemption resume and preemption repeat models increases as the ratio between primary users service time and secondary ones decreases, i.e., the probability of preemption increases.

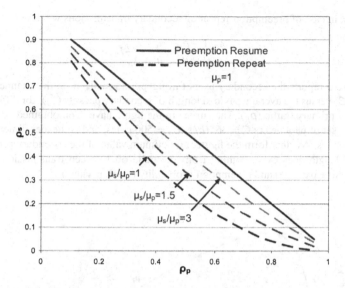

Fig. 2 *Secondary traffic (ρ_s) versus primary traffic (ρ_p). Primary and secondary users service time with negative exponential distributions.*

4 Packet Length Optimization for Secondary Transmissions

The analysis proposed in the previous section can be leveraged to select the packet length of secondary transmissions in order to optimize their throughput. Note that the throughput values obtained in Section 3 refer to the gross throughput, including physical and MAC headers. To measure the nominal throughput relevant to secondary users, let us define the average payload length (or duration[3]) of secondary packets , $\bar{L}_s$, and the header length (or duration), h_s. We observe that while h_s is associated to specific communication protocols (PHY/MAC/L3 headers), the value of $\bar{L}_s$ depends on the specific application running at the secondary users.

Furthermore, let C be the channel capacity shared by primary and secondary transmissions, $\bar{L}_p$ the average primary packet length, and $\mu_s = C/\bar{L}_s$ and $C/\mu_p = \bar{L}_p$ the average frequency of service for primary and secondary packets, respectively. The nominal throughput of secondary transmissions, in the case of work-conserving service model is given by: [4]:

$$\lambda_s < (1 - \rho_p) \frac{\bar{L}_s}{\frac{h_s}{C} + \frac{\bar{L}_s}{C}}, \tag{10}$$

---

[3] if normalized to the channel bandwidth

[4] Calculation details are skipped since calculation comes directly from the analysis proposed in the previous section.

whereas, in case of preemption-repeat of secondary transmissions we have:

$$\lambda_s < \frac{\lambda_p(1-\rho_p)(\mu_s-\lambda_p)}{\mu_s e^{\lambda_p h_s/C} - \mu_s + \lambda_p}\bar{L}_s, \tag{11}$$

Figure 3 reports the secondary users throughput normalized on the channel capacity (C) versus the average payload length of secondary packets ($\bar{L}_s$), for different values of primary traffic (ρ_p). The curves in the figure have been obtained considering the set of parameters $C = 36Mb/s$, $\bar{L}_p = 500$ bytes, and an header dimension $h_s = 40$ bytes. As clear form the figure, an optimum value of the secondary packets payload length does exist, coming from the trade off between transmission efficiency (large payload) and preemption probability (small packets).

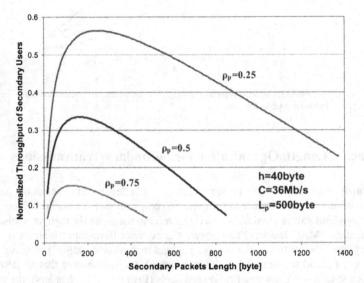

Fig. 3 *Normalized Throughput of Secondary transmissions versus the average payload length $\bar{L}_s$; $C = 36Mb/s$, $\bar{L}_p=500$ bytes, and $h_s=40$ bytes.*

Such optimum value, $\bar{L}_s^{\bar{o}pt}$, is formally characterized by the following equation:

$$\bar{L}_s^{\bar{o}pt} = argmax_{\bar{L}_s} \lambda_s \tag{12}$$

Figure 4 shows the behavior of $\bar{L}_s^{\bar{o}pt}$ when varying the traffic of the primary users for the same parameter setting as the one of Figure 3. As clear from the figure, the optimal payload dimension for secondary transmissions decreases when increasing the primary traffic intensity (ρ_p) and tends to level off for high values of it.

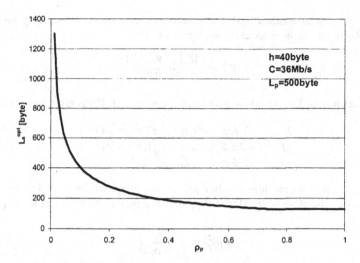

Fig. 4 *Optimal value of the secondary transmissions payload length* $L_s^{\bar{o}pt}$; $C = 36Mb/s$, $\bar{L}_p = 500$ *bytes, and* $h_s = 40$ *bytes.*

5 Delay Analysis

The system delay defined as the total time spent in the system by a secondary packet is also an important performance figure to evaluate cognitive transmissions. To this end, we derive hereafter closed form expressions for the system delay distinguishing again between the two cases of preemption resume and preemption repeat for the secondary users transmissions.

In case of preemption resume and assuming Poisson statistics for primary and secondary transmissions, the system can be modelled as an M/G/1 queue with two-classes priority users and preemption. Thus, the average waiting times of primary ($E[V_p]$) and secondary ($E[V_s]$) packets can be written as [23]:

$$
\begin{aligned}
E[V_p] &= m_{X_p} + \frac{\rho_p}{1-\rho_p} E[Z_p] \\
E[V_s] &= \frac{m_{X_s}}{1-\rho_p} + \frac{\sigma_p}{(1-\sigma_p)(1-\rho_p)} \sum_{i \in \{s,p\}} \frac{\rho_i}{\sigma_p} E[Z_i]
\end{aligned}
\tag{13}
$$

In case of preemption-repeat, we observe that the imbedded process of secondary transmissions can be modelled as an M/G/1 queue with service time C_s. Consequently, the average waiting time of secondary packets can be expressed using the Pollaczek-Khintchine result [23]:

$$
E[V_s] = \frac{\rho_s E[Z_s]}{1-\rho_s} + E[C_s]
\tag{14}
$$

where $E[Z_s]$ is the residual service time seen by secondary packet entering the system. According to the renewal theory, we can write:

$$E[Z_s] = \frac{E[C_s]}{2} + \frac{Var[C_s]}{2E[C_s]}.$$ (15)

$E[C_s]$ is given by Eq. (4), whereas a closed formula for $E[C_s^2]$ is given by [21]:

$$E[C_s^2] = 2(E[B_p] + E[I_p])^2[E(e^{\lambda_p X_p} - 1)^2] +$$
$$(E[B_p^2] + 2E[B_p]/\lambda_p + 2/\lambda_p^2)(E[e^{\lambda_p X_p}] - 1)$$ (16)
$$-2(E[B_p] + 1/\lambda_p)E[X_p e^{\lambda_p X_p}]$$

All the terms in the previous equation are known except for the second moment of the busy period of primary traffic, $E[B_p^2]$, which however, can be expressed as [23]:

$$E[B_p^2] = \frac{E[X_p^2]}{(1 - \rho_p)^3}$$ (17)

By substituting Eq. (16) into Eq. (15) we get $E[Z_s]$, which inserted into Eq. (14), leads to the closed form expression for the secondary packets waiting time.

Figure 5 reports the average time spent in the system by secondary packets normalized to the average service time, when varying the traffic intensity of primary and secondary users. From the figure, the total time spent in the system by secondary packets increases when increasing the traffic intensity of both primary and secondary users. In the former case, the delay increase is mainly due to higher preemption probability and longer busy periods of primary users, whereas, in the latter case, the queuing delay within secondary users'queues is the main contribution to the overall delay.

6 Concluding Remarks

This paper leverages queuing theory to provide upper bounds to the throughput/delay performance of cognitive scenarios where primary licensed users coexist with secondary opportunistic ones. Namely, we derived closed form expressions for the achievable throughput of secondary users and the corresponding delay performances, and we discussed on the quality of the proposed bounds under different traffic conditions. Finally, we have shown how the throughput model can be used to optimize the payload length of secondary transmissions.

The utility of the proposed bounds on throughput and delay is twofold:

- *Performance Evaluation*; the models can be obviously adopted to evaluate and predict the performance of cognitive scenarios, providing a benchmark to evaluate the efficiency of MAC protocols and cooperative sensing approaches for cognitive radio

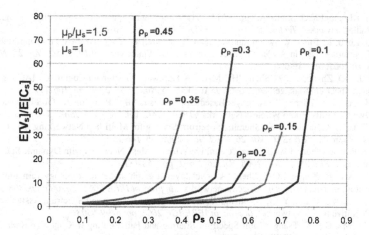

Fig. 5 *Average Time spent in the system by secondary packets normalized to the average extended service time; C = 36Mb/s, L_p=500 bytes, and h_s=40 bytes.*

- *Performance Optimization and dimensioning*; the model has clearly shown that the performance of secondary transmissions (throughput and delays) is favored by the knowledge of primary traffic statistics (ρ_p); therefore, the proposed model for the calculation of the nominal throughput and delay can be combined with techniques to estimate primary traffic statistics to design dynamic and adaptive dimensioning tools for secondary transmissions.

Natural follow ups of this work include the modelling of non-perfect sensing and collisions detection schemes, and the extension to partially connected scenarios where the channel statistics of the primary transmissions are spatially different throughout the cognitive network scenario.

References

1. Fereral Communications Commission, "Spectrum policy task force report," *FCC 02-155, Nov. 2002.*
2. J. Mitola, "Cognitive Radio: An Integrated Agent Architecture for Software Defined Radio", *PhD Dissertation, KTH, Stockholm, Sweden, Dec. 2000.*
3. S. Haykin, Cognitive Radio: Brain-Empowered Wireless Communications, *IEEE JSAC, Vol. 23, No. 2, February 2005, pp. 201-220.*
4. I.F. Akyildiz, W.Y. Lee, M.C. Vuran, S. Mohanty, "NeXt Generation/Dynamic Spectrum Access/Cognitive Radio Wireless Networks: A Survey", *Computer Networks Journal, (Elsevier), September 2006.*
5. A. Ghasemi, E.S. Sousa, "Collaborative spectrum sensing for opportunistic access in fading environment," *in proc. of IEEE DySPAN 2005, November 2005, pp. 131-136.*

6. H. Kim, and K.G. Shin. "Adaptive MAC-layer Sensing of Spectrum Availability in Cognitive Radio Networks", *Technical Report, CSE-TR-518-06, University of Michigan*

7. Q. Zhao, L. Tong, A. Swami, and Y. Chen "Decentralized Cognitive MAC for Opportunistic Spectrum Access in Ad Hoc Networks: A POMDP Framework" *IEEE JSAC, Vol. 25, No. 3, April 2007, pp. 589-600.*

8. J. Jia, Q. Zhang, and X. Shen, "HC-MAC: A Hardware-constrained Cognitive MAC for Efficient Spectrum Management", *IEEE JSAC, Vol. 26, No. 1, Jan. 2008, pp. 106-117.*

9. H. Su, and X. Zhang, "Cross-Layer Based Opportunistic MAC Protocols for QoS Provisioning Over Cognitive Radio Wireless Networks", *IEEE JSAC, Vol. 26, No. 1, Jan. 2008, pp. 118-129.*

10. T. Hou, Y. Shi, and H. D. Sherali, "Spectrum Sharing for Multi-hop Networking with Cognitive Radios", *IEEE JSAC, Vol. 26, No. 1, Jan. 2008, pp. 146-154.*

11. K.R. Chowdhury, I.F. Akyildiz, "Cognitive Wireless Mesh Networks with Dynamic Spectrum Access", *IEEE JSAC, Jan. 2008, Vol. 26, No. 1, pp. 168-181.*

12. C. Xin, B. Xie, and C.C. Shen, "A novel layered graph model for topology formation and routing in dynamic spectrum access networks", *in proc. of IEEE DySPAN 2005, pp. 308-317.*

13. G. Cheng, W. Liu, Y. Li, W. Cheng, "Joint On-Demand Routing and Spectrum Assignment in Cognitive Radio Networks", *in proc. of IEEE ICC 2007, pp. 6499-6503.*

14. M. Ma, D.H.K. Tsang, "Joint Spectrum Sharing and Fair Routing in Cognitive Radio Networks", *in proc. of IEEE CCNC 2008, pp. 978-982.*

15. N. Devroye, P. Mitran and V. Tarokh, "Achievable Rates in Cognitive Radio Channels", *IEEE Trans. Info. Theory, Vol. 52, May 2006, pp. 1813-1827.*

16. A. Jovicic and P. Viswanath, "Cognitive Radio: An Information-Theoretic Perspective", *IEEE International Symposium on Information Theory, July 2006, pp. 2413-2417.*

17. S.A. Jafar and S. Srinivasa, "Capacity Limits of Cognitive Radio with Distributed and Dynamic Spectral Activity", *IEEE JSAC, Vol. 25, No. 3, Apr. 2007, pp. 529-537.*

18. O. Simeone, I. Stanojev, S. Savazzi, Y. Bar-Ness, U. Spagnolini, and R. Pickholtz, "Spectrum Leasing to Cooperating Secondary ad hoc Networks", *IEEE JSAC, Vol. 26, No. 1, Jan. 2008, pp. 203-213.*

19. Z. Ji, and K.J. Ray liu, "Dynamic Spectrum Sharing: A Game Theoretical Overview", *IEEE Comm. Mag. , May 2007, Vol. 5, No. 5, pp. 88-94.*

20. O. Simeone, Y. Bar-Ness and U. Spagnolini, "Stable throughput of cognitive radios with and without relaying capability", *IEEE Trans. Commun., Vol. 55, No. 12, Dec. 2007, pp. 2351-2360.*

21. D.P. Graver, "A Waiting Line with Interrupted Services, Including Priorities", *Journal of the Royal Statistical Society, 1962, Vol. 24, No. 1, pp. 73-90.*

22. R.W. Wolff,"Work Conserving Priorities", *Journal of Applied Probabilities, August 1970, Vol. 7, No. 2, pp. 327-337.*

23. L. Kleinrock, "Queueing Systems: Computer Applications - Vol. 2", *Wiley, May 1976.*

Wireless Broadcast with Network Coding: Dynamic Rate Selection

Song Yean Cho and Cédric Adjih

Abstract Network coding is a novel method for transmitting data, which has been recently proposed. In this article, we study using network coding for one specific case of multicast, broadcasting. Precisely, we focus on (energy-) efficient broadcasting in a multi-hop wireless networks: transmitting data from one source to all nodes with a small number of retransmissions. It is known that the efficiency of network coding is essentially determined by the selected rates of each node. Our contribution is to propose a simple and efficient method for determining a rate selection. Our method adapts dynamically and uses only local dynamic information of neighbors: *Dynamic Rate Adaptation from Gap with Other Nodes (D.R.A.G.O.N.)*. The rationale of this rate selection method is detailed from some logical arguments. Experimental results illustrate the behavior of the method, and its excellent performance.

1 Introduction

Seminal work from Ahlswede, Cai, Li and Yeung [1] has shown that *network coding*, where intermediate nodes mix information from different flows, can achieve higher throughput for multicasting than classical routing. Since then, network coding has been shown to be specially useful in the context of wireless communications and in the context of multicast.

In this article, we will focus on using network coding as an *efficient* method to broadcast data to the entire wireless network, where the cost is the total number of transmissions. For single source broadcast, results from information theory indicate that optimality may be achieved by a simple coding

S. Y. Cho
Hipercom Team, LIX, École Polytechnique, France, e-mail: Cho@lix.polytechnique.fr

C. Adjih
Hipercom Team, INRIA Paris-Rocquencourt, France, e-mail: Cedric.Adjih@inria.fr

Please use the following format when citing this chapter:

Cho, S. Y., Adjih, C., 2008, in IFIP International Federation for Information Processing, Volume 265, Advances in Ad Hoc Networking, eds. Cuenca, P., Guerrero C., Puigjaner, R., Serra, B., (Boston: Springer), pp. 191-202.

method, *random linear coding* [2]. Then the key parameter for a given instance of a network   is essentially the average retransmission rate of the nodes — established on the entire duration of the stream (even for packet networks, see [3] for a recent synthesis of such results): the broadcast efficiency in terms of the number of transmissions can be evaluated with the average rates.

As a result, finding an optimal solution to minimize the cost consists of finding the optimal average rate of every node [6]: a *rate selection*. The problem is then reformulated:

- Problem statement: how to find a rate selection with good performance?

In fact, [4–6] have shown that optimal rate selection may be effectively obtained by solving linear programs – thus in polynomial time; and possibly in a distributed fashion.

However, a different, even simpler, approach is possible: previous work [7] has explored a simple strategy that essentially sets the same rate on every node, and had shown that it is asymptotically optimal (and at least 64 % more efficient than any method not using network coding). However this is an asymptotic result for networks with infinitely increasing density and area.

For actual networks, this rate selection may be adjusted with simple heuristics using local topology: such heuristics have been explored in [8]. They performed well; however in special cases such as sparse networks, it was found that the performance decreased, and local topology information does not seem sufficient to detect such cases.

In this article, we start from the same general idea of finding not necessarily an optimal rate selection, but a simple and efficient rate selection. We also start from the logic used in methods in [8], but with the novel approach of using simple dynamic information to adapt the rates, rather than static topology information: the rate of each node is set from the current state of the network. There are several advantages in doing so; first, the problematic cases which cannot be detected from static local topology information, may be discovered from dynamic information. Second, in a real network, the network itself evolves dynamically (for instance packet loss rate or topology may change), and hence the rate selection can no longer be a fixed constant rate. These dynamic features require dynamic adaption in any case.

Our key contributions are the proposal of a new heuristic for rate selections, its analysis, and an experimental investigation of the performance with simulations.

The rest of the paper is organized as follows: section 2 details the general framework, section 3 provides some background about network coding, section 4 details the new heuristic, DRAGON, section 5 analyzes performance with experimental results and section 6 concludes.

2 Framework

As indicated in the section 1, this article focuses on an efficient network coding method to perform broadcast.

We assume that a fixed number of nodes are present in a multi-hop wireless network. Inside the network, there is one source which will transmit a finite number of packets (referred to as the *generation size*). Other nodes are retransmitting the packets with network coding (as described in section 3).

The objective is broadcasting: eventually every node will have obtained a copy of the packets originated from the source.

The metric for efficiency is defined as the total number of transmitted packets per source packet. In general terms, as further described in section 5.1, the performance of a network coding method is derived from the average rates of the nodes. We focus on methods which explicitly select rates of the node: rate selection (see section 3.3).

In this article, we introduce a heuristic for selecting rates: DRAGON. It does not assume a specific type of network topology. However, it is suitable for networks where one transmission reaches several neighbors at the same time, that is, for wireless networks.

3 Network Coding Background

3.1 Random Linear Coding

Network coding consists in performing *coding* inside the network. One notable method of coding is *linear coding* [10] (see also [11]).

Starting with the assumption that all packets have identical size, with linear coding, the packets can viewed as vectors of coefficients of a fixed Galois field $\mathbb{F}_q^n$. Then this makes possible to compute linear combinations of them: this is the coding operation in linear coding. Since all packets originate from the source, at any point of time a node v will possess a set coded packets, every of which is a linear combination of the original source packets:

$$i^{th} \text{coded packet at node } v : p_i^{(v)} = \sum_{j=1}^{j=k} a_{i,j} P_j$$

where the $(P_j)_{j=1,\ldots,k}$ are k packets generated from the source. The sequence of coefficients, $[a_{i,1}, a_{i,2}, \ldots, a_{i,n}]$ is the *coding vector* of coded packet $p_i^{(v)}$.

With linear coding, an issue is selecting coefficients for the previous linear combinations. Whereas centralized deterministic methods exist, [2] presented a coding method, which does not require coordination of the nodes, *random linear coding*: when a node wishes to transmit a packet, computes a linear combination of all the coded packets that it possess, with randomly selected coefficients (α_i), and sends the coded packet: coded_packet $= \sum_i \alpha_i p_i^{(v)}$ This approach is made practical, with the proposition in [12], to add a special header containing coding vector of the transmitted packet.

3.2 Decoding, Vector Space, and Rank

The node will recover the source packets $\{P_j\}$ from the packets $\{p_i^{(v)}\}$, considering the matrix of coefficients $\{a_{i,j}\}$ from section 3.1. Decoding amounts to inverting this matrix, for instance with Gaussian elimination.

Thinking in terms of coding vectors, at any point of time, it is possible to associate with one node v, the *vector space*, Π_v spawned by the coding vectors, and which is identified with the matrix. The dimension of that vector space, denoted D_v, $D_v \triangleq \dim \Pi_v$, is also the *rank* of the matrix. In the rest of this article, by abuse of language, we will call *rank of a node*, that rank and dimension. Ultimately a node can decode all source packets when the rank is equal to the the total number of source packets (*generation size*). See also [13]. It is a direct metric for the amount of useful received packets, and a received packet is called *innovative* when it increases the rank of the receiving node.

3.3 Rate Selection

In random linear coding, the remaining decision is *when* to send packets. This could be done by deterministic algorithms; for instance, [13] proposes algorithms which take a decision of sending or not another packet upon reception.

In this article, we consider "rate selections": at every point of time, an algorithm is deciding the rate of every node. We denote $\mathcal{V}$ the set of nodes, and $C_v(\tau)$ the rate of the node $v \in \mathcal{V}$ at time τ. Then, random linear coding operates as indicated on algorithm 1. With this scheduling, the parameter

---

Algorithm 1: Random Linear Coding with Rate Selection

1.1 Source scheduling: the source transmits sequentially the D vectors (packets) of a generation with rate C_s.

1.2 Nodes' start and stop conditions: The nodes start transmitting when they receive the first vector but they continue transmitting until themselves **and their neighbors** have enough vectors to recover the D source packets.

1.3 Nodes' scheduling: every node v retransmits linear combinations of the vectors it has, and waits for a delay computed from the rate distribution.

---

which varies, is the delay, and we choose to compute it as an approximation from the rate $C_v(t)$ as: delay $\approx 1/C_v(t)$.

Notice that the performance, the number of transmissions per source packet, is identical after scaling the rates of all nodes (source and intermediate nodes), so we will assume that, in practice, such an adjustment is globally done so that the network operates below maximum channel capacity and with low loss rate. Furthermore, for convenience in the presentation, we assume that the unit of the rates $\{C_v\}$ is arbitrarily set so that source rate is $C_s = M$, where M = average number of neighbors.

3.4 Performance of Wireless Network Coding

One notable result relates to the performance of random linear coding, and is one of a series of information-theoretic results about network coding, starting with [1]. It is the following [3]: with random linear coding, when the rate of the other nodes are set, the source may transmit at a rate arbitrarily close to some fixed rate, the *maximum broadcast rate* and at the end of the broadcast, all the destinations can decode with a probability p_e. The error probability p_e may be made arbitrarily small, by increasing the generation size, (and independently of field size). As a result, in practice, an additional termination protocol may be used to ensure that all nodes can decode, but it has asymptotically negligible cost, and the performance is determined by the maximum broadcast rate.

The maximum broadcast rate of the source may be computed as the *min-cut of an hypergraph* using the average rates of other nodes [1, 6, 14].

Precisely, it is known that the source s can transmit individually to any node in the network, with a rate, which may be computed as the capacity of the min-cut of the network (viewed as an hypergraph). Denote $C_{\min}(s, t)$ the capacity of the min-cut between s and t. This is the *min-cut max-flow theorem* [16] and does not require network coding.

The groundbreaking result from [1] and several following generalizations (for instance [3, 14]) is that the source may transmit to several nodes at the same time (multicast), using network coding, and at the rate of the bottleneck destination. Thus, denoting $C_{\min}^{\text{all}}(s)$ the maximum broadcast rate of the source s for broadcast, we have $C_{\min}^{\text{all}}(s) \triangleq \min_{t \in \mathcal{V} \setminus \{s\}} C_{\min}(s, t)$

The dynamic behavior of the rank of one node is also known: assume that the source is transmitting with a rate C_s lower or equal to the maximum broadcast rate . Then the rank of one node t, will grow linearly with time τ as: $D_t(\tau) \approx C_s \times \tau$. If the source is transmitting with a rate too large, then it will be bounded by the min-cut to the destination t: $D_t(\tau) \approx C_{\min}(s, t) \times \tau$.

4 Heuristics for Rate Selection

In this section, we describe related work, prior heuristics for rate selection in section 4.2, and the related proposed dynamic heuristic, DRAGON in section 4.3. Before, we introduce the general concept of *local received rate*, in section 4.1, from which all these heuristics are actually derived; they are also connected to the maximum broadcast rate obtained as in section 3.4.

4.1 Local Received Rate and Optimality

We define the *local received rate* as: the total rate received by one node from its neighbors. An example is represented on Fig. 1a: the local received rate of t is the total rate from its neighbors v_1, v_2, v_3, v_4. It is not difficult to see that the broadcast rate of the source cannot be larger than the local received rate of any destination node (see formal details in [9]).

(a) Local received   (b) Example topology (source is the   (c) Performance of different
rate of t larger node)   heuristics

Fig. 1

The maximum broadcast rate of the source is lower than any local received rate, but one result links closely the two in [7]: a specific rate selection was introduced (*"IREN/IRON": Increased Rate for Exceptional Nodes, Identical Rate for Other Nodes*), where all nodes have the same rate, except from the source and the nodes near the edge of the network. One result is that the maximum broadcast rate is asymptotically the average local received rate[1]. From another viewpoint, the viewpoint of one node transmitting one packet, one metric is to count the number of its receiving neighbors for which the packet is useful (precisely, innovative, section 3.2): when it is useful for several nodes, it is a *multi-benefit* transmission ; when it is useful for all receivers, it is an *maximal-benefit* transmission. From that viewpoint, "IREN/IRON" has the same asymptotic cost as a method where all transmissions are maximal-benefit transmissions. As a result, it is a method which is asymptotically optimal – for the metric of the total number of transmissions.

4.2 Prior Static Heuristics using Cut At Destination

From section 4.1, we saw that the maximum broadcast rate is related to the local received rate in some cases of homogeneous networks. However, when the nodes have different numbers of neighbors, a first step is to adjust it, in order that the local received rate would be at least the broadcast rate of the source, $C_s \triangleq M$, for every destination: indeed, every node in the network should receive at least a total rate M from its neighbors.

A heuristic was explored in [8], inspired from [13]. A simple way to ensure that the local received rate of every node is at least equal to M, is the following: when a node has h neighbors, every of its neighbors would have a rate at least equal to $\frac{M}{h}$. Then the local received rate is always at least the sum of h such rates; indeed greater or equal to M. This yields the following rate selection:

---

[1] for lattice networks where the size of the network area grows towards infinity or for random unit-disk networks where both density and network area grow towards infinity.

- IRMS (Increased Rate for the Most Starving node) [8]: the rate of a node v is set to a constant value C_v, with:

$$C_v = k \max_{u \in H_v} \frac{M}{|H_u|}$$

where H_w is the set of neighbors of w, $|H_w|$ is its size, and $k = 1$ is a global adjustment factor.

In [13], and in a slightly different context (not explicitly a rate selection, broadcast all-to-all), theoretical arguments were given for ability to decode in the case of general networks when $k \geq 3$; but again, [7] is showing that $k = 1$ is sufficient, asymptotically.

In [8], IRMS ($k = 1$) was explored experimentally, and although overall good performance was observed, in the case of sparser networks, phenomena occurred where only a few nodes would connect one part of the network to another, in a similar fashion to the center node in Fig. 1b. In networks similar to Fig. 1b, the rate of the nodes linking two parts of the network, would be dependent on how many of them are present: such information is not available from local topology information.

4.3 New Dynamic Heuristic, DRAGON

The previous heuristics for rate selection were static, using simple local topology information, and the rates would be constant as long as the topology would remain identical.

In this article, a different approach is chosen. The starting point is the observation that with fixed rates, the rank of a node v, will grow linearly with time, as $D_v(\tau) \approx C_{\min}(s, v) \times \tau$, i.e. proportionally to the capacity of the min-cut from the source s to the node (see section 3.4). With a correct rate selection, one would expect this min-cut to be close to the source rate $C_{\min}(s, v) \approx M$ in every node, and hence would expect that all the ranks of all nodes grow at the same pace. Failure to do so is a symptom that the rate selection requires adjustment.

From $D_v(\tau)$, the rank of a node v at time τ, let us define $g_v(\tau)$, the maximum gap of rank with its neighbors, normalized by the number of neighbors, that is:

$$g_v(\tau) \triangleq \max_{u \in H_v} \frac{D_v(\tau) - D_u(\tau)}{|H_u|}$$

We propose the following rate selection, DRAGON *Dynamic Rate Adaptation from Gap with Other Nodes*, which adjusts the rates dynamically, based on that gap of rank between one node and its neighbors, as follows:

- DRAGON: the rate of node v is set to $C_v(\tau)$ at time τ as:
  - if $g_v(\tau) > 0$ then: $C_v(\tau) = \alpha g_v(\tau)$ where α is some constant
  - Otherwise, the node stops sending encoded packets until $g_v(\tau)$ becomes larger than 0

This heuristic has some strong similarities, with the reasonings presented in section 4.2, and with IRMS. Consider the local received rate of node v: DRAGON ensures that every node will receive a total rate LocalReceivedRate(v) at least equal to the average gap of one node and its neighbors scaled by α, that is, formally, that the local received rate at time τ verifies:

$$\texttt{LocalReceivedRate}(v) \geq \alpha \left(\frac{1}{|H_v|} \sum_{u \in H_v} (D_u(\tau) - D_v(\tau)) \right)$$

This would ensure that the gap would be closed in time $\approx \leq \frac{1}{\alpha}$, if the neighbors did not receive new innovative packets.

Thus, we can observe that DRAGON is constructed as a feedback control: from the expected dynamic behavior of network coding (namely a linear increasing with time of the information received, see section 3.4), it will detect inadequacies in the rate selection, and will adjust it accordingly. As further detailed in [9], DRAGON is decreasing the amount of transmissions from nodes with lower rank to nodes with higher rank, as such transmissions might be non-innovative (whereas, in the opposite direction, they always are). DRAGON can be understood as an algorithm decreases the rates, hence cost, of nodes whose transmissions are not absolutely guaranteed to be beneficial, and adjust them back only when problems are evidenced by a growing gap in rank.

We provide further insights on the dynamic behavior of DRAGON in [9] by considering approximations on linear networks: differential equations show that the network would converge to steady state exponentially with a time on the order of magnitude of $\frac{1}{\alpha}$, and that in steady state, the gap between neighbors, from the source to the edge, would be a constant $\frac{2M}{\alpha}$. Notice that insights from linear networks apply to general networks, as a lower bound, by considering in isolation one path from the source to one destination.

5 Experimental Results

5.1 Model, Metrics, Environment and Scenarios

In order to evaluate the performance of DRAGON, we performed extensive simulations, which are detailed in this section. The focus of the DRAGON algorithm is on wireless ad hoc networks, and simulations were performed either for random uniform graphs (inside a square) or with the reference network of Fig. 1b, in which one node connects two parts. This last network is of special interest because it exemplifies features found in sparse networks, where static heuristics fail.

The default simulation parameters are the following: number of nodes = 200; range is defined by M, expectation of number of nodes in one neighborhood, $M = 8$ by default; position of the nodes: random uniform i.i.d -ornet. on Fig. 1b; generation size = 500; field $\mathbb{F}_p$ with $p = 1078071557$; $\alpha = 1$ (for DRAGON) The simulator used was self-developed, with an ideal wireless model with no contention, no collision and instant transmission/reception. For comparison purposes, NS-2 (version 2.31) was also used with its default parameters.

The metric for (energy-)efficiency that is used in simulations is: the total number of transmitted packets per source packet, and is denoted as E_{cost}. $E_{cost} \triangleq \frac{\text{Total number of transmitted packets}}{\text{Generation size}}$. As mentioned in section 1, the optimal rate selection may be computed from a linear program [6]: it is the rate selection which minimizes E_{cost}. In some scenarios, we computed numerically this minimum E_{cost} (by a linear program solver), to obtain a reference point.

We also implemented a termination protocol which uses the state of neighbors piggybacked on coded packets to decide to stop transmission ; the generation size was choosen to be sufficiently large to offset its cost.

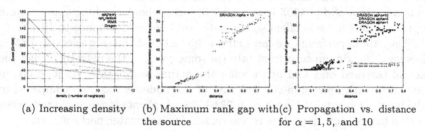

(a) Increasing density   (b) Maximum rank gap with(c) Propagation vs. distance
                              the source   for $\alpha = 1, 5$, and 10

Fig. 2

5.2 Efficiency of DRAGON

In this section, we start the analysis of the performance of various heuristics, by considering their efficiency from E_{cost}. Simulations were performed on several graphs with default parameters but $M = 6$ – relatively sparse networks – and with three rate selections: optimal rate selection, IRMS, and DRAGON. The Fig. 1c represents the results (for an average of 6 random graphs).

5.2.1 Theory and Practice

The first 3 bars, are unrelated with DRAGON, and in essence, attempt to capture the gap between theory and practice.

The first bar (label: $opt(th)$), is the optimal E_{cost} as obtained directly from the linear program solution, without simulation. The second bar (label: opt), is the actual measured E_{cost} in simulations in the ideal model wireless model, with optimal rate selection. The third bar (label: $opt - NS2$) is the actual measured E_{cost} in simulations with the simulator $NS - 2$ (packet size 512, coding vector headers included).

As one might see, with the default parameters, the measured efficiency when performing actual coding with optimal rates (and generation size = 500), gives a result rather close to numerical value of the optimal: within a few percents. Another result is that the impact of the physical and MAC layer, as simulated by NS-2 (with 802.11, two ray ground propagation, omni-antenna), is limited as one can see: $\approx 20\%$ (and the channel occupation rate was approximately of $1/3$).

The results are close. Therefore, because the purpose of our algorithm is not to perform congestion control (and because the parameters chosen would made some simulations operate above the channel capacity), in the remaining results, we will present results with the ideal wireless model.

5.2.2 Efficiency of different heuristics

The two last bars of Fig. 1c represent the efficiency of DRAGON and IRMS respectively. As one may see in this scenario, the ratio between the optimal rate selection, and DRAGON is around 1.6, but without reaching this absolute optimum, DRAGON still offers significantly superior performance to IRMS.

The gain in performance comes from the fact that the rate selection IRMS, has lower maximum broadcast rate (in some parts of the network), than the actual targeted one, and hence than the actual source rate. As a result, in the parts with lower min-cut, the rate of the nodes is too high compared to the innovation rate. Whereas with DRAGON such phenomena should not occur for prolonged durations: this is one reason for its greater performance.

5.2.3 Impact of Density

On Fig. 2a, simulations were performed on random graphs (avg. of 6), with default parameters and with increasing radio range. The modified parameter is M, the average number of nodes in one disk representing radio range. As one may see, DRAGON performs well, comparatively to IRMS in sparser networks which are the most problematic cases, for reasons explained previously. For denser networks, the gap between IRMS, DRAGON and the optimal rate selection closes.

5.3 Closer Analysis of the Behavior of DRAGON

5.4 Impact of α

In DRAGON, one parameter of the adaptation is α, and is connected to the speed at which the rates adapt. The table I indicates the total number of transmissions made, for the reference graph Fig. 1b, and for DRAGON with different values of α; and also for IRMS.

Value of α	$\alpha = 1$	$\alpha = 5$	$\alpha = 10$	IRMS
Total cost	16083	16272	17734	64411

Table 1

As one might see, first, the efficiency of IRMS on this network is rather low (1/4 of DRAGON): indeed, the topology exemplifies properties found in the cases of networks where IRMS was found to be less efficient: two parts connected by one unique node. For various choices of α, it appears that the performance of DRAGON decreases when α increases. This evidences the usual tradeoff between speed of adaptation and performance. However the decrease in performance is rather limited: we ascribe this fact to two factors. The first one is, again, that for identical average rates, different rate selections will asymptotically have identical performance, whether the rates are oscillating dramatically or not. The second one, is that in DRAGON, the nodes stop sending encoded packets, whenever they are unsure if its transmissions are beneficial to their neighbors.

5.4.1 Comparison with Model

On Fig. 2b, some results are represented, when running DRAGON, with $\alpha = 10$ on the reference network in Fig. 1b. Consider one node. At every time, it has a rank, and this rank can be compared with the number of packets already sent by the source: the difference between the two should be ideally 0, and a larger value is an indication of the delay in in propagation of the source packets. Hence that difference can be taken as a metric. We make the following statistics: for each node, we identify the maximum value of that difference over the entire simulation. We then plot one point on the graph: the x coordinate is the distance of the node to the source, whereas the y is this difference.

Therefore the graph indicates how the "gap of rank with the source" evolves with distance. First, we see that there is a large step near the middle of the graph: this is the effect of the center node, which is the bottleneck and which obviously induces further delay. Second, two linear parts are present on each side of the step: this confirms the intuitions given by the models in [9] about a linear decrease of the rank of the node from the source to the edge of the network.

Finally, one may find simulations results for $\alpha = 1, \alpha = 5$, and $\alpha = 10$ on Fig. 2c. As previously, one dot represents a node in the network, and the x coordinate is the distance of the node to the source ; but this time the y-coordinate is the time at which the node has received exactly half of the generation size. This yields further indication on the propagation of the coded packets from the source. Indeed if we compare the difference of time between nearest node from the source, and furthest node, we get a propagation time. It is around 35 for $\alpha = 1$, 6 for $\alpha = 5$ and 4 for $\alpha = 10$: roughly, it is inversely proportional to α, as expected. In addition, one sees that with higher values of α (greater reaction to gaps), the impact of the bottleneck in center node, is dramatically reduced.

6 Conclusion

We have introduced a simple heuristic for performing network coding in wireless multi-hop networks: DRAGON. It is based on the idea of selecting rates of each node, and this selection is dynamic. It operates as a feedback control, whose target is to equalize the amount of information in neighbor nodes (the rank), and hence indirectly in the network. The properties of efficiency of DRAGON are inherited from static algorithms, which are constructed with a similar logic. Experimental results have shown the excellent performance of the heuristics. Further work includes addition of congestion control methods.

References

1. R. Ahlswede, N. Cai, S.-Y. R. Li and R. W. Yeung, *"Network Information Flow"*, IEEE Trans. on Information Theory, vol. 46, no.4, Jul. 2000
2. T. Ho, R. Koetter, M. Médard, D. Karger and M. Effros, *"The Benefits of Coding over Routing in a Randomized Setting"*, International Symposium on Information Theory (ISIT 2003), Jun. 2003
3. D. S. Lun, M. Médard, R. Koetter, and M. Effros, *"On coding for reliable communication over packet networks"*, Technical Report #2741, MIT LIDS, Jan. 2007
4. Z. Li, B. Li, D. Jiang, L. C. Lau, *"On Achieving Optimal Throughput with Network Coding"* Proc. INFOCOM 2005.
5. Y. Wu, P. A. Chou, and S.-Y. Kung, *"Minimum-Energy Multicast in Mobile Ad Hoc Networks using Network Coding"*, IEEE Trans. Commun., vol. 53, no. 11, pp. 1906-1918, Nov. 2005
6. D. S. Lun, N. Ratnakar, M. Médard, R. Koetter, D. R. Karger, T. Ho, E. Ahmed, and F. Zhao, *"Minimum-Cost Multicast over Coded Packet Networks"*, IEEE/ACM Trans. Netw., vol. 52, no. 6, Jun. 2006
7. C. Adjih, S. Y. Cho and P. Jacquet, *"Near Optimal Broadcast with Network Coding in Large Sensor Networks"*, 1st Workshop Information Theory for Sensor Networks, Sante Fe, Jun. 2007 (WITS'07).
8. S. Y. Cho, C. Adjih and P. Jacquet , *"Heuristics for Network Coding in Wireless Networks"*, Proc. International Wireless Internet Conference (WICON 2007), Texas, USA, October, 2007, Accepted.
9. S. Y. Cho and C. Adjih *"Network Coding for Wireless Broadcast: Rate Selection with Dynamic Heuristics"*, INRIA RR-6349, Nov 2007.
10. S.-Y. R. Li, R. W. Yeung, and N. Cai. "Linear network coding". IEEE Transactions on Information Theory , Februray, 2003
11. R. Koetter, M. Medard, *"An algebraic approach to network coding"*, IEEE/ACM Transactions on Networking, Volume 11, Issue 5, Oct. 2003
12. P. A. Chou, Y. W, and K. Jain, *"Practical Network Coding"*, Forty-third Annual Allerton Conference on Communication, Control, and Computing, Monticello, IL, October 2003
13. C. Fragouli, J. Widmer, and J.-Y. L. Boudec, *"A Network Coding Approach to Energy Efficient Broadcasting"*, INFOCOM 2006
14. A. Dana, R. Gowaikar, R. Palanki, B. Hassibi, and M. Effros, *"Capacity of Wireless Erasure Networks"*, IEEE Trans. on Information Theory, vol. 52, no.3, pp. 789-804, Mar. 2006
15. D. S. Lun, M. Médard, R. Koetter, and M. Effros, *"Further Results on Coding for Reliable Communication over Packet Networks"* International Symposium on Information Theory (ISIT 2005), Sept. 2005
16. Ravindra K. Ahuja, Thomas L. Magnanti, and James B. Orlin, *"Network Flows: Theory, Algorithms and Applications"*, Prentice Hall, 1993.

A Reactive Wireless Mesh Network Architecture

Bachar Wehbi, Anis Laouiti and Ana Cavalli

Insitut TELECOM, TETECOM & Management SudParis, SAMOVAR CNRS
{bachar.wehbi, anis.laouiti, ana.cavalli}@it-sudparis.eu

Abstract. The future of wireless networks evolves toward more simple ways for users to get connected while on the move. In this perspective, Wireless Mesh Networks constitute one of the key technologies for new generation wireless networks. In this paper we present a reactive solution for routing and client management in an infrastructure-based wireless mesh network. The solution is based on DYMO[1]/AODV adhoc routing protocol; it performs on-demand path setup for clients and supports their mobility by introducing a light mechanism. Our solution is designed to minimize memory and bandwidth overhead by exchanging only mandatory information for client management and route establishment.

Keywords : *Mesh network, client management, wireless, DYMO/AODV.*

1 Introduction

Wireless mesh networks [2] are flexible and self-organized networks composed of a set of nodes equipped with wireless communication capabilities. Communications in a wireless mesh network are multi-hop where communicating nodes may not be in their direct radio range and rely on the cooperation of intermediate nodes to establish end-to-end routes.

Wireless mesh networks can be classified into infrastructure and infrastructureless based networks according to the capabilities of end user devices. Infrastructureless mesh networks are one-tier network architecture where user devices are part of the routing architecture as they have routing capabilities to relay packets on behalf of other nodes. Infrastructure based mesh networks, which are the focus of this work, are two-tier network architecture composed of a backbone of interconnected mesh routers. A mesh router may be equipped with additional wireless card functioning as an *Access Point* to offer network connectivity for user devices. Mesh routers are responsible for the routing function along with providing network access to user devices. Those are simple clients in the architecture and therefore have no special routing capabilities. Figure 1 illustrates a basic infrastructure based wireless mesh network.

Wireless mesh networks have been the focus of many research studies in the last decade. Most of the proposed solutions focus on routing on the mesh backbone, on capacity estimation of mesh networks and on channel allocation algorithms to exploit multi-channel capabilities [1, 5, 10].

---

[1] DYMO is the new version of the well known AODV routing protocol.

Please use the following format when citing this chapter:

Wehbi, B., Laouiti, A., Cavalli, A., 2008, in IFIP International Federation for Information Processing, Volume 265, Advances in Ad Hoc Networking, eds. Cuenca, P., Guerrero C., Puigjaner, R., Serra, B., (Boston: Springer), pp. 203-214.

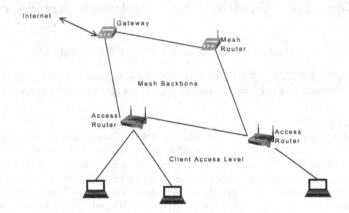

Fig. 1. Wireless Mesh network architecture.

We are interested in designing a wireless mesh architecture that serves for client-to-client and internet communications. The architecture must support client mobility while maintaining low traffic overhead. In addition, the solution should require no modification to client nodes. A client equipped with from the shelf wireless card should take full advantage of the network.

Our approach is based on a reactive mesh architecture in both routing and client management. Mesh routers are not required to keep track of all client nodes in the network. Each mesh router on the communication path involving client nodes maintains a list of these nodes. This partial client information base reduces memory and traffic consumption. We extend existing DYMO adhoc routing protocol to efficiently support the client access level of the mesh architecture.

The reminder of the paper is composed as follows: Section 2 describes some related work. Section 3 discusses the system architecture and its different building blocks. Section 4 concludes the paper.

2 Related Work

The concept of combining the properties of infrastructure and adhoc based networks has been the topic of many recent studies. One approach consisted of building an overlay over adhoc networks in order to improve the performance and increase the scalability of these networks. Other approaches try to exploit the mesh architecture and propose interesting technical solutions.

Hierarchical OLSR (HOLSR) [8] is designed for heterogeneous networks where nodes with different communication capabilities coexist. HOLSR dynamically organizes nodes, all running OLSR, into cluster levels. The objectives of HOLSR are to reduce the amount of exchanged topology control information at different levels of the hierarchical network topology and to use efficiently high capacity nodes. Our approach differs in that it does not require clients to run any particular routing protocol. The communications are transparent for our clients that think destinations are on the local network. Second, in HOLSR higher level nodes need to add routing entries toward all lower level nodes; this fact will explode their routing tables. Using our approach, a mesh router adds routing entries toward communicating nodes only if it is on the communication path.

For MIT's Roofnet Project [4] mesh clients are directly connected to Ethernet ports on the mesh routers. Network Address Translation is used to mask client addresses from the rest of the network. Contrarily, client nodes in our architecture are mobile; they are connected to the mesh routers using WIFI cards. Client mobility is supported thanks to additional functionalities incorporated into the routing protocol.

The MeshDV [9] protocol uses IP-in-IP encapsulation on end-mesh routers. Intermediate mesh routers see the traffic as being between the end-mesh routers; client communications are transparent for them. Our approach differs from MeshDV in that it requires no encapsulation mechanism. Only intermediate mesh nodes between communicating clients need to know about the communication. This reduces processing complexity implied by IP encapsulation/decapsulation and allows supporting client mobility within the routing protocol. The price is slightly more routing entries on mesh nodes.

The authors in [7] propose an extension to OLSR for mesh networks by using the Association Discovery Protocol (ADP) in order to distribute periodically the *Client Association Base* throughout the mesh network. Each mesh router maintains a Global Association Base recording which client is associated to which mesh router in the entire network.

SMesh [3] presents a mesh system that offers seamless handover to support VoIP and other real-time applications. Seamless handover is achieved by having a group of access routers (called Client Data Group) serving each mobile client. This group of access routers multicasts traffic to the mobile host during handover transitions cutting the handover latency to zero at the cost of higher bandwidth use. The problem of SMesh is that it requires all the access points to work on the same channel; consequently the mobile client can talk to multiple access points simultaneously. This significantly reduces the capacity of the client access level.

3 System Architecture

In this paper we propose a two-tier network architecture composed of a mesh backbone level and a client access level (see fig. 1). The backbone level can be seen as a wireless adhoc network of mesh nodes connected in a multihop manner. Some of the mesh nodes are equipped with additional wireless interface playing the role of access point to offer connectivity to standard WIFI clients; in the following we call these mesh nodes *access routers*. The set of access routers will form an extended basic service set (EBSS) allowing transparent client handover from one access router to another. Clients configure their SSID and join the network as they do in a classical WLAN. We use a centralized DHCP server that can run on one of the mesh nodes to configure the network with IP addresses. In addition, we rely on DHCP relay agents on each access router to relay DHCP message exchange between the clients and the server. Internet connectivity could be provided by one of the mesh nodes acting as a gateway for the network.

Connectivity in such network requires building routes between different mesh nodes and locating client nodes. An adhoc routing protocol can be used to construct routing tables for mesh nodes. The designed architecture can support proactive or reactive routing protocols. Proactive routing protocols like OLSR have the advantage of providing high knowledge about the network topology. However, the routing control overhead is high as control messages are periodic. The topology on the backbone level is stable as mesh nodes are not mobile in general; therefore there is no need to continue transmitting control messages once we have the topology of the network. Reactive routing protocols like DYMO/AODV have the advantage of low traffic overhead in a low mobility networks. In fact the mesh backbone is stable as mesh routers do not move. On the client access level, client nodes move from one access router to another. After a handover, reactive protocols try to find new routes to the moving nodes if they have active communications while proactive protocols wait until a new route is available in order to be able to contact the moving node. Both reactive and proactive routing protocols have their advantages and drawbacks. In this work we are not comparing them in a mesh topology; on the contrary we are designing a flexible mesh network architecture that can be used with a proactive or a reactive routing protocol. In the rest of this paper we will detail the system architecture assuming a reactive routing protocol is used.

On the backbone level, the routing protocol will build routes between mesh nodes. This routing information is insufficient to find paths between client nodes. To overcome this problem, access routers have to advertise their associated clients to complement the routing information with client locations. We use a reactive approach that consists on advertising client associations only when it is needed. This means when the client is involved in an active communication.

In our architecture, client nodes equipped with standard WIFI devices can take full advantage of the network without any modifications. Client nodes associates with access routers as in a WLAN; the mesh nature of the network is totally transparent for the clients. In order to offer the desired connectivity using the wireless mesh backbone, access routers need to implement the modules illustrated in figure 2. The aim is to link the data link layer client associations with the network layer routing protocol. Each access router runs the following modules:

- Client Management Module
- Routing Module
- DHCP Relay Agent
- ARP Request Handler

A client association with an access router will trigger an entry in the Client Management Module of the access router. The routing protocol consults the

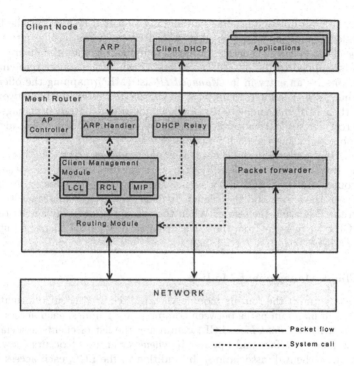

Fig. 2. System architecture: interaction between the different modules

Client Management Module to build and maintain routes toward client nodes. The ARP request handler at the access router will give local client nodes the illusion that the mesh network is a simple broadcast local network. While the DHCP relay agent relays messages between the server and the clients allowing the DHCP service to cover the whole network. We should note here that mesh routers (which doesn't provide client connectivity) run the routing module only. In the following sections we detail each of the mentioned modules before we run through an example illustrating the steps for a communication setup.

3.1 DHCP and MAC to IP Mapping

We propose a simple mechanism to map between IP and MAC addresses of client nodes. In fact, at the client access level, client associations require the MAC addresses of associated nodes whereas routing information at the backbone level requires the IP addresses of communicating clients. For this reason, client nodes IP to MAC addresses mapping is required at the access routers. We changed the IP allocation mechanism of DHCP in order to satisfy this requirement. When the DHCP server receives a request from a client identified by its MAC address, it computes the IP address by applying a hash function to the client's MAC address. If the hash function produces an already allocated IP address, the DHCP server selects an IP address from a managed IP range and sends it to the requesting client. Then it generates a message indicating that the client's MAC address is mapped to the offered IP address. Each access router receiving this message, inserts an entry in its *Managed IP* list (MIP) mapping the offered IP to the client's MAC address. This way, all the access routers in the network will have in their MIP the complete list of client nodes that obtained managed IPs. For the rest of the client nodes the mapping between the IP and MAC addresses can be obtained using the hash function.

The DHCP server and the clients exchange messages using local broadcasts, thus the server should exist locally. To overcome this limitation, we let each access router run the DHCP relay agent. The relay agent acts as an intermediate between the server and the clients. It relays the DHCP messages exchange between the client and the server. When the access router (relay agent) receives the DHCP offer message from the server it forwards it to the client and updates its *Local Client Table* (see section 3.2).

3.2 Client Management Module

In order to support the routing module with the required client information to establish and maintain paths between communicating nodes, each access router maintains a *Local Client List* (LCL) containing the list of clients associated to its access point interface and updates it whenever an event occurs (new client association or client disassociation). In addition to the LCL, each access router maintains a *Remote Client List* that contains the list of discovered remote client nodes and their responsible access routers. The RCL list is constructed when the access router receives a routing message containing information about a client that is in communication with a local client (see section 3.4).

LCL holds the list of client nodes associated with the access router. The LCL format is represented in table 1; each entry represents the mapping between the MAC and IP addresses of a given associated client node. This table is updated to reflect the new associations and disassociations of client nodes. In the LCL list, the mapping between the client's IP and MAC addresses is performed as follows: The client node association provides the client's MAC address to the *Client Management Module*. This module checks if the MAC address matches an entry in the *Managed IP* list. If a match exists, the access router inserts in its LCL the mapping between the client's MAC and IP addresses obtained from the MIP list. If no match exists, the access router applies the same hash function used by the DHCP server on the client MAC address to obtain the IP address and inserts the obtained mapping in the LCL list. RCL holds the list of remote clients in communication with local clients. These remote clients are mapped to their responsible access routers. Each entry in the RCL contains the IP address of the remote client node mapped to the IP address of its correspondent access router. The format of RCL is represented in table 2. The LCL and RCL tables, coupled with the routing protocol, allow to discover and to maintain routes between communicating client nodes. If a client node is not involved in any

Local Client List	
Client node IP	**Client node MAC**
Associated client IP 1	Associated client MAC 1
Associated client IP 2	Associated client MAC 2
...	...
Associated client IP n	Associated client MAC n

Table 1. Local Client List Format.

communication, it will appear only in the LCL list of its responsible access router.

Remote Client List	
Remote Client IP	**Remote access router IP**
Client IP 1	Access router IP 1
Client IP 2	Access router IP 2
...	...
Client IP n	Access router IP n'

Table 2. Remote Client List Format.

3.3 ARP Request Handler

The Address Resolution Protocol (ARP) [11] allows the mapping of a network address to a hardware address. In a 802.11 WLAN network, a node can communicate with another node inside the same network only if it knows its MAC address. Given a destination IP address, if its corresponding MAC address mapping is not present in the ARP cache of the client, the ARP module broadcasts an ARP request packet. All the nodes on the local network receive the packet and compare the destination IP with their own IP address. The node for which the IP address matches issues an ARP reply.

In our architecture, access routers will give the client nodes the illusion that the mesh network is a local broadcast network. For this end, each access router runs on its client access interface the *ARP Request Handler* module which is a modified ARP proxy. When a client node needs to communicate with a destination IP for which it has no IP to MAC mapping in its ARP cache, it broadcasts an ARP request.The access router's *ARP Request Handler* checks the LCL list in the *Client Management Module* to see if the destination is an associated client. If this is the case, the access router transmits the same ARP request on its access point interface. The communication between the two client nodes will be automatically bridged. If the destination is not a local associated node, the access router replies with an ARP reply message indicating that the access router's MAC address is associated with the destination IP address. By *faking* its identity, the access router accepts responsibility for routing packets to the *real* destination.

3.4 Routing Module

We extend Dynamic MANET On-Demand (DYMO)[2] [6] routing protocol to establish and maintain routes between communicating nodes in the mesh network. In the following we overview DYMO's operation, then we describe how access routers advertise their associated client nodes within routing messages and we end this section by explaining the DYMO extended operation for a mesh network.

DYMO overview: DYMO is a reactive adhoc routing protocol based on a RREQ/RREP route discovery. When a source node has data packets to send, it generates a *Route Request* (RREQ) message that floods throughout the wireless network. Upon receiving the RREQ the destination node sends in unicast a *Route Reply* (RREP) message to the source node. The propagation of the RREQ and RREP messages creates a bidirectional route between the source and the destination nodes. Once the route is set up, the source node starts delivering data packets. To detect the freshness of routing information and to guarantee a loop free operation, each node participating in DYMO maintains a sequence number. When a DYMO node generates a new routing message, it increments its own sequence number and inserts it in the routing message. Intermediate nodes compare the message sequence number with the node's last known sequence number to decide if received information is stale or not. Any of the wireless links can be lost at any time. This occurs when a node moves, crashes or is temporarily shut down, or due to the inherent variability of wireless links. Therefore, every node must monitor the link status with each of its neighbors to detect link breaks and invalidate the routing table entries which use those links. The most common strategy to accomplish this is by exchanging periodic HELLO messages.

Advertising client nodes: Client nodes see the network as a typical wireless LAN; routing on the mesh backbone is transparent for them. Since access routers provide network access to client nodes, they will be responsible for discovering routes on behalf of their associated clients. DYMO specification allows to append additional routing information to a routing message. We will exploit this option to allow access routers to advertise associated client nodes as these nodes don't have any routing capability. As clients are non DYMO nodes, they do not maintain sequence numbers to be used by the access routers when appending their addresses to routing messages. This implies that the access routers will either maintain a separate sequence number for each of their associated clients or use their own sequence number for the appended client node IP address. Both options are risky in practice. The freshness of routing information is identified by checking the value of the sequence number. A higher sequence number value means fresher information. DYMO nodes increment their sequence number value before issuing a new routing message allowing network nodes to detect

---

[2] DYMO is designed for flat topology adhoc networks. It cannot be directly applied in 2-tier Mesh networks.

valid from stale routing messages. This property cannot be satisfied when access routers maintain separate sequence numbers or use their own sequence numbers for client nodes. After a handover, a client may get a lower sequence number by its new access router.

To overcome this problem, we propose to use a new option that we call *Associated Node* to allow access routers to advertise their associated client nodes when required. The *Associated Node* option will be appended to DYMO routing messages. This option contains the IP address of the client node and a timestamp generated by the access router at the moment of building the routing message. The use of a timestamp allows to indicate the freshness of the client's related information. When a mesh node receives a routing message containing an *Associated Node* option, it treats the timestamp the same way it does with a sequence number. This means that mesh nodes maintain the association between the client IP address and the last received timestamp. When a mesh node receives a routing message with *Associated Node* option, it compares the received timestamp with its last known timestamp associated with the same client IP (if available) to decide whether the message is stale or not. Using timestamps for the *Associated Node* option relaxes the requirement of maintaining separate sequence number per client node. For this end, a synchronization mechanism should be implemented within the network. We use our synchronization mechanism described in [12] to synchronize the mesh nodes on the backbone level. This mechanism provides a synchronization accuracy in the order of few μsec in a multihop network. It is based on receiver to receiver synchronization to provide network wide synchronization with respect to one reference node in the network. Two mesh nodes receiving the same synchronization control message will compare the reception times to adjust their local clocks. Using this accurate time synchronization mechanism allows intermediate mesh nodes to detect the freshness of client's appended routing information by looking to the timestamp field. This remains true when client nodes move from one access router to another.

Extending DYMO operation: In this section we describe the modifications imported to DYMO to operate in the mesh environment. Mesh routers are responsible for discovering and maintaining routes on behalf of their communicating client nodes. To understand the extended routing operation, consider that client node C_1 associated with access router M_1 wants to communicate with destination client C_2 associated with access router M_2. When M_1 receives from C_1 a data packet destined to destination node C_2, it checks the RCL list of the *Client Management Module* to check for a match with the destination IP C_2. If no match exists, the routing module is contacted to discover a route to the destination IP C_2. The routing module then builds a Route Request message containing an *Associated Node* option. The route request message contains the following information[3]:

---

[3] DYMO uses the generalized packet format described in packetbb, however, for sake of simplicity we only show the information of interest contained in the routing messages.

$$Target\ Node : C_2\ IP\ \text{-}\ C_2\ sequence\ number^4$$
$$Originator\ Node : M_1\ IP\ \text{-}\ M_1\ own\ Sequence\ number$$
$$Associated\ Node : C_1\ IP\ \text{-}\ timestamp\ T_1$$

The message is flooded on the backbone level. When a mesh node receives the RREQ message, it updates its RCL list by adding that the client address C_1 associated with access router M_1; the routing table is also updated accordingly. Then the mesh node checks its LCL to see if the target node C_2 is an associated client. Only access router M_2 has a match; it issues a RREP message comporting an *Associated Node* option and containing the following information:

$$Target\ Node : C_1\ IP\ \text{-}\ timestamp\ T_1\ (from\ the\ RREQ)$$
$$Originator\ Node : M_2\ IP\ \text{-}\ M_2\ own\ Sequence\ number$$
$$Associated\ Node : C_2\ IP\ \text{-}\ timestamp\ T_2$$

The RREQ and RREP messages allow mesh nodes on the path between M_1 and M_2 to update their RCL lists and their routing tables with the required entries. Now when M1 receives the RREP message it updates it's RCL list with an entry indicating that C_2 is associated with M_2.

3.5 Handoff and Mobility Support

The access point interfaces of the access routers form an extended basic service set (EBSS) allowing transparent client handover from one access router to another. Handover is initiated by the client node when it receives a stronger signal from a new access router. On the backbone level, routes toward client nodes must be updated following a client handover. DYMO routing protocol has the RERR functionality to announce that certain destinations are not available. When a mesh node receives a packet from another mesh router destined to a target node for which there is no available route, a RERR message is initiated. After issuing a RERR, a new route discovery procedure is required to build the new path between the communicating nodes.

This reactivity in the route re-establishment may not be suitable for time constrained applications. To limit the effect of route re-establishment delay, when an access router receives an event on its client management module indicating that a new client has just associated, it issues a Hello message including the *Associated Node* option to inform its neighbors that the new associated node is reachable through it. This message allows neighbor nodes and potentially the previous access router responsible for the newly associated node [5] (if the node has moved from one access router to another) to update their RCL tables and their routing entries.

---

[4] The last known sequence number of the target node if any.

[5] Generally, a client moves between neighboring access routers. If this is not the case, the route re-establishment will follow the RERR as described in DYMO specification.

3.6 Communication Handling

Communications involving client nodes in the mesh network can be classified into: communication between two clients associated with the same access router, communications between two clients associated with different access routers and communications between clients and the Internet.

Clients associated with the same access router: The client access interface of the access router bridges automatically packets between the two clients as they are attached to an access point. No further attention is needed here as the communication will not affect the mesh backbone.

Clients associated with different access routers: When a client node C1 associated with access router M1 wants to communicate with client node C2 associated with access router M2, the following setup takes place.

1. C1 broadcasts an ARP Request asking for the MAC address corresponding to C2's IP.
2. M1's ARP request handler replies with an ARP reply claiming that its MAC address is associated with IP C2.
3. C1 can start now sending data packets to C2. Upon receiving data packets from C1, M1 checks for a valid route toward C2. If a route exists no more processing is required. If no route exists go to step 4.
4. M1 generates a RREQ message including an *Associated Node* option to discover a route to destination node C2 and floods it within the network.
5. M2 receives the RREQ checks its LCL list for a match with the target node C2. If a match exists, M2 sends in unicast a RREP message including an *Associated Node* option.
6. M1 receives the RREP inserts an entry in its RCL indicating that C2 is associated with M2.
7. The route from C1 to C2 is set up. The data flow between the two nodes can flow now.

In addition to the previously listed steps, each access router updates its routing table whenever a change occurs in its RCL. For example, when receiving a RREQ or a RREP message including an *Associated Node* option.

Communication with the Internet: Communications from a client to an Internet destination follows the same rules as for two clients associated with different access routers except that the network's gateway is responsible for responding to RREQs for the destination node. Similarly, when the data traffic is from the internet to an internal client, the gateway will be responsible for discovering a route toward the client. In both cases, the gateway inserts as *Associated Node* option in the generated routing messages.

4   Conclusion and Ongoing Work

In this paper we presented the architecture of a reactive infrastructure based wireless mesh network. It is based on the DYMO/AODV routing protocol with a new extension, *Associated Node*, to advertise client nodes. We use timestamps to detect the freshness of clients' related routing information. We use an ARP request handler, an ARP proxy like module, to give the clients the illusion of a local network. DHCP is used to configure client nodes and to map between network and hardware addresses. Each access router maintains a list of its associated clients and the list of remote clients which are in active communications with its local clients. The work is ongoing to implement the proposed system on a real platform in the LOR department at Telecom SudParis in order to study its performance.

References

1. A. Agarwal and P. R. Kumar. Capacity bounds for ad hoc and hybrid wireless networks. *Computer Communication Review*, 34(3):71–81, 2004.
2. I. F. Akyildiz, X. Wang, and W. Wang. Wireless mesh networks: a survey. *Computer Networks*, 47(4):445–487, 2005.
3. Y. Amir, C. Danilov, M. Hilsdale, R. Musaloiu-Elefteri, and N. Rivera. Fast handoff for seamless wireless mesh networks. In *MobiSys*, pages 83–95, 2006.
4. J. Bicket, D. Aguayo, S. Biswas, and R. Morris. Architecture and evaluation of an unplanned 802.11b mesh network. *MobiCom 05*, pages 31–42, 2005.
5. S. Biswas and R. Morris. ExOR: Opportunistic multi-hop routing for wireless networks. In *SIGCOMM*, pages 133–144, 2005.
6. I. Chakers and C. Perkins. Dynamic manet on-demand (dymo) routing. *IETF Internet-Draft draft-ietf-manet-dymo-06 (work in progress)*, 'Oct. 2006.
7. S. Y. Cho, C. Adjih, and P. Jacquet. Association discovery protocol for hybrid wireless mesh networks. Rapport de Recherche Num: 5853, INRIA Rocquencourt, France, 'March 2006.
8. Y. Ge, L. Lamont, and L. Villasenor. Hierarchical OLSR : A scalable proactive routing protocol for heterogeneous ad hoc networks. In *WiMob 2005*, Canada, August 2005.
9. L. Iannone and S. Fdida. MeshDV: A distance vector mobility-tolerant routing protocol for wireless mesh networks. *IEEE ICPS Workshop on Multi-hop Ad hoc Networks: from theory to reality (REALMAN)*, 'July 2005.
10. P. Kyasanur and N. H. Vaidya. Routing and link-layer protocols for multi-channel multi-interface ad hoc wireless networks. *Mobile Computing and Communications Review*, 10(1):31–43, 2006.
11. D. C. Plummer. Ethernet address resolution protocol: Or converting network protocol addresses to 48.bit ethernet address for transmission on ethernet hardware. *IETF RFC 826*, 'Nov. 1982.
12. B. Wehbi, A. Laouiti, and A. R. Cavalli. Accurate and efficient time synchronization mechanism for wireless multi hop networks. *Under publication*.

MEA-DSR: A Multipath Energy-aware Routing Protocol for Wireless Ad Hoc Networks

Floriano De Rango, Paola Lonetti, Salvatore Marano
D.E.I.S. Department University of Calabria
{derango, marano}@deis.unical.it

This paper presents a novel multipath energy aware routing for wireless ad hoc network. A deep analysis of different routing metrics such as MBCR, MMBCR and MDR have been led out and the Minimum Drain Rate metric has been selected as energy metric to integrate in the Multipath DSR protocol. Performance comparison with an energy efficient DSR (DSR-MDR) has been presented showing the benefits of the multiple route selection. An update mechanism and a simple data packet scheduling among the energy efficient paths have also been implemented to update the source route cache and for improving the traffic and energy load balancing. Comparison of Multipath DSR with MDR, cache update and round robin scheduling (MEA-DSR) has been also compared with Multipath DSR with MDR metric without cache update mechanism (MDSR-MDR). Simulation results confirm the improvements associated to multipath extension with energy aware metric with respect to the MDR-DSR (unipath routing).

"**Keywords**" Multi-path routing, Ad Hoc Networks, Energy, MDR.

I. INTRODUCTION

Numerous studies in literature have focused on multi-path routing, proposing different solutions and ways to see and solve the problem [2-18]. The multi-routes between a source and a destination can be used to transmit the information over all the paths at the same time in order to maximize the flow of data info as well as to split the bandwidth request of a flow over multi-paths in order to increase the success rate of the bandwidth request [2]. Another approach with a different purpose is to use the multi-routes not at the same time, but where one route is used as the primary route and the others as back-up routes in order to reduce the number of route recoveries [5]. Both of these approaches are improvements over uni-path routing protocols, because they have greater resilience to the host mobility in comparison with the relative uni-path version, reducing the delay and increasing the throughput. There are also some multi-path routing protocols that reduce the routing overhead through a single route discovery process able to build more links or node-disjoint routes towards the destination, such as Ad Hoc On Demand Multi-path Distance Vector Routing [10].

In literature there are a lot of works about multipath and power-aware routing protocol. The basic idea of this work is to join these two concepts in a unique protocol: MEA-DSR (Multipath Energy Aware DSR). The MEA-DSR is an extension

Please use the following format when citing this chapter:

De Rango, F., Lonetti, P., Marano, S., 2008, in IFIP International Federation for Information Processing, Volume 265, Advances in Ad Hoc Networking, eds. Cuenca, P., Guerrero C., Puigjaner, R., Serra, B., (Boston: Springer), pp. 215-225.

to the DSR protocol for computing multiple node-disjoint paths [8], where the "best" path is the most energy-efficient. We chose DSR as unipath routing protocol to extend, because it can be suitable from an energetic point of view for its reactive nature [6]. In multipath extension of DSR (Multipath DSR) Route Discovery mechanism of DSR was modified to implement a multipath and energy-aware routing. Moreover, a Caching Update Mechanism through probe packets was included to have always updated information in routing cache and a simple round robin data scheduling among multiple selected routes is also implemented in order to balance the traffic load and the energy consumption.

The paper is organized as follows: section II gives a brief overview of multipath routing in MANET; the adopted energy model and metric is introduced in section III; the energy extension to Multipath DSR is explained in section IV; at the end performance evaluation and conclusions are presented in section V and VI.

II. RELATED WORK

In the literature, there is much research on multi-path routing for ad hoc networks [2-5, 7-18]; in [2] there can be found a useful overview of this research activity. Multi-path routing offers the advantages of reducing the number of route discovery processes and the end-to-end data packet delay, while increasing the data packet throughput. There are several philosophies that approach the problem of multi-path in a different way. One of them is to use the multi-path routing to make load balancing between the paths [3]; another approach, in the case of QoS support, is to split the bandwidth request among more paths towards the destination in order to increase the success rate of finding routes in the route discovery phase, thus offering QoS guarantees. Multipath routing using a cross-layering approach have also been proposed such as in [10].

In [4] Lee and Gerla propose a multi-path routing algorithm called Split Multipath Routing (SMR) that represents an extension of the Dynamic Source Routing protocol. SMR uses two link-disjoint paths where the traffic is split. The traffic is distributed between the two paths through a per-packet allocation technique. The proposed scheme outperforms DSR because the multi-path routes provide robustness to mobility. The benefits of multi-path are more evident for high mobility speed. Also in [4] an extension of DSR to the multipath case has been proposed. However, in this paper, among many proposed routing schemes, we selected the work proposed by authors in [14] which has been shown to be very efficient and it was extended to the multipath case, investigating the performance of the protocol and energy load balancing under different network scenarios.

III. ENERGY-AWARE MODEL AND MDR METRIC

In this section some details about the energy model adopted in accordance with [12], and the energy aware metric will be given.

Energy model

A generic expression to calculate the energy required to transmit a packet p is: $E(p) = i \cdot v \cdot t_p$ Joules, where: i is the current consumption, v is the voltage used, and t_p the time required to transmit the packet. It is supposed that all mobile devices are equipped with IEEE 802.11b network interface cards (NICs). The energy consumption values were obtained by comparing commercial products with the experimental data reported in [12].

The values used for the voltage and the packet transmission time were: $v = 5V$ and $t_p = \left(\dfrac{p_h}{6 \cdot 10^6} + \dfrac{p_d}{54 \cdot 10^6} \right)$ s, where p_h and p_d are the packet header and payload size in bits, respectively.

We calculated the energy required to transmit and receive a packet p by using: $E_{tx}(p) = (280mA \cdot v \cdot t_p)$ and $E_{rx}(p) = (240mA \cdot v \cdot t_p)$ respectively. Since receiving a packet and just being idle, i.e., when simply powered on, are energetically similar [15], we assumed $E_{idle}(p) = (240mA \cdot v \cdot t_p)$, where t is the NIC idle time.

MDR Metric

An energy aware metric can be considered such as explained in [15]. However, in this section we recall just the cost function considered in our Multipath DSR extensions. It is the *Minimum Drain Rate* (MDR) and it permits a cost associated with a node to be calculated as referred to in (1):

$$C_i = \frac{RBP_i}{DR_i} \qquad (1)$$

where RBP_i denotes the residual battery energy at node n_i, and it indicates when the remaining battery energy of node n_i is exhausted, i.e., how long node n_i can keep up with routing operations with current traffic conditions based on the residual energy. DR_i is calculated by utilizing the well-known exponential weighted moving average method (see (2)) applied to the drain rate values DR_{old} and DR_{curr}, which represent the previous and the current calculated values.

$$DR_i = \alpha \cdot DR_{old} + (1 - \alpha) \cdot DR_{curr} \qquad (2)$$

The maximum lifetime of a given path r_p is determined by the minimum value of C_i over the path, that is $L_p = \min_{\forall n_i \in r_p} C_i$.

The Minimum Drain Rate (MDR) mechanism is based on selecting the route r_M, contained in the set R of all possible routes between the source and the destination nodes, that presents the highest maximum lifetime value, that is: $r_M = r_p = \min_{\forall r_i \in R} L_i$.

IV.MEA-DSR PROTOCOL

To have all possible paths between a source-destination pair, the destination replies to all ROUTE REQUESTs (RREQ)s that arrive, and the source stores all the paths of received ROUTE REPLY (RREP)s. Among all the stored paths, only node-disjoint routes are considered in accordance with [8]. The paths are ordered not just *by path length* (*minimum hop count* metric), but by an *energetic metric*. This energetic metric is computed while the RREP crosses the network from destination to source and it is stored in the routing table at source. The value of this metric is updated for all stored paths to avoid using an incorrect value that could compromise the performance of the protocol.

Route Discovery Mechanism

When a node s originates a new packet destined to some other node d, it places in the header of the packet a *source route* giving the sequence of hops that the packet should follow on its way to d. Normally, s will obtain a suitable source route by searching its *Route Cache* routes previously learned, but if no route is found in its cache, it will initiate the Route Discovery protocol to dynamically find a new route to d.

To initiate the Route Discovery, s transmits a RREQ message as a single local broadcast packet, which is received by (approximately) all nodes currently within its wireless transmission range.

When another node receives a RREQ, if it is d, it returns a message RREP to s. Otherwise, if this node is an intermediate node it forwards the RREP if it has no path toward destination in its own cache. If an intermediate node knows a route to destination, replies to s with a RREP, in which it copies the records stored in the RREQ and appends the rest of the path that is in its cache.

To have energy information, in accordance with [15], we have introduced a new field in DSR packet, such as referred in fig.1. The field C_i contains the cost function value. Before the destination sends back a RREP, it inserts in field C_i its cost function value. While the RREP is propagating to source, each node calculates its C_i, checks it with the value contained in RREP and , if it is necessary, replaces C_i contained in RREP with its one.

In source Route Cache the path will be stored as an entry <path, C_i >, where the path contains all the *nodes ID* and C_i is the cost function of the entire path. The paths to the same destination are ordered from the "best" to the "worst"; where the best stay owing to their greater energy-efficiency according with the chosen energy metric. In this case as a first step more energy metrics were considered such as in [15] and the best performers were selected.

Multiple paths store in the cache are only node-disjoint and this means that the routes have no nodes or links in common. Disjoint routes offer certain advantages over non-disjoint routes. For instance, non-disjoint routes may have lower aggregate resources than disjoint routes, because non-disjoint routes share links or nodes. In principle, node-disjoint routes offer the most aggregate resources, because neither links nor nodes are shared between the paths. Disjoint routes provide also higher fault-tolerance. When using non-disjoint routes, a single link or node failure can cause multiple routes to fail. In node or link disjoint routes, a link failure will only cause a single route to fail.

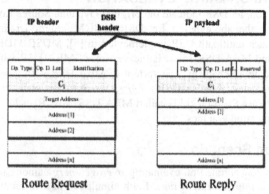

Route Request   **Route Reply**

Figure 1: Modified DSR PDU

The number of node-disjoint paths is smaller than non-disjoint paths, but if a node is shared among different routes, energy consumption balancing decreases.

Update Mechanism

As stated, when a source receives a RREP it stores path information and C_i *value*. Since nodes receive and transmit packets all time, they consume their energy, so the value of C_i of each node changes in time and information in source route cache become inconsistent with the real conditions of the network.

An update mechanism is needed because the following situation can occur. In cache there is a path that seems to have sufficient energy to support a given traffic load, while really this path   will run down soon if high data traffic crosses through itself. The Update Mechanism consists in a periodic updating of the cache through probe packets that are sent on all active paths of the set R.

Periodically all the nodes send a unicast probe request packet, called RREQ-PROBE, for all paths $p \in R$ in cache. The RREQ-PROBE is similar to a RREQ packet, but it is not sent in broadcast, because there is already a path to destination. When a RREQ-PROBE arrives at destination, a RREP-PROBE is sent back. The RREP-PROBE is a simple RREP with a set flag *probe*. Since the RREP-PROBE is a kind of RREP, it contains the destination C_i value. When it is received by an intermediate node, the node calculates its C_i, it checks this value with the value contained in the RREP-PROBE and, if it is necessary, it replaces the current cost with its calculated value. When the source receives an RREP-PROBE it simply updates information in its cache. This simple mechanism will allow the update of the set R of the active path, erasing the path from R that drains their energy too much.

V. PERFORMANCE EVALUATION

In this section, let DSR indicate the original Dynamic Source Routing Protocol, DSR-MDR is the abbreviation for DSR with Minimum Drain Rate (MDR). MDSR indicates multipath DSR implemented in [5], MDSR-MDR is for MDSR with MDR and MEA-DSR-MDR is the version of MEA-DSR with MDR metric and with Update Mechanism. The variant of MEA-DSR with other energy aware metrics is indicated as MEA-DSR-(*energy metric*). For example in the case of MBCR metric use the protocol is called MEA-DSR-MBCR such as referred in the legend of simulation graphics.

Simulation Scenario

This study is concentrated on evaluating *average energy* among nodes over time and the *connection expiration time*. Each simulation has a duration of 451 seconds. During each simulation, 8 constant bit rate (CBR) connection were generated, producing 4 packets/seconds with a packet size of 64 bytes. The transmission range used is fixed at 250 meters for all nodes.

The "random waypoint" model was used to simulate node movement. The motion is characterized by two factors: the maximum speed and the pause time. Each node starts moving from its initial position to a random target position selected inside the simulation area. When a node reaches the target position, it waits for the pause time, then it selects another random target location and moves again.

The ns-2 energy model was modified to allow the measuring of the battery energy.

Comparison among different metrics (MBCR, MMBCR, MDR)

This sub-section compares the performance of the MDR mechanism against MBCR (*Minimum Battery Cost Routing*) and MMBCR (*Min-Max Battery Cost Routing*) mechanisms (details of these metrics can be found in [14,15] and an extensive simulation under DSR can be found in [6]) using ns-2 simulator with the CMU wireless extension. The MEA-DSR-MDR protocol was considered. A network consisting of 40 mobile nodes distributed over a 1850x1850 meters area is considered. MEA-DSR was used to evaluate the behaviour of the MBCR, MMBCR and MDR mechanisms when all the nodes maintain their initial position for the simulations duration and when all the nodes move around the network. Figure.2 shows the comparison of average energy among all the nodes remaining at the end of the simulation for different mechanisms.

The MEA-DSR-MBCR approach attempts to maximize the lifetime of each host. Since cost function of the path is the sum of all the cost functions of the nodes, a route containing nodes with lower remaining battery capacity may still be selected if the other nodes along other routes have a greater remaining capacity; so the use of run-down nodes is not prevented, therefore in the network there will be nodes with more residual energy and nodes that are not alive, so the average energy will be a lower value.

The MEA-DSR-MMBCR approach tries to distribute evenly the energy consumption among nodes by using their residual battery capacity. However, since it allows nodes to accept all the connection requests if they temporarily have enough battery regardless of current traffic condition, the nodes will eventually experience lack of battery. The absence of some particular nodes owing to the traffic overload, forces the current connection to attempt to establish a new route. Therefore MEA-DSR-MMBCR suffers from the short lifetime of connections. On the other hand MEA-DSR-MDR seems to use longer routes among a few paths even in the sparse network to balance energy consumption among nodes. As some nodes die over time, the total number of possible routes between the source and destination nodes decreases. Moreover, the node movement allows new routes to appear. Therefore, MEA-MMBCR and MEA-MDR can balance traffic by alternating the use of existing routes with different hops.

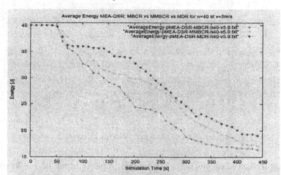

Figure 2: Average Energy MEA-DSR: MBCR –MMBCR –MDR v=5m/s

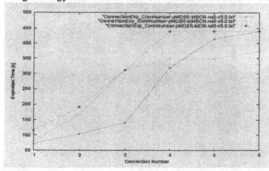

Figure 3: Expiration of Connections MEA-DSR: MBCR –MMBCR –MDR with v=5m/s.

The MEA-DSR-MDR approach can properly extend the lifetime of nodes and of connections (see Figure.3) by evenly distributing the energy expenditure among nodes. It avoids the over-dissipation of specific nodes by taking into account the current traffic condition and by utilizing the drain rate of the residual battery capacity. The main goal of MEA-MDR is to avoid the over-dissipation of energy at critical nodes in order to extend the lifetime of connections. After all those simulation analysis, MDR is chosen as the energy metric of the Multipath DSR. With the addition of round robin scheduling scheme and the cache update through probe packets, the protocol is called MEA-DSR-MDR .

MEA-DSR-MDR and Update mechanism evaluation

Figure 4 illustrates the lifetime of connections is longer for a value of 20 seconds. Updating every 20 seconds means having more current information instead of updating in 40 seconds, but it also means inserting in the network almost double of the probe packets. The difference between a timer value of 20 seconds and 40 is more evident for low mobility (Figure. 4) than high mobility (Figure. 5). The reason is that high mobility takes more frequent route breakage and this determines an implicit updating of cache made by new route discovery processes.

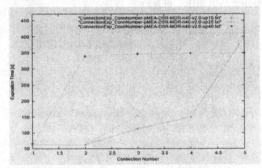

Figure 4: Expiration of connections MEA-DSR: update timer 10-20-30 sec and v=2m/s.

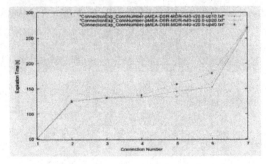

Figure 5: Expiration of connections MEA-DSR: update timer 10-20-30 sec and v=20m/s

Comparison of MEA-DSR-MDR with DSR and MDSR

Up to now it has been discussed how to implement MEA-DSR-MDR, the effect of the update rate and what energy metric is more efficient. Now DSR-MDR, MDSR-MDR, MEA-DSR-MDR are also considered for comparison purpose. MDSR has been implemented with the addition of probing packets to test and update multiple routes state and round robin scheduling for sending data packets over multiple routes.

Multiple paths between source and destination node pairs can be used to compensate for the dynamic and unpredictable nature of ad hoc networks. Spreading the traffic among multiple routes can improve load balancing, alleviate congestion and bottlenecks, and prolong nodes and connections lifetime, thereby saving more energy .

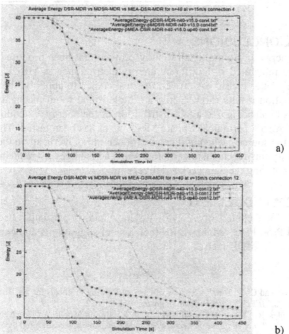

a)

b)

Figure 6: Average Energy DSR MDSR MEA-DSR v=15m/s a) 4 connection and 64 bytes packet length; b) 12 connection and 64 bytes packet length;

For high mobility (Figure 6), the update mechanism penalizes MEA-DSR-MDR compared with MDSR-MDR, this is caused by the amount of unnecessary probe packets sent on the network. The overhead is bigger for MEA-DSR-MDR than MDSR-MDR. It is truth for all considered speeds, but its weight is more evident for high mobility. The nodes movement determines frequent route breakages and forces new Route Discovery processes. More rapidly the nodes move, more frequently route discoveries start causing overhead increase. In MEA-DSR-MDR overhead caused by probe packets must be added. So in MEA-DSR, nodes spend more energy because they transmit and receive more packets.

On other hand, delivery data packet increases and end to end delay decreases in MEA-DSR-MDR with respect to MDSR-MDR such as shown in Table I for a probing time of 20s. However, the control overhead is increased for the probe packet forwarding.

TABLE 1: PERFORMANCE EVALUATION OF UNIPATH AND MULTIPATH ROUTING WITH MDR METRIC

	DSR	MDSR	MEA-DSR
Overhead (%bytes)	2.4	2.8	3.5
E2E delay (ms)	20ms	14ms	10ms
Data Packet Delivery ratio (%)	80%	85%	90%

VI. CONCLUSIONS

A novel energy aware multipath routing protocol has been proposed (MEA-DSR). It has been integrated with different energy metrics such as MBCR, MMBCR and MDR. This latter metric has proved the best choice to apply on the MDSR protocol. Simulation results showed how a simple round robin mechanism permits an energy load balancing and a fair distribution of the energy, extending the connection time. Also a periodical Update Mechanism has been tested. This permits one to update the source cache but it can introduce more overhead on the network. For low mobility this mechanism can offer some advantages by reducing the E2E delay and increasing the data packet delivery ratio.

ACKNOWLEDGEMENT

We thank Polytechnic University of Valencia and, in particular, Prof. Juan Carlos Cano and Prof. Pietro Manzoni for their useful suggestions and explanations provided about the MDR metric.

REFERENCES

[1] E. Royer and C.-K. Toh, "A Review of Current Routing Protocols for Ad Hoc Mobile Wireless Networks," *IEEE Personal Comm.Magazine*, vol. 6, no. 2, Apr. 1999.

[2] S. Mueller, R.P.Tsang, D.Ghosal, "Multipath Routing in Mobile Ad Hoc Networks: Issues and Challenges," *Invited paper in Lecture Notes in Computer Science*, Edited by Maria Carla Calzarossa and Erol Gelenbe, 2004.

[3] M.R.Pearlman, Z.J.Haas, P.Sholander, S.T. Tabrizi, "On The Impact of Alternate Path Routing for Load Balancing in Mobile Ad Hoc Networks," *in Proc. of 1 ACM International Symposium on Mobile Ad Hoc networking & Computing*, Boston, Massachussets, pp.3-10, 2000.

[4] Lee, S.-J., Gerla, M., "Split Multipath Routing with Maximally Disjoint Paths in Ad Hoc Networks," *IEEE International Conference on Communications*, Vol. 10 (2001)

[5] Marina, M.K., Das, S.R, "On-demand Multipath Distance Vector Routing in Ad Hoc Networks," *Proceedings of ICNP*, 2001.

[6] M.Fotino, et al., "Evaluating Energy-aware Behaviour of Proactive and Reactive Routing Protocols for Mobile Ad Hoc Networks," in *SPECTS'07*, 16-18 July, San Diego, CA, USA.

[7] Z., Krishnamurthy, S.V., Tripathi, S.K, "A Framework for Reliable Routing in Mobile Ad Hoc Networks," IEEE INFOCOM (2003).

[8] A. Mohammad Abbas, B.N.Jain, "Mitigating Overheads and Path Correlation in Node-Disjoint Multipath Routing for Mobile Ad hoc Networks" in *Proc. of 1st IEEE COMSWARE*, New Delhi, January 8-12, 2006.

[9] C.Chen, W. Wu, Z. Li "Multipath Routing Modelling in Ad Hoc Network" *IEEE ICC*, 16-20 May 2005.

[10] V.Loscrì, F. De Rango, S. Marano, "Ad Hoc On Demand Distance Vector Routing (AOMDV) over a Distributed TDMA MAC Protocol for QoS support in Wireless Ad Hoc Networks: Integration Issues and Performance Evaluation," *ETT Journal*, Vol.18, Issue 2, 2007.

[11] J. Gomez, A.T. Campbell, M. Naghshineh, and C. Bisdikian, "Conserving Transmission Power in Wireless Ad Hoc Networks," Proc. *Ninth Int'l Conf. Network Protocols*, 2001.

[12] L. Feeney and M. Nilsson, "Investigating the Energy Consumption of a Wireless Network Interface in an Ad Hoc Networking Environment," Proc. *IEEE INFOCOM*, 2001.

[13] S. Singh, M. Woo, and C.S. Raghavendra, "Power-Aware with Routing in Mobile Ad Hoc Networks," Proc. Fourth Ann. ACM/ *IEEE Int'l Conf. Mobile Computing and Networking*, 1998.

[14] C.-K. Toh, "Maximum Battery Life Routing to Support Ubiquitous Mobile Computing in Wireless Ad Hoc Networks," *IEEE Comm. Magazine*, June 2001.

[15] D.Kim, et al., "Routing Mechanisms for Mobile Ad Hoc Networks Based on the Energy Drain Rate" *IEEE Trans.on Mob. Comp*, vol. 2, no. 2, Apr-June 2003

[16] J. Li, D.Cordes and J. Zhang "Power – Aware Routing Protocols in Ad Hoc Wireless Network" *IEEE Wireless Communication* – December 2005

[17] W. Kim, X. Yu-long, C. Guo-liang and W. Ya-feng, "Power-aware On-demand Routing Protocol for MANET," in *Proc. of the 24th Int. Conf. on Distributed Computing Systems*, March 2004.

[18] C.F. Chiasserini and R. R. Rao, "Routing Protocols to Maximize Battery Efficiency," Proc. *21st Century Military Commun. Conf.*, vol. 1, Oct. 2000, pp. 496–500.

A New Energy Efficient Multicast Routing Approach in MANETs

Mehdi Nozad Bonab[1], Jalil Jabari Lotf[2], Bager Zarei[3], Mehdi Dehghan[4]

[1]Dep. of Computer Engineering, Islamic Azad University,Marand Branch, IRAN,
M.Nozad@gmail.com

[2]Dep. of Computer Engineering, Islamic Azad University, Ahar Branch, IRAN,
J-Jabbari@iau-ahar.ac.ir

[3]Dept. of Computer Engineering, Islamic Azad University, Shabestar Branch, IRAN,
Zarei_Bager@yahoo.com

[4]Dept. of Computer Engineering, Amirkabir University, Tehran, IRAN,
Dehghan@ce.aut.ac.ir

Abstract. Multicasting in mobile Ad hoc networks (MANETs) is transmission of packet to a group of nodes that identified by a single address. In ad hoc networks because of the non-existence of fixed infrastructure and also unavailability of the unlimited source of energy during operation of the system, one of the common problems is the limitation of the energy consumption in each node. Therefore, offering effective ways for better usage of energy in this type of networks seems necessary. In this article an effective way for energy efficient consumption has been proposed through the introduction of the quality of service (QOS) classes for multicasting group in ODMRP[1] protocol, which in turn it causes an increase in the networks life time which is one of the most important parameters in this type of networks. The simulation results show that life time of network, increase up to 5.45 percent in average. However, this improvement doesn't negative affect on other parameters. So that end-to-end delay remained fixed and the delivery rate increased. The only control overhead increase up to 1/10000 byte, which can be ignored because of the significant increase in the life time of the network.

Keywords: Ad Hoc Networks, Multicast Routing, Life Time, Energy Efficient

1. Introduction

Mobile ad hoc networks are formed dynamically by an autonomous system of mobile nodes that are connected via wireless links without using the existing net-

---

[1] More information about ODMRP can be found in [5].

Please use the following format when citing this chapter:

Bonab, M. N., Lotf, J. J., Zarei, B., Dehghan, M., 2008, in IFIP International Federation for Information Processing, Volume 265, Advances in Ad Hoc Networking, eds. Cuenca, P., Guerrero C., Puigjaner, R., Serra, B., (Boston: Springer), pp. 227-238.

work infrastructure or centralized administration [1]. These networks include the connection of mobile nodes on a shared wireless channel, and nodes that act as the routers. Ad hoc networking is a technique which has been considered very important in resent years. These networks controlled always, they have no owner, and every body can use them. The significant advantages of ad hoc networks are: quick improvements, ability, scalability, and support of mobility which are used in a wide range of applications. In other words, the non-existence of fixed infrastructure and topology has caused these networks useable for many applications. As an example, these networks are appropriate in areas where natural disasters may cause destructions in the common infrastructures; and also there are suitable in war environments.

Multicasting is an efficient communication service for supporting multi-point applications (e.g., software distributions, audio/video conferencing) in the Internet. In MANET, the role of multicast services is potentially even more important due the bandwidth and energy savings that can be achieved through multicast packet's delivery [6]. Since MANETs exhibit severe resource constraints such as battery power, limited bandwidth, dynamic network topology and lack of centralized administration, multicasting in MANETs become complex [1].

A multicast packet is delivered to multiple receivers along a network structure such as tree or mesh, which is constructed once a multicast group is formed.[2] However, the network structure is fragile due to node mobility and thus, some members may not be able to receive the multicast packet. In order to improve the packet delivery ratio, multicast protocols for MANETs usually employ control packets to refresh the network structure periodically. It has been shown that mesh-based protocols are more robust to mobility than tree-based protocols [7], due to many redundant paths between mobile nodes in the mesh. However, a multicast mesh may perform worse in terms of energy efficiency because it uses costly broadcast-style communication involving more forwarding nodes than multicast trees [2].

In mobile ad hoc networks, energy efficiency is as important as general performance measures such as delay or packet delivery ratio since it directly affects the network life time [2]. Moreover, in these networks because of wireless communications between hosts, energy constraint has been more underlined. The existing multicast routing protocols concentrate more on quality of service parameters like end-to-end delay, jitter, and bandwidth, but they do not stress on the energy consumption factor of the multicast [3]. Thus, offering effective ways for the best usage of energy in these protocols is necessary.

In this article an effective way for energy efficient consumption has been proposed through the introduction of the quality of service (QOS) classes for multicasting group in ODMRP protocol, which in turn it causes an increase in the networks life time which is one of the most important parameters in this type of networks. The simulation results show that life time of network in proposed method increased remarkably. However, this improvement doesn't negative affect on other parameters. So that end-to-end delay remained fixed and the delivery rate increased. The only control overhead increase worthlessly, which can be ignored.

2. Energy efficient multicast routing protocols in MANETs

Two approaches have been proposed for energy efficient multicast in MANETs. The first is based on the assumption that the transmission power is controllable. Under this assumption, the problem of finding a tree with the least consumed power becomes a conventional optimization problem on a graph where the weighted link cost corresponds to the transmission power required for transmitting a packet between two nodes. The second approach for energy efficiency comes from the difference of tree-based multicast from mesh-based multicast. One general idea of the power-saving mechanism is to put a mobile node in sleep (low power) mode while it is not sending or receiving packets [2]. The two approaches are discussed in Sections 2.1 and 2.2, respectively.

2.1. Energy efficiency via adaptive transmission power control

Network performance in a MANET greatly depends on the connectivity among nodes and the resulting topology. To create a desired topology for multicast, some multicast protocols adjust the nodes' transmission power assuming that it is controllable.

2.1.1. Broadcast Incremental Power (BIP) and Multicast Incremental Power (MIP) [8, 9]

The object of BIP is the determination of the minimum-cost (in this case, minimum-power) tree, rooted at the source nod e, which reaches all other nodes in the network. The total power associated with the tree is simply the sum of the powers of all transmitting nodes. Initially, the tree consists of the source node. BIP begins by determining the node that the source node can reach with minimum power consumption, i.e., the source's nearest neighbor. BIP then determines which new node can be added to the tree at minimum additional cost (power). That is, BIP finds a new node that can be reached with minimum incremental power consumption from the current tree node. This procedure is repeated until there is no new (unconnected) node left. BIP is similar to Prim's algorithm in forming the MST (minimum spanning tree), in the sense that new nodes are added to the tree one at a time on the basis of minimum cost until all nodes are included in the tree. Unlike Prim's algorithm, however, BIP does not necessarily provide minimum-cost trees for wireless networks.

To obtain the multicast tree, the broadcast tree is pruned by eliminating all transmissions that are not needed to reach the members of the multicast group. That is, the nodes with no downstream destinations will not transmit, and some nodes will be able to reduce their transmission power (i.e., if their distant downstream neighbors have been pruned from the tree). MIP is basically source-initiated tree-based multicasting of session (connection-oriented) traffic in ad hoc wireless networks. In both BIP and MIP, for simplifying trade-offs and evaluation of total power consumption, only the transmission energy is addressed, and it is assumed that the nodes do not move and that a large amount of bandwidth is available. Advantages over traditional network architectures come from the fact that the performance can be improved by jointly considering physical layer issues and network layer issues (i.e., by incorporating the vertical integration of protocol layer functions). That is, the networking schemes should reflect the node-based operation of wireless communications, rather than link-based operations originally developed for wired networks.

2.1.2. Single-Phase Clustering (SPC) and Multi-Phase Clustering (MPC) [10]

The two distributed, time-limited energy conserving clustering algorithms for multicast, SPC and MPC, minimize the transmission power in two-tiered mobile ad hoc networks. In SPC, each master node pages the slave nodes at the same maximum power, and each slave node acknowledges the corresponding master node having the highest power level. The highest power at a slave node means that the paging master node is nearest to it; hence transmission power could be saved when the slave node selects the master node that provides the highest receive power. When slave nodes send acknowledgments to each master node, the master nodes set the transmission power level to support all acknowledged slave nodes.

MPC consists of the dropping-rate-down phase and the power-saving phase. In the dropping-rate-down phase, master nodes search the slave nodes that could receive the multicast packets from only one master node. The corresponding master nodes set the transmission power level to support those slave nodes, and then the searched slave nodes belong to the corresponding master node. In the subsequent power saving phase, each master node pages the information about current power level. Paged slave nodes must have two or more candidate master nodes; hence each slave node selects one master node based on the difference of the current power (P_0) and the power to support the master node (P_n). When the master node is selected, the slave node acknowledges the master node with P_n, and each master node resets the transmission power level with the maximum value between the acknowledged P_n values.

The schemes are motivated by the fact that the most hierarchical networks such as Bluetooth scatternet are two-tier networks. The amount of energy consumption in two-tier mobile ad hoc networks could be varied with cluster configuration (e.g., the master node selection). However, an optimal cluster configuration cannot be obtained within a limited time for running a heuristic multicast algorithm. It is assumed that a slave node is connected to only one master node, and direct connection between the master node and a slave node is prohibited. MPC is desirable when energy conservation is more important than computation speed. Otherwise, SPC is preferable.

2.2. Energy savings by avoiding broadcast-based multicast

Recent wireless LAN standards usually adopt sleep mode operation in order to reduce power consumption, i.e., a communication subsystem goes into energy conserving sleep mode if it has no data to send or receive. If a node sends a packet in unicast mode specifying a receiving node, other nodes except the receiver can continue to sleep. However, when a node sends a packet in broadcast mode, all neighbor nodes have to wake up and receive the packet even though they may eventually discard it. But, receiving is not that simple because a node does not know when others will send packets to it-self. Aforementioned power saving mechanisms solves the problem by providing each node with information about when to wake up and receive packets and to sleep rest of the time. Since mesh-based multicast protocols depend on broadcast-style communication, they are not suitable in an energy constraint environment. Based on this observation, the following multicast protocol employs a multicast tree but tries to improve the packet delivery ratio to the level achieved by mesh-based protocols.

2.2.1. Two-Tree Multicast (TTM) [4]

This protocol tries to reduce the total energy consumption while alleviating the energy balance problem without deteriorating the general performance. Since TTM is based on multicast trees, it inherits all the advantages of tree-based multicast protocols in terms of total energy consumption. TTM adopts shared tree multicast rather than per-source tree multicast in order to avoid the tree construction overhead. It consumes less energy than mesh-based protocols by employing multi-destined unicast-based trees. As for the energy balance problem found in conventional single shared tree-based multicast (STM), TTM uses two trees called primary and alternative tree. When the primary tree becomes unusable or overloaded, the alternative tree takes the responsibility of the primary tree, and a new alternative tree is immediately constructed. By doing this, TTM maintains only two trees at a particular time instance, but, in fact, it uses many trees per multicast group as time advances. This is in contrast with a multicast mesh, which can be regarded as a superposition of a number of trees at a time instance. TTM is similar to the relocation scheme [12], where the root node is periodically replaced with the one nearest the center location to achieve the shortest average hop distance from the root to all receiver nodes. In TTM, a group member with the largest remaining battery energy is selected to replace the root node, and the corresponding alternative tree is constructed and maintained to replace the primary tree. The selection of an alternative root is made in advance to provide a better quality of communication service. Using the example of Fig. 1, and Fig. 2 shows the two trees constructed for a multicast group of eight members (one sender and seven receiver nodes). The primary tree consists of a primary root (r_p), four forwarding nodes (p, q, s, and t), and seven receiver nodes, while the alternative tree consists of an alternative root (r_a), four forwarding nodes (p, r_p, s, and t), and seven receiver nodes.

232

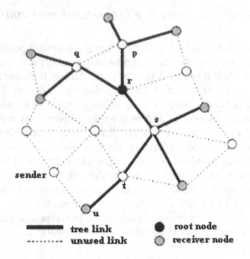

Fig. 1- An example of tree-based multicast

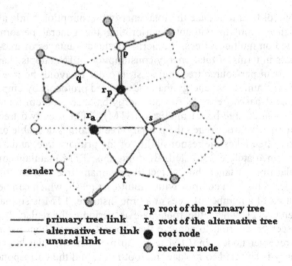

Fig. 2- An example of two trees in TTM

The TTM protocol performs as follows: Two trees are periodically recon-structed (e.g., every 3 seconds) by periodic join messages (with the information on remaining battery energy) sent by all receiver nodes to r_p and r_a. The two root nodes in dependently construct multicast trees based on the forwarding paths that the join messages traverse. When a sender node intends to send a multicast message, it forwards the multicast message to r_p to be broadcast by the root node as in most shared multicast tree protocols.

3. Suggested method

Considering the point that, MANET life time is defined as the duration of time until the first node (or some percent of nodes) in the network to fail due to battery energy exhaustion. As it mentioned earlier in introduction section, in this article a method is offered to increase network life time, which explained in this section thoroughly.

Suggested solution to increase network's life time is the offer of the concept of service classes with three priority levels and use of it in ODMRP protocol. In this method, every multicast session is assigned a priority based on the type of application and QoS requirements such as bandwidth, delay and jitter. The multicast source assigns the priority for the session and it is assumed to be genuine. The proposed method takes the multicast requests with three different classes of priority level namely class A, class B and class C. Each packet takes its generator session class.

The class A multicast session is assigned high priority that has very stringent QoS requirements in terms of delay, bandwidth and the minimum number of receivers. High-profile multicast sessions such as real-time applications are grouped into service type class A. The class C multicast session is treated as low-priority service as that of normal best effort service. Low-profile multicast sessions such as chatting are grouped as class C. The class B multicast session is assigned medium priority that is in between class A and C services. Multicast sessions with moderate QoS requirements such as file and multimedia transfer are classified as class B.

In suggested method different amounts of threshold is considered for each node of network. Each node correspond to class of received packet to it, decides to send or not to send that packet. For example, if we assume that threshold amount for each node is 80 and 60 units for C and BC classes respectively, this node sends all packets (packet with class A, B, C) if its energy is more than 80 units; Else, if this node's energy is between 60 and 80 units then due to the limitation of the energy, it will not transfer packets with class C and just transfers packet with class A and B, otherwise (the existing energy of node be less than 60 unit) because of the intensity limitation of the energy, doesn't transfer packets with class B, C and only transfers packet with class A. This, in turn, causes the node energy which has reached to its threshold amount gets zero later. Consequently the rest of nodes can have more roles in the transmission of data packets and use their energy in a best way. Generally it can be said that those nodes whose energy has been limited don't send any type of packets, thus their energy don't end early and causes an increase in network life time.

Essential point which should be mentioned have is that ODMRP protocol operates on mesh-based protocols, therefore, unlike tree-based protocols, they don't need having a rerouting for dropped packets; because there is different routes for transferring pockets to certain destination with more probability.

4. Performance evaluation of suggested method

4.1. Simulation environment

The simulator is implemented within the Global Mobile Simulation (GloMoSim) library. The GloMoSim library is a scalable simulation environment for wireless network systems using the parallel discrete-event simulation capability provided by PARSEC [11]. Our simulation models a network of 50 mobile hosts placed randomly within a 1000m × 1000m area. Radio propagation range for each node is 250 meters and channel capacity is 2 Mbits/sec. Each simulation executes for 300 seconds of simulation time. Multiple runs with different seed numbers are conducted for each scenario and collected data is averaged over those runs.

One multicast group with a single source is simulated. The source sends data at the rate of 20 packets/second. The size of data payload is 512 bytes. Multicast member nodes are randomly chosen with uniform probabilities. Members join the multicast group at the start of the simulation and remain as members throughout the simulation. Random waypoint is used as the mobility model. A node randomly selects a destination and moves towards that destination at a predefined speed. Once the node arrives at the destination, it stays in its current position for a pause time between 0 and 10 seconds. After being stationary for the pause time, it selects another destination and repeats the same process.

In simulations, mobility speed is varied from 1 km/s to 70 km/s, and the number of nodes is considered from 2 to 30. In additional, quantities of 20-30, 40-50, and 60-80 used as BC and C threshold limits respectively for nodes; and the quantities of 600-1200, 800-1500, 1000-1800, 1400-2500, and 8000-4000 were considered as primary energy of normal nodes and traffic generator nodes respectively.

In simulation of the suggested method, the following parameters were evaluated:

Life Time: Life time is defined as the duration of time until the first node (or some percent of nodes) in the network to fail due to battery energy exhaustion.

Packet Delivery Ratio: The number of data packet delivered to multicast receivers over the number of data packets supposed to be delivered to multicast receivers.

Control Overhead: Number of control bytes transmitted per data byte delivered. In addition to bytes of control packets (e.g., JOIN REQUESTS, JOIN TABLES), bytes of data packet headers are included in calculating control bytes transmitted. Accordingly, only bytes of the data payload contribute to the data bytes delivered.

End-to-End delay: The time taken for a packet to be transmitted across a network from source to destination.

4.2. Simulation results

The results of simulation regarding the setting of section 4.1 are as follows:
In simulations, we considered three cases NON_Restrict, C_Restrict, and BC_Restrict for comparing proposed method with primary ODMRP protocol. In NON_Restrict case, the nodes don't have any restriction for packets transferring; in other words the nodes transfer all packets (packets with class A, B, and C). In C_Restrict case, the packets with class C dropped if nodes energy reaches to C threshold. The BC_Restrict is similar to C_Restrict with this difference that packets with class B also dropped if nodes energy reaches to BC threshold.

Fig. 3 show the average network life time for different thresholds. As such it can be observed, by increasing the threshold values and also by increasing the intensity of constraints, the network life time is increased; because the nodes are reached to their energy thresholds, only transfer packets with higher classes, thus their energy finished later, consequently the network life time is increased.

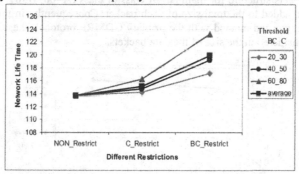

Fig. 3- Average network life time for different thresholds

As there was not any energy parameter in primary ODMRP protocol, it is equivalent to NON_Restrict case with infinite energy values for nodes, which in this case network life time was equal to the end time of simulation (300 second).

On the basis of the obtained results, network life time in average for NON-Restrict case is 113.7 and for BC-Restrict is 119.9, which it shows that the network life time of proposed method rather than primary ODMRP protocol increases about 5.54%.

As the increase in the network life time may cause decrease of the quality of the other parameters in network, we evaluated some of theses parameters.

In fig. 4, the average delivery rate is shown for different thresholds. As such it can be observed, by increasing the intensity of constraints, the network life time is increased, thus the number of received packets and consequently delivery rate increases. It should be noted that the obtained results for the primary ODMRP protocol is constant due to there was no restrict on it.

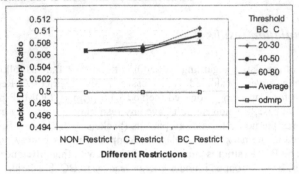

Fig. 4- Average delivery rate for different thresholds

In fig. 5, the average control overhead is shown for different thresholds. Regarding that in the implementation of the proposed method, one field is added to the data packets structure for maintain of class of class (A=00, B=01, C=10) two bits are also added to the total size of each packet. Consequently, in the comparison of the suggested method with the primary ODMRP protocol, these two added bites are considered in the size of the data packets.

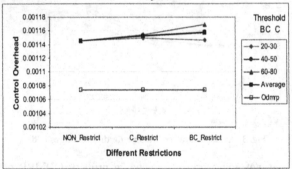

Fig. 5- Average control overhead for different thresholds

Regarding fig. 5, by increasing the intensity of constraints, the number of the control packets and consequently the control overhead increased. Also by increasing the threshold values, because of the act of dropping packets start early then the number of received packets decreases, and consequently control over head increases.

As it can be considered, control overhead of the proposed method in comparison to primary ODMRP protocol has increased up to 1/10000 bits, which it is ignorable in practice.

In fig. 6, the average end-to-end delay is shown. In simulations initial energy, threshold values, and intensity of constraints had no effects for this parameter, only the number of participated nodes in simulation and also the speed of mobility of these nodes had some effects on this parameter. As it can be seeing in fig. 6, by increasing the number of nodes, the end-to-end delay decreases and increasing the network life time had no effect on this parameter.

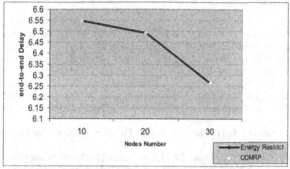

Fig. 6- Average end-to-end delay for different number of nodes

On the basis of the obtained results from fig. 3 to 6 we can conclude that the proposed method increases the network life time considerably; also this increase does not have any negative effect on the other parameters. Of course it is possible to increase the network life time by increasing threshold values as much as it has no negative effect on other parameters.

5. Conclusion and future works

The energy efficient consumption in MANETs is a necessity for each node and as a whole for the total network. The performed researches show that the on de-mand tree-based protocols in which the topology of network changes frequently can not be the best choice in a dynamic environment. Considering this point that usability of alternative routes allow information to be delivered to all or most of the multicast receivers even though a link is broken seems that mesh-based proto-cols is effective than tree-based protocols. In mesh-based protocol, one of the im-portant problems is energy efficient consumption in these types of networks. The reason for this is unavailability to infinite sources of energy during the operation of network in directly.

Our proposed method is based on energy efficient consumption in order to in-crease network life time by classifying multicast sessions. Using GloMoSim soft-ware the performance of the proposed method and other parameters which were probability affected by the proposed method were evaluated. The result showed that proposed method increases network life time remarkably, and do not negative effect on other parameters. Future attempts should be focused on the scalability of multicast routing by increasing the number of multicast sessions and number of multicast sources.

6. References

1. Chlamtac I, Conti M, Liu J J (July 2002) "Mobile ad hoc networking: imperatives and challenges", Elsevier, Amsterdam, 1000 AE, Netherlands, PP. 13-64
2. Ilyas M (2002) "The Handbook of Ad hoc Wireless Networks", Florida Atlantic University Boca Raton, CRC Press, FL, U.S.A.
3. Manoharan R, Thambidurai P, Ramesh R (December 2006)"Power aware scalable multicast routing protocol for MANETs", International Journal of Communication Systems, John Wiley and Sons Ltd, Chichester, West Sussex, PO19 8SQ, United Kingdom, PP. 1089 - 1101, vol. 9, No. 10
4. Moh S, Yu C, Lee B (2001) "Energy Efficient Two-Tree Multicast for Mobile AdHoc Networks", IEEE INFOCOM
5. Lee S J, Su W, Gerla M (December 2002) "On-Demand Multicast Routing Protocol in Multihop Wireless Mobile Networks", Kluwer Academic Publishers, Dordrecht, 3311 GZ, Netherlands, PP. 441-453, VOL. 7, NO. 6
6. Chlamtac I, Weinstein O (April 1987) " The wave expansion approach to broadcasting in multi-hop radio networks, in: Proceedings", IEEE INFOCOM, San Francisco, CA
7. Lee S, S u W, Hsu J, Gerla M, Bagrodia R (March 2000) " A Performance Comparison Study of Ad Hoc Wireless Multicast Protocols", IEEE Infocom 2000, Tel Aviv, vol. 2, PP. 565–574
8. Wieselthier J, Nguyen G, Ephremides A (November 1999) "Algorithms for Energy-Efficient Multicasting in Ad Hoc Wireless Networks", Military Communication Conference (MILCOM 1999), Atlantic City, NJ, VOL. 2, PP. 1414–1418
9. Wieselthier J, Nguyen G, Ephremides A (May 2001) "Energy Efficiency in Energy-Limited Wireless Networks fo r Session-Based Multicasting", IEEE Vehicular Technology Conference (VTC 2001), VOL. 4, PP. 2838–2842
10. Ryu J, Song S, Cho D (September 2000)"A Power-Saving Multicast Scheme in Two-Tier Hierarchical Mobile Ad-Hoc Ne tworks", IEEE Vehicular Technology Conference (VTC 2000), VOL. 4, PP. 1974–1978
11. UCLA Parallel Computing Laboratory and Wireless Adaptive MobilityLaboratory, GloMoSim: A Scalable Simulation Environment for Wireless and Wired Network Systems.
12. Gerla M, Chiang C, Zhang L (1999) "Tree multicast strategies in mobile, multihop wireless networks", Baltzer/ACM Journal of Mobile Networks and Applications (MONET), VOL 3, PP. 193–207